Through a Trauma

Through a Trauma Lens aims to understand and highlight successful examples of health, mental health, substance abuse treatment, and other service delivery systems that have implemented an integrated trauma-informed service model. This innovative volume draws on the author's first-hand experience working alongside a number of local and state organizations as well as a nationwide survey of notable trauma-informed models. Structured around illustrative case studies, chapters that correspond to stage of adoption, and strategies for cultivating staff support, this valuable new resource include examples and strategies to be applied in any treatment or service setting.

Vivian Barnett Brown, Ph.D. is the founder and former CEO of Prototypes: Centers for Innovation in Health, Mental Health and Social Services, a multi-facility, multi-service non-profit agency with services located throughout Southern California. Dr. Brown has more than 40 years of experience developing innovative, community-based services, including: community mental health centers; community health programs; substance abuse treatment services; mental health and specialized co-occurring disorders treatment; trauma-informed and trauma-specific services; domestic violence prevention and intervention services; HIV/AIDS outreach, prevention, and treatment services; and services for incarcerated women and recently released men, women, and youth.

Through a Trauma Lens

Transforming Health and
Behavioral Health Systems

Vivian Barnett Brown

 Routledge
Taylor & Francis Group

NEW YORK AND LONDON

First published 2018
by Routledge
711 Third Avenue, New York, NY 10017

and by Routledge
2 Park Square, Milton Park, Abingdon, Oxon, OX14 4RN

Routledge is an imprint of the Taylor & Francis Group, an informa business

© 2018 Taylor & Francis

The right of Vivian Barnett Brown to be identified as author
of this work has been asserted by her in accordance with
sections 77 and 78 of the Copyright, Designs and Patents Act
1988.

Library of Congress Cataloging-in-Publication Data
Names: Brown, Vivian B. (Vivian Barnett), 1939– author.
Title: Through a trauma lens : transforming health and behavioral
   health systems / by Vivian Barnett Brown.
Description: New York : Routledge, 2017. | Includes bibliographical
   references and index.
Identifiers: LCCN 2017011989| ISBN 9781138648937 (hbk) |
   ISBN 9781138648951 (pbk) | ISBN 9781315626109 (ebk)
Subjects: LCSH: Psychic trauma–Treatment.
Classification: LCC RC552.T7 B76 2017 | DDC 616.85/21–dc23
LC record available at https://lccn.loc.gov/2017011989

ISBN: 978-1-138-64893-7 (hbk)
ISBN: 978-1-138-64895-1 (pbk)
ISBN: 978-1-315-62610-9 (ebk)

Typeset in Bembo
by Apex CoVantage, LLC

To Gloria

Contents

PART III

PART IV

Preface

Many years ago, when I wrote my application to the University of Southern California Graduate School in Psychology, I discussed my wish to learn more about substance abuse. My wish came true when I entered my internship in the early 1960s at the Brentwood Veterans Administration Hospital, where I spent half my time at the Psychiatric Hospital on the last locked ward and half my time at the Wadsworth Medical Hospital, working with Dr. Sidney Cohen, famous drug researcher. While no one talked much about alcohol and other drugs in my course work, my internship was filled with wonderful discussions about substance use and treatment/prevention. I was also honored to do assessments on patients before surgery and for brain/cognitive issues. On the psychiatric ward I saw the impact of trauma on men who had been sent into war, as well as the impact of the new anti-psychotic medications on patients. After those experiences, my career path was set; I would work with both mental health and substance abuse disorders.

My next internships were at the Los Angeles Psychiatric Service (later to become the Didi Hirsch Community Mental Health Center) and at the Reiss-Davis Child Study Center. Through those internships, I developed skills in crisis intervention and in long-term psychotherapy for adults and children. My training and work with crisis intervention taught me to ask, "What brought you here today?" and "What happened?" rather than "What's wrong with you?" My first full-time job as a psychologist was at the Los Angeles Psychiatric Service/Didi Hirsch CMHC, where I developed the Consultation, Education and Prevention (CEP) Division, the Substance Abuse Treatment Division, the Liaison Inpatient Division, and Ethnic Minority Programs. As part of the Substance Abuse Treatment Division, I designed and implemented one of the first treatment programs for women and children (Via Avanta) and, under the CEP Division, the Southern California Rape Prevention Study Center.

More than 20 years later, in 1986, when I felt Community Mental Health Centers were no longer meeting emerging community needs, my colleague, Maryann Fraser, LCSW, MBA and I founded a new organization, PROTOTYPES, Centers for Innovation in Health, Mental Health, and Social Services. The agency was designed to develop new models of treatment to meet emerging needs, to test and refine the models, and, then, to disseminate them. HIV/AIDS was on the rise, so we developed a residential drug treatment program for women and children living with HIV/AIDS, as well as mental health and substance abuse disorders. With funding from the National Institute on Drug Abuse, we also created an outreach program for women at risk for HIV/AIDS. It was a wonderful journey of discovery and integration, during a time of crisis. By the late 1980s and early 1990s, we at PROTOTYPES had integrated treatment for substance use, mental disorders, HIV/AIDS and other health problems, and trauma. I also began writing about my concept of the level of burden.

PROTOTYPES was chosen as one of nine sites in the five-year national Women with Co-Occurring Disorders and Violence Study (WCDVS) funded by the Substance Abuse and Mental Health Services Administration (SAMHSA). In addition, we were one of the four sites that worked with and studied the children of the women who participated in WCDVS. During the WCDVS study, SAMHSA invited Drs. Felitti and Anda to present their ACE Study to all the sites. After the WCDVS, the site directors and consumers formed the National Trauma Consortium (NTC) and developed a number of monographs and publications, as well as training curricula on trauma and trauma-informed care, over the next ten years. PROTOTYPES also developed a domestic violence shelter for women with substance use disorders, mental illness, and HIV/AIDS.

Throughout all these years, I was also fortunate to serve on numerous federal, state, and local advisory committees and to contribute to changing our systems. Since my retirement as PROTOTYPES' Chief Executive Officer in 2008, I have been consulting on system change and helping programs and systems around the country to become "trauma-informed." Much of that work has been with Family Drug Treatment Court Systems. (See Chapter 11 for a discussion about the research done on these court systems.) Even though we still have a long way to go, it has been a wonderful experience to work with others who are enthusiastic about becoming trauma-informed.

Acknowledgements

I want to acknowledge the many people who have taught me, supported me, and joined me on my journey of discovery and implementation. Sidney Cohen, M.D., Ernest Lawrence, Ph.D., Mortimer Meyer, Ph.D., Gertrude Baker, Ph.D., Hedda Bolgar, Ph.D., for teaching me in my early years and supporting me throughout my career. Gerald Jacobson, M.D., for being an important mentor and supporting my efforts to expand community mental health. David Ruja, Ph.D. and Dorothy Semenow, Ph.D., for their therapeutic magic. Anna Freud, for spending one glorious day with me at her home in Hampstead, London and sharing her wisdom. Maryann Fraser, LCSW, MBA, for being my incredible co-founder in PROTO-TYPES and my dear friend; her calm nature, brilliant insights, and willingness to join me on every adventure made her a real partner in systems change. Areta Crowell, Ph.D., Irma Strantz, DPH, and Margy Gatz, Ph.D., for their expert guidance and support throughout my career. The staff of the Southern California Rape Prevention Study Center, the Board of Directors and staff of PROTOTYPES, for trusting me and joining me on efforts to meet community and individual needs in new ways. George Huba, Ph.D. and Lisa Melchior, Ph.D., Principals of The Measurement Group, for their research and evaluation expertise, as well as their ongoing support for all of PROTOTYPES' programs. Suzanne Sanchez, for her brilliance, her outstanding feedback, and willingness to implement my ideas, no matter how outrageous they seemed to her. Ruth Slaughter, for her sensitivity to and with women who have experienced domestic violence and her openness to finding new ways of reaching and helping people living with HIV; she is truly a pioneer. The clients/patients of Didi Hirsch CMHC and PROTOTYPES, who constantly taught me how to be a better clinician and researcher. The outstanding WCDVS teams, who really demonstrated the way to fully integrate trauma into our work and how to become "trauma-informed." Nancy Poole, Ph.D. and the wonderful team at the British Columbia Centre for Excellence in Women's Health, for their insights and interest in the WCDVS and my work. The Family Drug Treatment Court Systems, who have worked with me and enthusiastically embraced the work necessary to become trauma-informed. My friends and colleagues, Laurie Drabble, Ph.D., Nancy Young, Ph.D., Sid Gardner, Ph.D., Harold Pruett, Ph.D., and Tom Backer, Ph.D., for encouraging me to "write a book." My friends Barrie Levy, LCSW and Linda Garnets, Ph.D., for supporting so many of my efforts and for always being willing to engage in long and productive discussions about our work. My friend and colleague, Michael Gross, Ph.D., for all his encouragement, for interviewing me on PROTOTYPES for this book, and for his many thoughtful insights. I wish to thank all the individuals I interviewed—Nancy Paull, MA, Maxine Harris, Ph.D., Roger Fallot, Ph.D., Edward Machtingher, M.D., and Nancy Kassam-Adams, Ph.D.—for sharing their paths to becoming trauma-informed. Marge Tischer, for her work in transcribing the interviews. My partner-in-crime, Gloria Weissman, for being there through all the good and hard times, for her brilliance and humor, for reminding me that a "book is not a grant application" and for her all her suggestions about the book. My children and grandchildren, for being their wonderful selves. I hope they will carry on this work. Katie, Chloe, and Jason certainly have made contributions already to better health and behavioral health, and I am hoping that one or more of the five grandchildren will discover new and improved ways to help their fellow human beings.

Part I

Introduction

I would like you to meet Mary, a 25-year-old African American woman from South Central Los Angeles. She has used heroin in the past, but most recently has been using crack cocaine numerous times each day. She is homeless and has one child, a 2-year-old boy. She was living with her son's father, who introduced her to drug use and beat her throughout the time they were together. In order to feed herself and her son and be able to maintain her drug use, she now participates in sex work.

Outreach workers found Mary in a park, bleeding from wounds inflicted by her former partner and trying to comfort her frightened son. The outreach workers fed her and her son and spoke to Mary about getting help. She was interested in getting off the streets and protecting herself and her child, but she was not sure about any drug treatment program, especially if it meant having her son taken away. The outreach workers called the residential treatment program (the Women's Center) run by their agency and scheduled an appointment for Mary that afternoon. After driving her to the emergency room to ensure that her wounds were taken care of immediately, the outreach workers took her and her son to her intake appointment.

Because the outreach workers had some basic information about Mary and knew she needed some assistance immediately, she did not have to go through a phone screening or any waiting period before she could be seen at the treatment program. At the Women's Center, the psychiatric social worker doing the intake screening detected signs of a thought disorder in Mary. After exploring Mary's history, the social worker found that she had been hospitalized for mental illness on a number of occasions since her adolescence. She also had received psychiatric medications, which she always failed to continue taking after returning home from the hospital because of the side effects.

Because the Women's Center is designed as a comprehensive, trauma-informed treatment program for women with substance use disorders, mental illness, trauma (including domestic violence), and health problems (including HIV/AIDS), Mary was not only welcomed, but ensured that all her needs would be addressed. The medical staff met with her and her son to get a full medical history and do a basic examination, and the consulting psychiatrist spoke with her about taking medications.

When Mary realized that she and her son could both be in the residential treatment program, she relaxed and said that now she felt her son would be safe. When asked by the nurse practitioner if she was ready to move in that day,

Mary said, "Yes." A "mentor mom" (a senior resident) then greeted her and her son, took them to her room, and then took them on a tour of the facility. Mary and her son were then given a meal and introduced to the Children's Center Coordinator. Mary's son was just in time for afternoon nap, so he stayed in the Children's Center.

Next, Mary was introduced by the mentor mom to the leader of the Orientation Group, a group for all newcomers to the program. In the group, Mary learned about all the components of the treatment program and the procedures and schedules (including phases of the program). She had time to share what she wants to receive from the program and express what she fears about being in treatment.

The next day, when Mary was participating in a more comprehensive assessment with the social worker, she was asked about the domestic violence she had experienced and then about any other experiences in her life that might have been traumatic. Mary revealed that she had been sexually abused as a child by a family friend who lived in the projects.

After meeting her primary counselor, an initial treatment plan was constructed with Mary's input. It included an ongoing psychiatric consultation, a trauma-specific intervention group, a substance use educational group, and a Mommy and Me group. For her son, there would be the Children's Center and the Early Head Start program. The counselor went over the plan with Mary and asked her if it seemed to cover what she might want in the program. Mary was also told that, over the period of time of her stay in treatment, she would have a number of opportunities to see her schedule changed.

Now, let me introduce you to Joe, a 24-year-old war veteran, who served in Afghanistan. Joe came to the outpatient treatment program for assistance with his alcohol and methamphetamine problems. During his intake appointment, it became clear that he was also struggling with flashbacks, hypervigilance, and anger toward his wife. When asked why he did not go to the VA program, he responded that the waiting list was too long and that he didn't trust the VA to really help him. When he was asked if he had ever been seen by the VA or a military health care provider, he said that he was seen once and was told about some therapy for his symptoms, but that he "didn't like the sounds of it" (it was exposure therapy[1] for trauma) and didn't return for care.

When the medical staff in the outpatient program, including the consulting psychiatrist, met with Joe, they recommended to him that his medical records be obtained in order to: (1) understand his whole medical history; (2) see if he had been evaluated for traumatic brain injury (TBI); and (3) find out if he had been prescribed any medications. Joe was then introduced to the staff of the outpatient program, who explained all the program components, including family treatment (if he wanted it), vocational training, etc. He and his primary counselor went over his initial treatment plan.

Mary and Joe are like patients/clients that our health care, mental health, and substance abuse treatment systems encounter every day. As you read their stories, you might well have thought about how they would have been treated in your system and how difficult it can be to take care of patients and clients with a history of trauma. You may have noticed that they have overlapping and complex problems that preclude simple solutions from traditional systems of mental health, substance abuse, and medical treatment. Their problems can be overwhelming, not only for them, but for their providers. They need more services—and better-integrated services—to help them enter care and follow recommendations. Their priorities for themselves may differ from the ones we have for them. And, perhaps hardest of all, they don't trust us because they have been harmed and are fearful.

I ask you, as you begin reading this book, to think of it as undertaking a "journey through the trauma lens." I ask you to come with me on a walk through the health care system, the mental health system, and the substance abuse treatment system. I ask you to look through a trauma lens as we take that walk together and to keep Mary and Joe in mind. If you look at the individuals who cross our thresholds, trauma is everywhere. It pervades their histories and their lives. However, most of our systems have not come to terms with this, and the result is high numbers of dropouts from treatment, poorer outcomes, and higher costs. At the same time, the reactions and challenges of trauma-affected patients frustrate and exhaust their providers, who want to help them and who sometimes cannot see the reasons why their most sincere and dedicated efforts to do that are not enough to keep patients coming back or to do what they need to do to get better. This book is about the "exceptions": organizations that have transformed their programs, services, staff, and approaches to care to become trauma-informed.

The first part of the book (Chapters 1 to 5) introduces a trauma perspective, i.e., that trauma is ubiquitous and that it takes a toll and adds burdens to both patients and providers. It discusses why trauma needs to be addressed by each of our systems and introduces some of the adaptations that can help systems of care provide effective, equitable, and cost-effective services to the large numbers of patients and clients who have been affected by trauma.

Part II of the book (Chapters 6 to 8) describes, in depth, exemplary trauma-informed programs and allows us to hear the perspectives of their directors in their own words. Those who designed and implemented them discuss the core components of these programs, as well as the barriers and facilitators they experienced in adopting trauma-informed practice.

In the third part of the book (Chapters 9 to 10), I discuss the core components and specific recommended practice changes for each system (health care, mental health, substance abuse treatment) in order for them to become trauma-informed. Finally, I describe how the programs interviewed have demonstrated their successes through research.

Part IV (Chapter 11) describes steps already taken by other systems—including child welfare, education, criminal justice, and the military—to become trauma-informed.

I believe that, as the role of traumatic life experiences in our patients' developing and overcoming health and behavioral problems/conditions becomes increasingly clear, trauma-informed practice will become "standard practice." I also believe that this will lead to enhanced patient-provider relationships, improved outcomes, better provider morale, and lower costs. I hope this book adds to the important changes happening in our health and behavioral health systems. Improvement depends on our collective wisdom. It is not easy to give up the culture in which we were trained, but, if we decide to make it happen and learn from each other about how to make it happen, it will happen.

Note

1 Exposure therapy for PTSD involves having the client describe and explore trauma-related memories and emotions; intense emotions are evoked, with the intention of desensitizing the client through repeated exposure. However, some patients may show an exacerbation of symptoms.

Chapter 1

Trauma as a Core Component of Care

Dramatic changes are taking place in our health care and behavioral health care systems. Attention to issues related to comorbidity, health care reform, and fragmentation of care have led to greater awareness of the urgent need for integrated care. Defined simply, integrated care is the working together of medical and behavioral health providers so that both providers and patients experience *one* seamless treatment plan, with several steps for the array of problems the patient brings, implemented by one treatment team (Blount 1998). Integrated care models are the best laboratories for the development and refinement of services for complex problems.

In Western medicine, we have perpetuated the dichotomy of mind and body in our biomedical model, in our organization of services (separate health, mental health, and substance use disorders systems), and in our practice. This has led to both fragmentation and duplication of effort. We need to do better with and for patients who have co-occurring mental and physical problems, particularly patients who have experienced trauma.[1] As will be discussed below and in later chapters, there is now increasing recognition that traumatic experiences are pervasive in the lives of our patients and clients. Because of this, trauma-sensitive and trauma-informed care must be a core component of integrated systems; it is an important link that has been missing in much of our work. As providers, agencies, and entire systems look at the best strategies for providing collaborative, patient-centered care, implementing trauma-informed practice is another important step toward transformation. In fact, I believe that we cannot and will not truly attain the aims of enhancing our patients' experience of care, improving the health of our diverse population, and reducing costs of care unless we adopt a trauma-informed approach. Trauma should be seen as the expectation, not the exception.

In fact, research during the past two decades has demonstrated that a large percentage of children and adults in our human service systems have experienced trauma at some point(s) in their lives. As defined by the Substance Abuse and Mental Health Services Administration, trauma is: "an event, series of events, or set of circumstances that is experienced by an individual as physically or emotionally harmful or life threatening and that has lasting adverse effects on the individual's functioning and mental, physical, social, emotional, or spiritual well-being" (SAMHSA 2014, p. 9). Estimates of lifetime exposure to traumatic events in the general population in the U.S. ranges from 60 to 70 percent (Kessler et al. 1995). Overall, 20 to 30 percent of those exposed to trauma will develop posttraumatic stress disorder (PTSD). The more one is exposed to trauma, in terms of severity and duration, the higher the likelihood of a PTSD diagnosis (e.g., veterans' exposure to heavy levels of combat and trauma). However, millions of individuals who are experiencing PTSD and other sequelae of trauma go unrecognized and untreated.

The traumatic event may be re-experienced in one or more of the following ways: recurrent and intrusive recollections of the event or the feeling as if the event was recurring; avoidance of stimuli associated with the trauma and detachment from others; dissociative symptoms; symptoms of increased arousal (e.g., bursts of anger); physical symptoms (e.g., pain). Comorbid disorders such as depression may be the survivor's primary reason for coming into treatment, while the history of trauma is easily overlooked. Because of shame, memory difficulties, fear of ongoing danger (domestic violence), and mistrust of the provider, the patient may not disclose any issue related to his/her trauma experiences.

As will be discussed in more detail in later chapters, studies have shown that violence and trauma can cause neurological damage, lead to adoption of risky behaviors, and result in a wide variety of health and behavioral health problems. This increases the demands on all health care and human services and costs the U.S. billions of dollars annually. The growing science base regarding trauma and PTSD is important as providers, legislators, and policymakers increasingly push for higher quality, increased accountability, and better outcomes. As our understanding has grown about the scope of and possible causal pathways for trauma-related syndromes, new trauma-specific services/interventions and trauma-informed approaches and practices have been developed and tested. Trauma-informed systems and services take into account knowledge about trauma—its prevalence, impacts, and interpersonal dynamics—and incorporate this knowledge thoroughly in all aspects of service delivery.

Trauma, Comorbidity, and Health Reform

As national health reform is implemented, the health care system is stepping up its efforts to improve quality and reduce costs. Since a small percentage of the population account for most of the health care spending (Stanton 2005), achieving these goals may require focusing on the subgroups most at risk of high costs and poor quality of care. Priority populations include children, aging adults, chronically ill patients, and those with comorbidity. In an important monograph funded by the Robert Wood Johnson Foundation entitled *The Synthesis Project: Mental Disorders and Medical Comorbidity*, comorbidity is defined as "the co-occurrence of mental and physical disorders in the same person, regardless of the chronological order in which they occurred or the causal pathway linking them" (Goodell, Druss, and Walker 2011, p. 2). At the present time, an increasing proportion of health care resources are directed toward an expanding group of patients with complex conditions and comorbidities.

In fact, most primary care visits by adults involve more than one health problem or disease. Based upon epidemiological data from the *2001–2003 National Comorbidity Survey Replication (NCS-R)* (Algeria et al. 2003), 34 million American adults (17% of the adult population) had comorbid mental health and medical conditions within a 12-month period. In addition, more than 68 percent of adults with a diagnosed mental health disorder reported having at least one medical disorder, and 29 percent of those adults with a medical disorder had a comorbid mental health disorder (Kessler et al. 2004).

When primary care has traditionally sought to coordinate care for patients with multiple morbidities, incentives have been used mainly to improve outcomes in specific diseases, rather than to manage comorbidity. The effects of comorbidity are excluded from most medical practice guidelines. For example, a physician following clinical guidelines could prescribe up to 12 medications for a patient with osteoporosis, diabetes, hypertension, and COPD. It should be noted that this same patient could be taking medications for behavior health issues, such as depression, anxiety, and/or severe mental illness.

At the systems level, fragmentation and separation (silos) among medical, mental health, and substance abuse systems result in patients with co-occurring conditions receiving care from multiple uncoordinated practices (Druss and Esenwein 2006). Fragmentation and separation is often made worse by the presence of competing and contradictory service approaches among service systems. Disciplinary silos have slowed the advance of progress in practice and research.

Concept of Level of Burden

Given that the number of U.S. adults with multiple conditions is projected to rise from 57 million in 2000 to 81 million by 2020 (Wu and Green 2000), it is important to redesign health care, mental health care, and substance abuse caretaking into consideration of patient illness burden and treatment burden. It is also important that this redesign includes the integration of trauma-informed practices designed to reduce treatment burden on clients and on staff. One of the components for accurately predicting those patients/clients at greatest risk of becoming overwhelmed by treatment burden is the experience of cumulative trauma; i.e., those patients who have experienced multiple traumatic events are most at risk.

In my own work on integrating substance use disorders, mental health disorders, HIV/AIDS, and trauma, I implemented a number of studies on the level of burden on clients caused by the number of problems/disorders they experienced. In the first study of women in residential substance abuse treatment (Brown, Huba, and Melchior 1995), we found that the majority of clients (more than 63%) had four or more problems, e.g., drug use, alcohol use, major health problems (cancer, diabetes, hepatitis, etc.), HIV/AIDS as a separate health problem, psychological issues, and cognitive impairment. We also found that women with higher levels of burden dropped out of treatment earlier than other women. However, if they were able to stay in treatment, they eventually had outcomes similar to the other women. Thus, not only was there a burden of illness for the clients, but also a burden of treatment on the clients; i.e., if the treatment were multileveled and complex, the women with higher levels of burden needed more support and fewer requirements from treatment than other women in order to succeed in the treatment.

In our second study (Brown, Melchior, and Huba 1999), trauma experiences were added to the list, as well as a diagnosis of serious mental illness. We examined the effects of severe mental illness, as well as the overall level of burden, on retention in treatment. Cox regression analyses revealed that severe mental illness (including PTSD) had a significant negative relationship to retention. An alternate model was tested to specifically address the relationship between the burden elements and program retention. Of all the possible burden elements, there were statistically significant main effects for severe mental illness, HIV status, and methamphetamine use. Women who had been diagnosed with severe mental illness and HIV tended to drop out early. This was not true of women with PTSD diagnosis and/or methamphetamine use.

It is possible that, for these women, the controlled structure of the modified therapeutic community and the emphasis on "safety first" outweigh the sometimes overwhelming nature of entering and remaining in a complex treatment environment. The women with severe mental illness and/or HIV may be more easily overwhelmed by participating with others in a community, changing behaviors, complying with procedures, etc. For such women, it is important to design better "treatment readiness" strategies, such as treatment readiness groups, visits to the program prior to intake, outreach workers accompanying the women for preadmission visits and intake, and stabilization of medications (if necessary and wanted) prior to admission. It was shown in this study that women with diagnoses of severe mental illness who did stay in treatment had outcomes similar to other women.

It should be noted that the PROTOTYPES program in which the studies were implemented was long-term residential treatment for up to 18 months. For many women with comorbid substance abuse, mental illness, trauma experiences, and health problems, the average stay was 12 months. A period of 18 months allowed us to treat pregnant addicted women—through their pregnancies and post-partum—and to help them bond with their babies and learn parenting skills. It also allowed women who had lost custody of their children, but wished to work toward reunification, sufficient time in treatment to do so. Finally, it allowed women with significant trauma histories and current trauma in their lives (e.g., domestic violence) sufficient time, safety, and slow enough treatment pacing to learn new coping skills of emotional regulation, self-care, and parenting.

For the third study (Brown 2000), we looked at traumatic experiences (with or without PTSD) and found that, of 286 women, 87 percent had a history of childhood and/or adult physical and/or sexual abuse, and 63 percent had four or more burden elements. Again, "high burden" women tended to leave earlier than "low burden women," but, if the high burden women remained in treatment, they did as well as low burden women. It should be noted that the high burden women had significant health disorders (cancer, diabetes, and HIV/AIDS).

My colleagues and I then extended the Stages of Change model (Prochaska, DiClemente, and Norcross 1992) for women with multiple, interrelated needs, particularly women who abuse substances and also have co-occurring problems of mental illness, histories of physical and sexual abuse, and HIV/AIDS. We believed that it was necessary to expand the Stages of Change model into a more complex Steps of Change model (Brown et al. 2000) of behavioral change for women entering residential treatment. This enhanced model takes into consideration that women may wish to make changes simultaneously in several aspects of their lives. For these women, there may be issues of substance abuse, current domestic violence, current issues of depression and anxiety, and current health risks (e.g., HIV/AIDS).

The four areas of readiness to change that we studied were domestic violence, sex risk behaviors, substance use behaviors, and emotional problems. We hypothesized that women would wish to address the most immediately threatening issue first (and to seek help for it) before addressing other problems. The study supported a step model of women's movement from needs to entry into drug treatment. Time urgency or "immediacy" appeared to be related to an underlying issue of seeking help; i.e., domestic violence was a more acute danger than substance abuse. However, while a woman may feel the urgency to do something about her safety, she may also fear the loss of her children if she reports violence in the home. If she enters a residential drug treatment program that also admits her children, she can attempt to resolve both her substance abuse and the domestic violence issue without having to admit the domestic violence. In this study, we hypothesized that "immediacy" was equivalent to "safety"; that is, by entering the treatment environment, the woman and her children were safer. We also wanted to point out that the woman's perception of need or immediacy may differ from that of a therapist, substance abuse counselor, or other treatment provider.

I, therefore, proposed a multi-leveled picture of the levels of burden as follows:

Burden of Problems on Client	Burden of Treatment	Burdens on Staff
Substance use	Time for appointments (waiting times)	Time pressures
Mental illness		Monitoring of all conditions
Trauma	Time pressures (15 minutes with MD)	EHRs
Cognitive impairment	Multiple providers/multiple appointments	Poor or inadequate communication among providers
High blood pressure	Triggered by procedures	Compassion fatigue/burnout
Cardiac problems	Costs	Limits on amounts of services
	Multiple locations	
Diabetes	Medications (adherence/non-adherence; side effects)	New priorities
Depression		Staff turnover
Domestic violence	Monitoring of all conditions (including urinalyses)	Trauma experienced by staff/secondary traumatization
Anxiety	Mistrust of providers and treatments	Lack of information about community resources
Stigma	Difficulty understanding instructions	
HIV/AIDS		Funding changes
Physical injury	Language/literacy issues	Mistrust of patients
Cancer	Self-care regimens	Patient emergencies
Poverty/ unemployment	Care transitions	Dealing with complexity/ comorbidity
	Loss of providers (turnover)	
Lack of social/ family support	Disrespectful providers	Productivity pressures
		Angry/hostile patients

Figure 1.1 Level of Burden

As can be seen, the first column is the burden of illness on the patient/client. The second column of the diagram is the burden of treatment on the patient; i.e., the more problems the patient has, the more complex the treatment plan. The third column in the diagram is the burden of illness/treatment on the staff; i.e., the more problems the client/patient has, plus the more complex the treatment plan, the greater is the level of burden on staff members trying to assist the client. Time pressures, new priorities, funding changes, patient emergencies, etc., all add to the burdens on staff, particularly those who have themselves experienced trauma, compassion fatigue, and burnout.

The concept of level of burden is closely related to the concept of "minimally disruptive medicine" (MDM) developed by May and colleagues (May, Montori, and Mair 2009). They also believe that the burden of treatment for many people with complex, chronic comorbidities reduces their capacity to collaborate in their care. However, they do not specifically mention trauma or traumatic experience. May and colleagues note that chronic illness requires taking on lifetime burden of management of complex treatment regimens, including medication management, self-monitoring, organizing doctor's visits and laboratory tests, and passing on information about their care to different health care providers and behavioral health providers. They argue that, in order to be effective, care must be "less disruptive" and treatment regimens tailored to the realities of patients' daily lives. In addition to patients with chronic conditions, patients with cognitive impairment also may have diminished capacity to adhere to therapeutic regimens. In my work this would include women who experienced cognitive impairment from domestic violence (e.g., having one's head bashed against a wall). This is an extremely important example, since it begins to add the component of trauma to the picture. High treatment burden may lead to poor adherence, missed appointments, poor outcomes, plus additional expenses for patients.

Acknowledging comorbidity, including trauma, is an important step in enhancing and improving practice. The effects of complexity and comorbidity are often systematically excluded from most practice guidelines. Establishing the weight of the burden on patients necessitates identifying all the patient's problems, including capacity problems.[2]

Minimally disruptive medicine (MDM) seeks to right-size and redirect care strategies to fit patient context and be minimally disruptive of their lives and maximally supportive. In the setting of multimorbidity, this often requires the adjustment of protocols and practice guidelines to fit patient needs, stated patient preferences, and complicated patient circumstances.

The capacity of patients includes physical, mental, social, financial, personal, and environmental domains—and is dynamic, changing with one's disease and life trajectory; e.g., heart failure exacerbation reduces physical capacity, the loss of a job impacts financial capacity, and traumatic experiences may lead to mistrust of the physician and/or an inability to tolerate some medical procedures. When workload exceeds capacity, patients feel the effects of treatment burden, and this can lead to de-prioritization of various aspects of care and ultimately result in poor fidelity to treatment plans, treatment failures, and readmissions to the hospital.

It is important to assess the patient's treatment burdens and the patient's values, preferences, and treatment goals in order to arrive at feasible and patient-focused care strategies. Patients and their caregivers need to report on the burden of treatment and should participate in deciding which conditions to tackle next. The next step is improving the efficiency of interacting with health care from the patient's perspective (e.g., shortening waiting times and/or streamlining administrative hurdles) and engaging community navigators or peer supports who can support and connect patients to community resources.[3]

Gallagher and colleagues (Gallagher et al. 2011) performed an analysis of qualitative interview data from 47 patients with chronic heart failure in the UK. The number of medications prescribed for each patient ranged from four to 13, and the number of comorbidities ranged from one to seven. Patients in this study frequently described a laborious regimen with many medications, often with troublesome adverse effects. It was clear that dealing with both the medications and these adverse effects consumed vast amounts of the patients' time and energy. Patients reported the considerable work of attending appointments, with multiple visits to the hospital for tests and clinic appointments, recurrent admissions, and frequent visits to their family practitioner. The burden was worsened by poor communication at the primary-secondary care interface, as patients had to make numerous appointments with family practitioners until contact had been made with their specialist in order to alter management plans. Patients also described difficulties accessing a range of services, including health and social services.

In a review of the literature published between 2002 and 2011, Sav and colleagues in Australia (Sav et al. 2015) found that, although the burden associated with chronic illness is well documented, the burden associated with treatment has not been well defined. The dimensions of treatment burden included: undesirable physical effects of treatment (side effects); economic burden imposed by treatment (financial burden); time required to obtain, receive, monitor, and manage treatment (time burden); and psychosocial aspects of burden, including the impact on family and lifestyle (personal burden). Some of the elements of treatment burden, such as the number of medications and physical side effects, were a significant source of the burden. In discussing patient characteristics, authors suggest that gender seemed to be a key antecedent of burden, with women experiencing more treatment burden than men; women also reported more caregiver burden when their children were ill. In addition, the authors found that comorbidity and particular chronic conditions such as diabetes and schizophrenia were associated with greater treatment burden. Trauma exacerbates the already complicated and overlapping burdens of illness and treatment for the client and the burden of treatment on the providers, and trauma is an important link between the three types of burden. Trauma keeps patients from trusting providers, keeps them isolated and fearful, keeps them from adhering to treatment recommendations, particularly medications, and keeps them from being able to self-manage. Therefore, it is important for providers: to decrease the burdens in all three spheres; to increase our sensitive, trauma-informed practices; to give additional support to the patients to help them follow through on treatment recommendations; to make it easier/less burdensome to adhere to treatments; to understand their angry, fearful, disassociated responses and respond in a caring, supportive way, while also taking care of ourselves as providers. I therefore advocate for "trauma universal precautions," i.e., seeing trauma as the expectation, not the exception.

The Role of Trauma in Achieving Health Equity

In 2001 the Institute of Medicine published its important report, *Crossing the Quality Chasm: A New Health System for the 21st Century*, and described "six aims for improvement."

According to the report, health care systems must aim to be safe, effective, patient-centered, timely, efficient, and equitable. In a recent post by the Institute for Healthcare Improvement (IHI), Derek Feeley (2016) reported that in the 15 years since the Chasm report, "meaningful progress" has been made on five of the six aims. However, progress on the sixth aim, viz., equity, has lagged behind.

In 2008, Donald Berwick and colleagues (Berwick, Nolan, and Whittington 2008) first described the "Triple Aim" of: improving the patient's experience of care; improving the health of populations; and reducing the per capita cost of health care. The Institute of Healthcare Improvement (IHI) developed the Triple Aim as a statement of purpose, and it has become the organizing framework for the National Quality Strategies of the U.S. Department of Health and Human Services and for other public and private health organizations.

IHI's Innovation Team produced a new white paper, *Achieving Health Equity: A Guide for Health Care Organizations*, which offers a conceptual framework and steps for organizations to take in mitigating health inequities (Wyatt et al. 2016). The authors state, "Health equity is not a fourth aim, but rather an element of all three components of Triple Aim. The Triple Aim will not be achieved until it is achieved for all" (Wyatt et al. 2016, p. 3). The white paper also notes that: "Currently, most health systems are designed to produce inequitable outcomes" (Wyatt et al. 2016, p. 11).

A paper by Browne and colleagues (Browne et al. 2012) identified four key dimensions of equity-oriented primary health care services, as well as strategies for operationalizing these services for marginalized populations. The authors also state that "focusing on the health effects of inequities necessitates attention to the concept of trauma." Traumatizing experiences include discrimination, poverty, emotional abuse, race-based violence, loss of homeland, forced attendance at residential schools, disruption of families, etc. These experiences can be historical and intergenerational, such as the experiences of the Aboriginal people in Canada and the American Indian people in the U.S. Research on primary health care delivery highlights several problems: (1) inverse care, i.e., those who are most marginalized and have the greatest health and behavioral health problems have the least access to care; (2) fragmentation and under-resourcing of care for marginalized populations; and (3) policy and funding environments that do not address these problems.

The four dimensions are interrelated and overlapping:

1. Inequity-responsive care: explicitly addressing the social determinants of health.
2. Trauma- and violence-informed care: recognizing that most people affected by systemic inequities and structural violence have experienced, and often continue to experience, varying forms of traumatic events. "Such care consists of respectful, empowerment practices informed by understanding the pervasiveness and effects of trauma and violence rather than 'trauma treatment' such as psychotherapy."
3. Contextually-tailored care: expanding the concept of patient-centered care to include services that are explicitly tailored to the populations served and local contexts.
4. Culturally-competent care: taking into account not only the cultural meaning of health and illness, but also people's experiences of racism, discrimination, and marginalization, as well as the ways in which those experiences shape health, life opportunities, access to health care, and quality of life.

Their eighth strategy focuses on trauma-informed care. It recommends that organizations "tailor care, programs and services to populations' individual and group histories, with an emphasis on trauma- and violence-informed care" (Browne et al. 2012, p. 10).

Trauma-informed care is about creating a safe environment based on an understanding of the effects of trauma, so that health care encounters are safe, affirming, and validating. For example, in recognition of the devaluing of Aboriginal culture as a result of Canada's colonial history, one of the PHCs featured signage in a local indigenous dialect to convey that the staff valued Aboriginal identity. Trauma-informed care requires that organizations integrate comprehensive and continuing education for all staff, including receptionists, direct care staff, and management. Equally important are supports for staff who may be dealing with vicarious trauma when working with patients with significant trauma histories and/or have experienced their own trauma experiences.

Notes

1 Throughout the book, I will be focusing on a broad range of traumatic experiences and traumatic responses, not just on posttraumatic stress disorder (PTSD).
2 In most research, disease burden is expressed in terms of "disability-adjusted life years" (DALY), representing an estimation of the gap between current health status and an ideal situation of the whole population living into old age in full health (Murray & Lopez 1996).
3 In this context, the example of simplification of antiretroviral therapy to a single-tablet regimen vs. unmodified antiretroviral treatment in virologically suppressed HIV-1-infected patients not only improved adherence and patient outcomes, but also helped reduce treatment burden on patients (May, Finch et al. 2009).

References

Algeria, M, Jackson, JS, Kessler, RC, and Takeuchi, D 2003, *National Comorbidity Survey Replication (NCS-R) 2001–2003*, Ann Arbor, MI, Inter-university Consortium for Political and Social Research.

Berwick, DM, Nolan, TW, and Whittington, J 2008, The Triple Aim: Care, Health, and Cost, *Health Affairs*, vol. 27, no. 3, pp. 759–769.

Blount, A (ed.) 1998, *Integrated Primary Care: The Future of Medical and Mental Health Collaboration*, New York, WW Norton & Co, Inc.

Brown, VB 2000, *Changing and Improving Services for Women and Children: Strategies Used and Lessons Learned*, Culver City, CA, PROTOTYPES Systems Change Center.

Brown, VB, Huba, GJ, and Melchior, LA 1995, Level of Burden: Women with More Than One Co-Occurring Disorder, *Journal of Psychoactive Drugs*, vol. 27, no. 4, pp. 339–346.

Brown, VB, Melchior, LA, and Huba, GJ 1999, Level of Burden Among Women Diagnosed with Severe Mental Illness and Substance Abuse, *Journal of Psychoactive Drugs*, vol. 31, no. 1, pp. 31–40.

Brown, VB, Melchior, LA, Panter, AT, Slaughter, R, and Huba, GJ 2000, Women's Steps of Change and Entry into Treatment: A Multidimensional Stages of Change Model, *Journal of Substance Abuse Treatment*, vol. 18, pp. 231–240.

Browne, AJ, Varcoe, CM, Wong, ST et al. 2012, Closing the Health Equity Gap: Evidence-Based Strategies for Primary Health Care Organizations, *International Journal for Equity in Health*, vol. 11, no. 59, pp. 1–15.

Druss, BG and Esenwein, SA 2006, Improving General Medical Care for Persons with Mental and Addictive Disorders: Systematic Review, *General Hospital Psychiatry*, vol. 28, no. 2, pp. 145–153.

Feeley, D, August 11, 2016, Equity: The Forgotten AIM, Institute for Healthcare Improvement, www.ihi.org/Topics/Health-Equity/Pages.

Gallagher, K, May, CR, Montori, VB, and Mair, FS 2011, Understanding Patients' Experiences of Treatment Burden in Chronic Heart Failure Using Normalization Process Theory, *Annals of Family Medicine*, vol. 9, pp. 235–243.

Goodell, S, Druss, BG, and Walker, ER 2011, *The Synthesis Project: Mental Disorders and Medical Comorbidity, Policy Brief No. 21*, Princeton, NJ, Robert Wood Johnson Foundation.

Kessler, RC, Berglund, P, Chiu, WT et al. 2004, The U.S. National Comorbidity Survey Replication: Design and Field Procedures, *International Journal of Methods in Psychiatric Research*, vol. 13, no. 2, pp. 69–94.

Kessler, RC, Sonnega, A, Bromet, E, Hughes, M, and Nelson, CB 1995, Posttraumatic Stress Disorder in the National Comorbidity Survey, *Archives of General Psychiatry*, vol. 52, pp. 1048–1060.

May, C, Finch, T et al. 2009, Development of a Theory of Implementation and Integration: Normalization Process Theory, *Implementation Science*, vol. 4, pp. 1–9.

May, C, Montori, VM, and Mair, FS 2009, We Need Minimally Disruptive Medicine, *British Medical Journal*, vol. 29, no. 339, pp. 485–487.

Murray, CJL and Lopez, AD 1996, *The Global Burden of Disease: A Comprehensive Assessment of Mortality and Disability from Diseases, Injuries, and Risk Factors in 1990 and Projected to 2020*, Cambridge, MA, Harvard School of Public Health Organization and the World Bank.

Prochaska, JO, DiClemente, CC, and Norcross, JC 1992, In Search of How People Change: Applications to Addictive Behaviors, *American Psychologist*, vol. 47, pp. 1102–1114.

Sav, A, King, MA, Whitty, JA et al. 2015, Burden of Treatment for Chronic Illness: A Concept Analysis and Review of the Literature, *Health Expectations*, vol. 18, no. 3, pp. 312–324.

Stanton, MW 2005, *The High Concentration of U.S. Health Care Expenditures*, Rockville, MD, Agency for Healthcare Research and Quality.

Substance Abuse and Mental Health Services Administration 2014, *SAMHSA's Concept of Trauma and Guidance for a Trauma-Informed Approach*, HHS Publication No (SMA) 14–4884, Rockville, MD, Substance Abuse and Mental Health Services Administration.

Wu, S and Green, A 2000, *Projection of Chronic Illness Prevalence and Cost Inflation*, Washington, DC, Rand Health.

Wyatt, R, Lederman, M, Botwinick, L, Mate, K, and Whittington, J 2016, *IHI White Paper, Achieving Health Equity: A Guide for Health Care Organizations*, Cambridge, MA, Institute for Healthcare Improvement.

Chapter 2

Significant Studies on Trauma/Stress and Its Impact

Shelly Taylor (2010) describes four phases of research efforts linking early life stress to adult health outcomes. Phase 1 (1930s to 1940s) was dominated by case histories, e.g., accounts of people whose lives were suddenly upended by a major tragic event and who rapidly succumbed to death, often from cardiovascular events. Phase 2 (1950s to1960s) studies provided better evidence for the relationship between stress and health, but little clarity on the underlying mechanisms of this relationship. For example, Holmes, Rahe, and Arthur (Holmes and Rahe 1967; Rahe and Arthur 1978) reported that when people experience accumulated stressors the likelihood of subsequent illness is increased. However, much of this research merely demonstrates these links without identifying pathways by which these links might occur. In Phase 3 (1980s to 1990s), studies concerned with the underlying pathways began to emerge. For example, studies of medical students facing exams and kindergarten children beginning school revealed changes in immune functioning among these individuals that were potentially prognostic for adverse health outcomes. Phase 4 (1990s to 2000s) studies, reflecting the more current state of the field, are guided by complex multivariate models over time (McEwen 1998).

Research most clearly demonstrating the relationship among early environment, biological functioning, and health outcomes includes evidence that low childhood socioeconomic status (SES) predicts adult health outcomes (Chen, Matthews, and Boyce 2002), as well as evidence that a harsh early family environment marked by abuse, conflict, harsh parenting, and/or neglect predicts adverse health outcomes (Repetti, Taylor, and Seeman 2002). Similarly, strong evidence now ties family environments characterized by adverse conditions to adult health risks. This is not "family blaming," but is a strong indication of the need for two-generation programs (e.g., family-centered programs) since many parents were themselves traumatized as children.

This chapter focuses on two major studies and their impact on a movement toward trauma-informed care. The Adverse Childhood Experiences (ACE) study and subsequent follow-up studies linked adverse childhood experiences to physical health in adulthood. The second major study is the Women with Co-Occurring Disorders and Violence Study (WCDVS), which began the national and international movement toward the implementation of trauma-informed care. In the chapter, I also discuss two prospective studies to address the ACE study's limitations as a retrospective study and to show that results from prospective studies demonstrate similar findings to it.

ACE Study

The largest and most widely disseminated study of the relationship between stressful and traumatic events in childhood and long-term health effects is the Adverse Childhood Experiences (ACE) study (Felitti et al. 1998). The ACE study was a collaborative effort between Kaiser Permanente (Felitti) in San Diego and the Center for Disease Control (CDC) (Anda). The idea for the study grew out of clinical observations and interviews with obese patients that pointed to significant adverse effects in the childhoods of these individuals as the possible precursors to their obesity and other health issues. The ACE study was conducted from 1995 to 1997 among 17,337 Kaiser Health Plan members. The purpose of the study was to determine the prevalence among this group of ten stressful, traumatic childhood (before the age of 18) events and the long-term medical effects of these experiences. The average age of the study participants was 52. The sample was almost evenly divided among men and women. Approximately 80 percent were White (Hispanic and non-Hispanic), 10 percent were Black, and 10 percent were Asian. Eight categories of adverse childhood events were studied in the first wave; two more categories (emotional neglect and physical neglect) were added in the second wave.[1]

The prevalence among the group for the ten ACEs were:

Psychological abuse (by parent)	11%
Physical abuse (by parent)	28%
Sexual abuse (by anyone)	22% (28% for women; 16% for men)
Emotional neglect	15%
Physical neglect	10%
Alcoholism or drug use in home	27%
Divorce or loss of a biological parent	23%
Depression or mental illness in family	17%
Mother treated violently	13%
Household member in prison	6%

An ACE score for each individual study participant was calculated by adding together the number of categories of adverse events reported by that participant. Women were 50 percent more likely than men to have a score of 5 or higher. It should be noted that multiple incidents within a category are not scored (beyond 1); thus, for example, having an alcoholic and a drug user in the same household score the same as having one alcoholic. This has the effect of definitely understating the findings. In addition, experiences such as encountering explicit racism are not included.

Felitti and Anda then looked at the correlation between these scores and a variety of health issues and risk behaviors in adulthood. In the area of addiction, the strongest relationship seen was between ACE scores and the injection of street drugs. At an ACE score of 6, there was a 4,600 percent increase in the likelihood of later becoming an injection drug user, as compared to an ACE score of 0. (See more on ACEs and addiction in Chapter 3.) When ACE scores were calculated for coronary artery disease, nine of the ten events were found to be associated with an increase in likelihood of coronary heart disease in adult life, even in the absence of Framingham risk factors.[2] In another analysis of 21 different autoimmune diseases,

Felitti and Anda (2014) found a strong relationship between ACE scores and the likelihood of developing autoimmune diseases decades later. "In recent years physicians have come to understand the role of major unrelieved stress in immunosuppression, both as a result of prolonged high levels of circulating cortisone analogues and by ultimate dysregulation of the hypothalamic-pituitary-adrenal axis with its effects on the immune system" (Felitti and Anda 2014, p. 208).

The relationships between ACE scores and depression, suicidality, chronic anxiety, amnesia, and hallucinations were also studied and showed similar results. In addition, the ACE study team documented the relationship of ACE scores to participants' having 50 or more sexual partners, a risk factor for HIV/AIDS and other sexually transmitted diseases. The findings of the ACE study made it clear that stressful and traumatic events experienced in childhood have a proportionate and long-lasting effect on emotional state, whether measured by depression or suicide attempts or by what Felitti and Anda refer to as "self-help attempts" such as smoking, alcohol use, and drug use, including injection drug use.

In terms of the links between traumatic/stressful childhood experiences and adult biomedical disease, one can look at the relationships between ACE scores and liver disease, chronic obstructive pulmonary disease (COPD), coronary artery disease, and autoimmune disease, as noted above. In the case of coronary artery disease, it may be thought that the relationship is a simple one; in other words, that ACEs lead to a coping behavior of smoking, which becomes the mechanism of damage to the coronary arteries. However, the authors of the ACE study believe that, while this hypothesis is true, it is also incomplete.

In their analysis in *Circulation*, Dong and colleagues (2004) found that there was a strong relationship between ACE score and coronary artery disease even after controlling for all conventional risk factors, such as smoking, high cholesterol, etc., Felitti and Anda hypothesize that ACEs are related to adult disease through two mechanisms: (1) risk factors (e.g., smoking, alcohol use, overeating) that are attempts to decrease the impact of the traumatic experience(s); and (2) effects of chronic stress as mediated through the mechanisms of "hypercortisolemia, pro-inflammatory cytokines, and other stress responses on the developing brain and body systems, dysregulation of the stress response, and pathophysiological mechanisms yet to be discovered" (Felitti and Anda 2010, p. 83). In addition, analysis of findings from the prospective phase of the ACE study has confirmed that individuals with ACE scores of 6 and higher had a life span almost two decades shorter than that of individuals with ACE scores of zero (Brown et al. 2009).

After the first wave of the ACE Study, Kaiser Permanente integrated the trauma-oriented ACE questions into the detailed biomedical questionnaire that patients filled out at home, before coming in for their comprehensive medical evaluation. They also added questions in the past history section about combat, living in war zones, murder of a family member, and suicide in the family. (Still missing are questions about neighborhood crime and violence and experiences with racist conditions and discrimination.) When Kaiser patients came in for their exams, the discussion included questions such as, "I see on the questionnaire that you experienced _____. Tell me, how that has affected you later in life?"

After this new procedure was implemented, an outside organization, using neural net analysis, carried out a study of more than 100,000 Kaiser patients. These findings showed a dramatic change that was not anticipated. In the year following the medical evaluation using the expanded questionnaire with trauma-oriented components, there was a 35 percent reduction in doctor office visits and an 11 percent reduction in ER visits among that cohort compared to the year before. It should be noted that almost none of these patients had been referred to psychotherapy and none had complained about being asked about the childhood experiences. In fact, many patients were complimentary and/or grateful. As Felitti said, "Gradually, we came to see that asking, listening, and enabling a patient to go home feeling still accepted is, in itself, a major intervention" (Felitti and Anda 2014, p. 212).

In 2008, the CDC developed the ACE questions for inclusion into the Behavioral Risk Factor Surveillance System (BRFSS). State health departments are using these questions in their BRFSSs. This ACE data will be used to design similar measures for other countries (Anda et al. 2010). Currently the CDC and the World Health Organization (WHO) are pilot testing the use of ACE questions in health surveys around the world.

The existing literature, particularly the ACE study, relies heavily on cross-sectional designs that cannot demonstrate that childhood adversities cause particular outcomes, but only that childhood adversities are associated with certain outcomes. In addition, a number of researchers have pointed out that reliance on retrospective self-reports of childhood abuse is problematic. While the ACE study measured adverse experiences retrospectively, it has an ongoing longitudinal/prospective follow-up that has also demonstrated increased risk for negative outcomes. However, there are two important prospective studies that add to the evidence for the relationship between traumatic events and health consequences.

Prospective Studies

In a 23-year longitudinal study, beginning in 1987, of the impact of intrafamilial sexual abuse on female development, Trickett and colleagues (2011) used a cross-sequential design. Six assessments took place over the course of the study, with participants at a median age of 11 years at the first assessment and median age of 25 at the sixth assessment. The prospective, longitudinal nature of the study provided a unique opportunity to look at the continued cycle of violence and revictimization. Results from analyses of the fifth and sixth assessments (at ages 20 and 25) indicated that sexually abused females were almost twice as likely to have experienced sexual and physical revictimization as females who had not been sexually abused. The abused females were more likely to have been abused by older non-peers and to have experienced physical injury, and they reported almost four times as many incidents of self-inflicted harm and suicidality than comparison females. Sexual revictimization was significantly and positively correlated with PTSD symptoms, dissociation, and sexual preoccupation. At the sixth assessment, domestic violence was assessed; more than 53 percent of sexually abused women reported at least one domestic violence experience versus 24 percent of women in the comparison group.

The study also showed that sexually abused females, as compared with matched, non-abused females, differed across a number of biopsychosocial domains. Those who had been sexually abused had: lower resting rates of cortisol; HPA (hypothalamic-pituitary-adrenal) dysregulation and attenuation; increased rates of obesity; and earlier onset of puberty. They were more likely to: be depressed; be diagnosed with PTSD and dissociative symptoms; be physically and sexually re-victimized; be involved with an abusive partner; become pregnant as an adolescent; engage in self-mutilation; engage in risky sexual activity; abuse drugs and/or alcohol; and experience more trauma during their lifetimes. In addition, the study found evidence of immune system dysfunction and increased levels of catecholamine among the women who had been abused, as well as more major medical illness, more medical visits, and more hospitalizations. Study subjects resembled the ACE group population as well as those people diagnosed as having "complex trauma."

The authors stated that their results "underscore the high probability of the emergence of sleeper effects[3] and increasingly deviant developmental trajectories ... treatment of childhood sexual abuse should either continue across development or, at the very least, be revisited at various points in development" (Trickett, Noll, and Putnam 2011, p. 470). In fact, they felt it could be important to enroll sexually abused girls into long-term prevention programs when the abuse is first identified.

Widom and colleagues (Widom et al. 2012) used a prospective cohort design to look at physical health outcomes in abused and neglected children. They matched children, ages 0 to 11, with documented physical and sexual abuse and neglect during 1967 to 1971 with children without documented maltreatment. Both groups completed a medical status examination and interview during 2003 to 2005 (mean age = 41.2 years). This study also had a large heterogeneous sample varied in terms of race and ethnicity.

Results showed physical health outcomes according to blood tests results in middle childhood. Child maltreatment predicted above normal hemoglobin A1C, indicating poor glycemic control and risk for diabetes, and lower levels of albumin (B = -0.11). Specific types of abuse and neglect were associated with different health consequences. Childhood physical abuse predicted increased risk for malnutrition, lower albumin levels, higher blood urea nitrogen levels, and above normal HbA1c. Physical abuse also predicted increased risk for above normal C-reactive protein, suggesting risk for heart disease. For sexual abuse, there were nonsignificant trends for Hepatitis C and HIV and a significant increased risk of malnutrition. Neglect predicted above normal HbA1c and lower levels of albumin. There was a significant interaction between child abuse/neglect and gender for individuals with above normal HbA1c. Maltreated females overall and neglected females in particular were at increased risk of above normal HbA1c, whereas the results for males were in the opposite direction.

This prospective, long-term investigation shows evidence of the impact of childhood experience of abuse and neglect 30 years later on important health indicators. These findings provide clear evidence that childhood abuse and neglect affect adult health status in terms of increased risk for diabetes, lung disease, malnutrition, and vision problems. These findings do not reflect the extent to which these participants may have disorders controlled by medication, diet, or other treatments.

Women with Co-Occurring Disorders and Violence Study (WCDVS)

The Women with Co-Occurring Disorders and Violence Study (WCDVS), a five-year study funded by the Substance Abuse and Mental Health Services Administration (SAMHSA), was designed to look at the best practices for women who were diagnosed with substance abuse and mental illness who had also experienced violence or trauma histories. The sample, drawn from nine sites around the U.S., was 2,729 women, all of whom had had two or more previous treatment episodes. The women were provided either integrated services (integrating mental health, substance use, and trauma) or, in the comparison sites, treatment-as-usual (TAU).

WCDVS was one of the first and one of the largest studies to implement and evaluate the effectiveness of trauma-specific interventions and trauma-informed care in addressing the needs of consumer/survivors. All nine sites needed to demonstrate four common elements: comprehensiveness of services provided (delivery of eight core services); integration at the clinical and organizational levels; delivery of trauma-specific interventions; and consumer/survivor/recovering person involvement. A cross-site methodology evaluated the effectiveness of the trauma-integrated interventions. Trauma-integrated interventions were defined as the simultaneous provision of substance abuse, mental health, and trauma services to women in the intervention condition. Outcome measures were levels of PTSD/ trauma, substance use, and mental health symptoms. Service utilization and consumer satisfaction were also measured.

The lessons learned included: (1) integrated care showed significant results in reducing substance use by six months and reduction in mental health and posttraumatic symptoms by 12 months; (2) consumer/peer staff played important roles in providing care and in participating in research design; (3) trauma-specific interventions showed significant results in outcomes; and (4) trauma-informed practice led to increased engagement and increased retention.

Meta-evaluations of all the WCDVS sites (Cocozza et al. 2005; Morrissey et al. 2005a) reported that women in the intervention group showed better outcomes on drug use severity, PTSD severity (statistically significant), and mental health symptoms than women in the comparison group. Morrissey and colleagues (Morrissey et al. 2005b) also studied the characteristics of all participants to identify person-level characteristics that moderated outcomes and found that women with more severe baseline measures on behavioral health tended to report better outcomes at six months. There was a significant reduction in drug use at six months for the intervention group; this reduction leveled off at 12 months (but levels of use did not rise).[4] Both the intervention and the comparison group showed significant reductions in alcohol use. At 12 months, mental health symptoms and PTSD severity showed statistically significant reductions in the intervention group. Further analyses (Cusack, Morrissey, and Ellis 2008) confirmed that, at 12 months, treatment effects were largest for women with the most severe substance abuse and PTSD presentation.

In addition, eight points of contrast between sites were developed (Cocozza et al. 2005) to identify which of these were most salient in explaining the differences seen between the intervention and comparison groups (program-level factors). The eight dimensions were: (1) resource coordination and advocacy; (2) parenting training services; (3) women-focused services based on a strength-based and empowerment perspective; (4) consumer/survivor/recovering involvement; (5) trauma-specific interventions; (6) comprehensive, integrated treatment; (7) integrated counseling; and (8) number of core services received. One of these elements was a key contributor to improved outcomes: integrated counseling, which was defined by how many of the three key components (mental health, substance use, trauma) women reported receiving. While integrated counseling showed to be an important element, it was also understood by the sites that there needed to be an organizational or system-level infrastructure to support this work; viz., a trauma-informed system.

Data from the WCDVS was also reanalyzed by grouping the women by their baseline PTSD and substance abuse presentation and assessing the differential response to the integrated intervention (Cusack, Morrissey, and Ellis 2008). Treatment effects were largest for subgroups characterized by high levels of PTSD and substance use. The women in the most severe presentation (severe comorbid group) who received the integrated intervention had the greatest amount of symptom reduction in PTSD relative to the comparison condition; they were followed by women with the PTSD/drug profile and those with the PTSD profile. These three subgroups represent a population of "difficult to treat" women and would be the ones most in need of integrated trauma-specific interventions. The fact that these women obtained significantly and clinically meaningful change is highly encouraging.

Two studies of WCDVS focused upon costs, one assessing costs at six-months follow-up (Domino et al. 2005a) and one at twelve-months follow-up (Domino et al. 2005b). In both studies there were no significant differences in total costs between intervention and usual care conditions. On the basis of previous costs analyses, the authors state that programs that successfully reduce substance use and mental health symptoms, including PTSD, among clients with complex and high-end service needs would result in fewer hospitalizations, decreased use of crisis/emergency room services, and a reduction in criminal justice involvement.

Some specific WCDVS site data also adds to the accumulating knowledge about trauma integration into service programs. In the PROTOTYPES site (Gatz et al. 2007), the women in the intervention group improved more on the posttraumatic symptoms and showed lower severity of substance use severity at both baseline and 12 months than did women in the comparison group. Another finding from the PROTOTYPES site was that the rate of retention in treatment was significantly higher in the trauma-informed integrated treatment group than in the comparison group. Dropout was higher in the comparison condition than in the intervention condition throughout the first 12 weeks of treatment.

In addition, the PROTOTYPES site added a measure of coping skills (adapted from an unpublished measure by Lisa Najavits, developer of *Seeking Safety*). In the intervention group, women's use of coping skills increased from baseline to 12 months, but, in the comparison group, women's use of these skills decreased slightly from baseline to 12 months. Three-way repeated measures ANOVA results suggested that improvement on coping skills mediated improvements in emotional distress and substance use outcomes. This finding echoes a study by Brown and colleagues (Brown, Read, and Kahler 2003) that found participants (with both substance use disorders and PTSD) who had "remitted from PTSD at follow-up" reported significantly greater levels of positive coping and lower levels of negative coping than those in the unremitted group. In addition, both positive and negative coping were found to contribute significantly to percentage of days abstinent from substances. In a process evaluation of implementation of *Seeking Safety* (the trauma-specific intervention chosen by PROTOTYPES), when clients were asked what they felt were the most beneficial parts of the treatment, the things most often mentioned were coping skills, safety, understanding PTSD/trauma, and understanding oneself. "The group helped me stay in the treatment program"; "It [the group] affected the way I dealt with everything else in the facility, to tolerate the changes I was going through."

In a study on implementing *Seeking Safety* in four of the nine WCDVS sites, Brown and colleagues (Brown et al. 2007) investigated the implementation decisions the different sites made to optimize the compatibility of the trauma-specific intervention with site/client needs. Also, a total of 157 clients and 32 clinicians reported on satisfaction with various aspects of the intervention. The adaptations included: the number of sessions,[5] which ranged from 12 to 31; cultural adaptations, which added examples from different cultural groups; reading handouts for clients who had low reading skills; and replacing the word "PTSD" with the word "trauma."

With regard to client and clinician responses, the women clients were extremely positive about the group intervention. In rating specific topics, the clients rated all of them very helpful. The sessions that received the highest ratings were: "Healthy Relationships," "Self-Nurturing," "Honesty," "Setting Boundaries," "When Substances Control You," "Safety," "Coping with Triggers," "Detaching from Emotional Pain," and "Asking for Help." The elements of *Seeking Safety* rated highest across sites included the learning of coping skills, the safe coping list, and safety as a priority of treatment. Consistent with the ratings, comments in the women's own words reflected the three most important parts of the group intervention: (1) the group experience, i.e., feeling safe and bonding with other women who had similar experiences; (2) learning about coping skills; and (3) receiving information about the connection between PTSD/trauma and substance abuse. Clients described *Seeking Safety* as uniquely touching on their needs in a way that previous treatments had not.[6]

Clinicians implementing the intervention were also uniformly enthusiastic about *Seeking Safety*. When asked how long it took them to feel comfortable facilitating the group and mastering the manual, about 60 percent of the clinicians indicated that it took less than a month (typically three weeks). Two sites expressed the value of using co-facilitators for the group sessions.

A second analysis on retention was implemented by two sites from the WCDVS, the Boston site and PROTOTYPES site (Amaro et al. 2007). In this analysis, after controlling for baseline differences, the intervention group was more likely than the control group to have longer treatment stays, with a 31 percent lower risk of dropping out from treatment than that of the comparison group. In addition, longer treatment stay was associated with greater symptom improvement for mental health and substance use at six months.

Strategies to enhance integration at the organizational level included the establishment of coordinating bodies in each site and the integration of consumer/survivor/recovering individuals on all levels of the work. With regard to the establishment of a coordinating body, PROTOTYPES formed a systems change planning body called the Local Expert Group (LEG), which brought together providers from multiple systems, consumers, policymakers, and researchers who helped steer the course of the five-years project in Los Angeles County, California. (It is important to note that L.A. County is larger in population than many states.)

Chaired by Areta Crowell, Ph.D., former L.A. County Department of Director of Mental Health, the group included the Directors of Mental Health (past and present), Directors of Alcohol and Drug Use Disorders, Director of the Department of Child and Family Services, Director of the Department of Social Services; service providers including mental health, substance use disorders, and domestic violence; consumers and researchers from UCLA and USC. Early on (1997) the group decided to focus upon how welfare reform could be used as a "crisis" point or strategic lever for the facilitation of integration of trauma efforts and broader systems change.

In an interview for one of a number of monographs PROTOTYPES Systems Change Center wrote and disseminated on the WCDVS project (Backer and Howard 1998), Crowell stated:

> While I think of myself as a leader who is open to continuous quality improvement of the services we deliver and to new ways of thinking about the system, the experience of bringing together leaders with very different information and experience for brainstorming and creative thinking sessions went far beyond my usual experience. Each participant was helped to break out of the separate organizational 'silos' in which we operate so much of the time, silos which reflect profound differences in assumptions, language used, funding and expectations. We shared a common goal of trying to overcome legislative/bureaucratic divisions, to create wholeness in service response to the many and diverse needs of whole persons (Backer and Howard 1998, p. 3).

One other study from the WCDVS is important to discuss, viz., the Children's Subset study implemented by four of the nine WCDVS sites. The primary goal of this study (Noether et al. 2007) was to assess the efficacy of a skills-based intervention for promoting resilience in children who have been exposed to interpersonal violence and whose mothers have histories of co-occurring substance use, mental health disorders, and trauma. The sample consisted of 253 mothers and 253 children. The children participated in a trauma-informed intervention that consisted of a clinical assessment, resource coordination/advocacy, and a skills-building intervention group adapted from Peled and Davis (1995).

Children in the comparison group received treatment-as-usual. A baseline and four follow-up interviews at three months, six months, nine months, and 12 months were conducted. At six months, the mothers' positive six-month outcomes on the larger WCDVS significantly predicted their children's positive outcomes, as measured by the Behavioral and Emotional Rating Scale (BERS). Specifically, children whose mothers had positive outcomes did well regardless of treatment assignment, while children in the intervention group showed general improvement regardless of their mothers' six-month outcomes. Involvement in the intervention group led to significant improvement in the specific domains of positive interpersonal relationships, knowledge about safety, and positive self-identity. At 12 months, the mothers' 12-month outcomes no longer appeared to play a significant role in predicting their children's positive outcomes.

Treatment condition, however, did play a significant role, with the intervention group showing more positive outcomes. Qualitative findings from interviews with the mothers supported the quantitative finding that children benefited from the skills-building intervention. The mothers commented that their children had made improvements in a number of behavioral and emotional areas, including improved ability to communicate and express themselves, reduced anger, more positive attitude, more honesty, and improved listening skills. For many of the children, their mothers' treatment and recovery represented a respite from a chaotic and dangerous lifestyle. In fact, particularly for those children and mothers entering residential treatment, admission into treatment may end, at least for a period of time, both domestic violence and the witnessing of domestic violence. Parental treatment offers a window of opportunity to reach children early in the development of childhood problems during a time when the parent is motivated to make dramatic life changes and is supported by a nurturing environment and supportive staff.

Trauma-informed organizational and systems change has been an important concept in changing the fragmented and siloes systems of care that individuals and families experience when accessing services in health, mental health, and substance abuse treatment systems. The ACE study and the WCDVS, as well as some recent prospective studies, have been of invaluable help in informing our first steps toward person-centered, trauma-informed collaborative care. The next chapters are meant to guide us further along on the journey toward transformation.

Notes

1 In a recent study, Wade and colleagues investigated the breadth of adverse experiences to which low-income, urban children are exposed. The stressors that were not found in the *ACE Questionnaire* included: community violence and crime; economic hardships; and discrimination (Wade et al. 2014).
2 Framingham risk factors include: age, gender, smoking, total cholesterol, HDL cholesterol, systolic blood pressure, and use of BP medication.
3 "Sleeper effects" as used here refers to effects of trauma that show up many years after the trauma experience itself.
4 A number of publications by other groups have indicated that there was no significant reduction in substance abuse. I believe this is because the authors of those publications only read the WCDVS's publications at 12 months and did not understand that the leveling off in substance abuse noted at that time was, in fact, a leveling off at the reduced level shown at six months, not at the original level of drug use.
5 This was recommended as a possible adaptation by the author/developer of *Seeking Safety*, Lisa Najavits.
6 The women in the study had a minimum of two previous treatment episodes (mental health and/or substance abuse treatment).

References

Amaro, H, Chernoff, M, Brown, V et al. 2007, Does Integrated Trauma-Informed Substance Abuse Treatment Increase Treatment Retention, *Journal of Community Psychology*, vol. 35, no. 7, pp. 845–862.

Anda, R, Butchart, A, Felitti, V, and Brown, DW 2010, Building a Framework for Global Surveillance of the Public Health Implications of Adverse Childhood Experiences, *American Journal of Preventive Medicine*, vol. 39 no. 1, pp. 93–98.

Backer, TE and Howard, EA 1998, *Integrated Service Programs for Women with Multiple Vulnerabilities*, Culver City, CA, PROTOTYPES System Change Center.

Brown, DW, Anda, RA, Tiemeier, H et al. 2009, Adverse Childhood Experiences and the Risk of Premature Mortality, *American Journal of Preventive Medicine*, vol. 37, no. 5, pp. 389–396.

Brown, PJ, Read, JP, and Kahler, CW 2003, Comorbid Posttraumatic Stress Disorder and Substance Use Disorders: Treatment Outcomes and the Role of Coping, in P Ouimette and PJ Brown (eds.), *Trauma and Substance Abuse: Causes, Consequences, and Treatment of Comorbid Disorders*, Washington, DC, American Psychological Association, pp. 171–188.

Brown, VB, Najavits, LM, Cadiz, S et al. 2007, Implementing an Evidence-Based Practice: Seeking Safety group, *Journal of Psychoactive Drugs*, vol. 39, pp. 231–240.

Chen, E, Matthews, KA, and Boyce, WT 2002, Socioeconomic Differences in Children's Health: How and Why Do These Relationships Change with Age, *Psychology Bulletin*, vol. 128, no. 2, pp. 295–329.

Cocozza, JJ, Jackson, EW, Hennigan, K et al. 2005, Outcomes for Women with Co-Occurring Disorders and Trauma: Program-Level Effects, *Journal of Substance Abuse Treatment*, vol. 28, no. 2, pp. 109–119.

Cusack, KJ, Morrissey, JP, and Ellis, AR 2008, Targeting Trauma-Related Interventions and Improving Outcomes for Women with Co-Occurring Disorders, *Administration and Policy in Mental Health*, vol. 35, no. 3, pp. 147–158.

Domino, ME, Morrissey, JP, Chung, S et al. 2005a, Service Use and Costs for Women with Co-Occurring Mental and Substance Use Disorders and a History of Violence, *Psychiatric Services*, vol. 56, no. 10, pp. 1223–1232.

Domino, M, Morrissey, JP, Nadlicki-Patterson, T, and Chung, S 2005b, Service Costs for Women with Co-Occurring Disorders and Trauma, *Journal of Substance Abuse Treatment*, vol. 28, no. 2, pp. 135–143.

Dong, M, Giles, WH, Felitti, VJ et al. 2004, Insights into Causal Pathways for Ischemic Heart Disease: Adverse Childhood Experiences Study, *Circulation*, vol. 110, no. 13, pp. 1761–1766.

Felitti, VJ and Anda, RF 2010, The Relationship of Adverse Childhood Experiences to Adult Medical Disease, Psychiatric Disorders, and Sexual Behavior: Implications for Healthcare, in RA Lanius, E Vermetten, and C Pain (eds.), *The Impact of Early Life Trauma on Health and Disease: The Hidden Epidemic*, Cambridge, England, Cambridge University Press, pp. 77–88.

Felitti, VJ and Anda, RF 2014, The Lifelong Effects of Adverse Childhood Experiences, in *Chadwick's Child Maltreatment, 4th Edition, Volume 2*, St. Louis, MO, STM Learning, Inc., pp. 203–215.

Felitti, VJ, Anda, RF, Nordenberg, D et al. 1998, Relationship of Childhood Abuse and Household Dysfunction to Many of the Leading Causes of Death in Adults: The Adverse Childhood Experiences (ACE) Study, *American Journal of Preventive Medicine*, vol. 14, no. 4, pp. 245–258.

Gatz, M, Brown, V, Hennigan, K et al. 2007, Effectiveness of an Integrated Trauma-Informed Approach to Treating Women with Co-Occurring Disorders and Histories of Trauma: The Los Angeles Site Experience, *Journal of Community Psychology*, vol. 35, no. 7, pp. 863–877.

Holmes, TH and Rahe, RH 1967, The Social Readjustment Rating Scale, *Journal of Psychosomatic Research*, vol. 11, pp. 213–218.

McEwen, BS 1998, Protective and Damaging Effects of Stress Mediators, *New England Journal of Medicine*, vol. 338, pp. 171–179.

Morrissey, JP, Ellis, AR, Gatz, M et al. 2005a, Outcomes for Women with Co-Occurring Disorders and Trauma: Program and Person-Level Effects, *Journal of Substance Abuse Treatment*, vol. 28, no. 2, pp. 121–133.

Morrissey, JP, Jackson, EW, Ellis, AR et al. 2005b, Twelve-Month Outcomes of Trauma-Informed Interventions for Women with Co-Occurring Disorders, *Psychiatric Services*, vol. 56, no. 10, pp. 1213–1222.

Noether, CD, Brown, V, Finkelstein, N et al. 2007, Promoting Resiliency in Children of Mothers with Co-Occurring Disorders and Histories of Trauma: Impact of a Skills Based Intervention Program on Child Outcomes, *Journal of Community Psychology*, vol. 35, no. 7, pp. 823–843.

Peled, E and Davis, D 1995, *Groupwork with Children of Battered Women*, Thousand Oaks, CA, SAGE Publications.

Rahe, RH and Arthur, J 1978, Life Change and Illness Studies: Past History and Future Directions, *Journal of Human Stress*, vol. 4, pp. 3–15.

Repetti, RL, Taylor, SE, and Seeman, TE 2002, Risky Families: Family Social Environments and the Mental and Physical Health of Offspring, *Psychology Bulletin*, vol. 128, no. 2, pp. 330–366.

Taylor, SE 2010, Mechanisms Linking Early Stress to Adult Health Outcomes, *Proceedings of the National Academy of Sciences of the United States*, vol. 107, no. 19, pp. 8507–8512.

Trickett, PK, Noll, JG, and Putnam, FW 2011, The Impact of Sexual Abuse on Female Development: Lessons from a Multigenerational, Longitudinal Research Study, *Development and Psychopathology*, vol. 23, no. 2, pp. 453–476.

Wade, R, Shea, JA, Rubin, D, and Wood, J 2014, Adverse Childhood Experiences of Low-Income Urban Youth, *Pediatrics*, vol. 134, no. 1, pp. 13–20.

Widom, CS, Czaja, SJ, Bentley, T, and Johnson, MS 2012, A Prospective Investigation of Physical Health Outcomes in Abused and Neglected Children: New Findings from a 30-Year Follow-Up, *American Journal of Public Health*, vol. 102, no. 6, pp. 1135–1144.

Chapter 3

Populations Needing Special Focus

There are a number of specific populations that are at high risk of experiencing traumatic events and at high risk of re-traumatization. These populations include: women (pregnant and postpartum women, women who have lost custody of a child/children, and women who experience domestic violence/intimate partner violence); men who are survivors of sexual and/or physical abuse; individuals living with HIV/AIDS; children (children in the child welfare system, children of incarcerated parents, and children experiencing childhood adversity); and lesbian, gay, bisexual, and transgender individuals.

Pregnant and Postpartum Women

Recently there has been increasing concern regarding childbirth trauma (Declerq et al. 2008; Olde et al. 2006; Mojab 2009). "Birth may be traumatic when a mother experiences an actual or perceived threat to her or her baby's life, serious injury to herself or her baby, threat to her or her baby's physical integrity, or her baby's death" (Mojab 2009, p. 67). It is estimated that up to one third of childbearing women report a traumatic birth experience (Mojab 2009). In a review of the literature, Bailham and Joseph (2003) found that 25 to 30 percent of women experienced PTSD symptoms at a subclinical level and/or met criteria for partial PTSD shortly after giving birth and that 1 to 6 percent develop full-blown PTSD. The combination of depression and trauma symptoms in the mother may negatively impact her interactions with the baby, causing breastfeeding problems, avoiding the baby, and anxiety about the baby; it may also cause her to avoid health care providers. Screening for maternal risk factors before birth of the child and screening again for symptoms of traumatic stress after birth will be helpful in identifying the need for additional psychological services for the mother. Three predictors of childbirth trauma have been reported: prenatal factors, include a history of sexual abuse and having a first child; characteristics of the birth experience, including emergency caesarean sections, medical complications concerning the mother or child, and extreme pain during delivery; and postnatal factors, including inadequate low social support.

With regard to maternal depression, the widespread absence of attention to the mother-child relationship in the treatment of depression in women with young children is another striking example of the gap between science and practice. Abundant clinical research indicates that the successful treatment of a mother's depression does not generally translate into comparable recovery in her young child, unless there is an explicit therapeutic focus on their dyadic relationship.

Payments mechanism that require (or provide incentives for) the coordination of child and parent medical and/or mental health services for the treatment of maternal depression offers a promising strategy for addressing this gap.

As part of an ongoing project, funded by SAMHSA, Brown and Melchior implemented screening for postpartum depression in a family-centered, trauma-informed residential drug treatment program for pregnant and postpartum women (PROTOTYPES Women's Center). Women were screened two weeks following the birth of their children, and those women whose scores indicated postpartum depression were seen immediately by the Clinical Director or Supervising Social Worker to enhance treatment planning. Of the women who were screened, 39.7 percent had scores indicating major postpartum depression. Another 27.9 percent had a score suggestive of significant symptoms of postpartum depression. Addressing co-occurring postpartum depression and substance use disorders while a woman is in treatment, particularly in a program with supports in place to help her bond with her child, may lead to improved outcomes for the mother and the child.

Women Who Have Lost Custody of Their Children

Women feel a devastating sense of grief and loss when they lose custody of their child to child welfare. This loss is complicated by feelings of shame, helplessness, anger, and emotional numbness. It is also important to recognize that women with trauma histories (the majority of women involved with child welfare) are more likely to experience subsequent grief as complex trauma. Many women who experience custody loss are vulnerable and disadvantaged; they are often marginalized because of poverty, socio-economic status, race, mental health issues, substance use problems, and immigration status. Many may have been removed from their own parents' care as children. Novac and colleagues (2006) describe a number of trauma responses to custody loss:

1. Numbing/self-punishment—women may increase their drug use to manage feelings of shame, guilt, isolation, hopelessness, helplessness, and anger.
2. Powerlessness—women may feel like they were not part of the court process of taking their child and did not have a voice in it. Their legal representatives may not always explain the legal proceedings in a way that the women can understand.
3. Betrayal—feelings of betrayal by the child welfare worker who used information in proceedings against them.
4. Shame—women feel judged as "not fit to parent."
5. Unrealistic expectations—for mothers to regain custody, they must respond to a barrage of expectations, e.g., urine tests, mental health assessments, drug treatment, parenting training, and supervised child visits.
6. Feeling "dead alone"—if their children are adopted, birth mothers are often left feeling devastated and re-traumatized. Often, they will have another child to heal the loss.

Overall, the real or perceived threat of losing custody of a child creates a situation of "power over" parents that would be very difficult for most people to manage, and, for those who have a history of traumatic events, it can trigger responses related to past situations over which they had no control (e.g., sexual and/or physical abuse) and which overwhelmed them.

Women Who Are Victims of Domestic Violence (DV)/ Intimate Partner Violence (IPV)

Intimate partner violence is an important public health problem. Approximately 42.4 million (35.6%) women in the U.S. have experienced rape, physical violence, and/or stalking by an intimate partner at some point in their lifetimes (Black et al. 2011). IPV refers to an ongoing pattern of coercive control maintained through physical, psychological, sexual, and/or economic abuse. Comprehensive reviews of the physical health consequences of IPV report multiple health outcomes, including chronic pain, cardiovascular problems, gastrointestinal disorders, head injuries, neurological problems (Stockman, Hayashi, and Campbell 2015), and disordered eating patterns in ethnic minority women. IPV intersects with HIV through multiple mechanisms, including forced sex with an infected partner. The psychological impact of IPV on ethnic minority women includes higher rates of depression, PTSD, and suicidality.

There is a relatively high likelihood that survivors of IPV have experienced many other types of trauma (e.g., child abuse, community violence, sexual harassment, sexual assault, and immigration-related trauma). One factor unique with regard to trauma for women with IPV is the likelihood of an ongoing, stressful contact/ relationship with the abuser, continuing even after separation if there are children (custody, visitation) or if the perpetrator continues to threaten her.

A centerpiece of the Affordable Care Act (ACA) of 2010, Section 2713, states a commitment to preventive services for women, and one of the key preventive services included in the guidelines for ACA implementation adopted by the U.S. Department of Health and Human Services (DHHS) is screening and counseling for intimate partner and interpersonal violence. In 2013, the DHHS Coordinating Committee for Women's Health convened the Intimate Partner Violence Screening and Counseling Research Symposium to identify research gaps related to IPV screening and counseling in primary health care settings and to develop enhanced guidelines. The system envisioned by the symposium was one in which each health care setting is the "right door" for screening and accessing IPV services. The participants recommended that IPV screening be part of a comprehensive assessment that considers the multiple health and behavioral risk factors associated with IPV, including history of trauma, substance abuse, sexual risk behaviors, symptoms of PTSD, and depression. Screening should also occur during follow-up visits so that providers can assess their patients for important changes in risk and/or safety. In addition, it was recommended that IPV screening and referrals be delivered in a medical home or other health care setting that follows a patient-centered, team-based, and coordinated care model. Ghandour and colleagues state, "we envision that all healthcare services are delivered using a trauma-informed approach" (Ghandour, Campbell, and Llyod 2015, p. 58). It is also important that health care providers inquire about the health and safety of children who may be exposed to IPV and other traumas. Providers need to acknowledge the fear among victims that disclosure of IPV might lead to the involvement of child welfare, criminal justice, and immigration.

The percentage of women seeking drug abuse treatment who have experienced recent IPV ranges from 25 to 57 percent, making this an important group to target for intervention (Gilbert et al. 2006). Findings from meta analyses of research in this area show consistent patterns of bidirectional relationships between alcohol use/abuse and exposure to IPV (Devries et al. 2014). Drug use also has been found to increase the odds of IPV; Moore and colleagues (2008) found three times greater odds of IPV occurring in couples where there was drug involvement. There is a complex relationship between IPV, drug use, and HIV risk due to: a dependence upon one's abusive partner for drugs; coerced sexual behavior to obtain drugs; and an impaired ability to negotiate condom use with an abusive partner at high risk for or infected with HIV. Substance abuse treatment programs need to screen for IPV and include interventions that address IPV and unhealthy/unsafe relationships. It should be noted that both substance use disorders (SUDs) and PTSD are elevated in women with histories of IPV (Dutton et al. 2006). SUDs and PTSD may both act to heighten risk of exposure to IPV by impairing judgment, increasing risk-taking, or triggering partner aggression.

Women are at increased risk for IPV during their pregnancies, and IPV during pregnancy has significant negative consequences for both the woman and her fetus. Experiencing IPV during pregnancy is associated with: missing prenatal care or waiting to enter care until the third trimester; poor nutrition; alcohol and drug use; depression; and, of course, maternal injury. IPV effects on the neonate include low birth weight and preterm birth. There are a number of studies that have also shown increased risk of perinatal death. Prenatal care presents a unique opportunity for health care providers to foster trusting relationships with women, thereby increasing the likelihood of IPV detection and mitigating its negative consequences to both mother and child. As discussed later in this chapter, home visiting is a targeted intervention designed to prevent or reduce IPV victimization.

Male Abuse Survivors

Male survivors of childhood sexual abuse have reported that health care providers show skepticism about the idea that they have been sexually abused, particularly if the abuser was a woman, and/or the providers minimized the seriousness of the abuse. If the abuse was by another man, the survivor may experience fear that he will be seen as homosexual. The image of the male as "strong and always in control" adds another difficulty for male survivors; they may deny that they have been abused, and they do not seek help for their abuse. I have seen this very clearly with men who have been in prison for their drug use and drug sales. In addition, when visiting a prison program as a member of a national advisory committee, the men did not acknowledge any trauma and talked about their very helpful "anger management" group (which was a trauma group renamed for the men); the women discussed openly how they felt their "trauma groups" were the most important groups. It should also be mentioned that the men who were abused sexually by clergymen not only had fears about their own sexual orientation, but had been abused at the hands of a trusted and beloved mentor (betrayal trauma).

Fallot and Bebout (2012) recommend that men should be asked about their "exposure to violence" in the intake process; framing trauma experience as exposure to violence is more likely to elicit disclosure. Also, they recommend prefacing questions with some data about the pervasiveness of violence to make it easier for men to discuss their histories. Whereas women may enter trauma services already able to acknowledge vulnerability, many men may find it difficult to label, describe, and perhaps experience a wide range of emotions, especially the "softer ones." The authors state that a man who is reluctant to talk about his emotional life is not necessarily "resistant" or "in denial"; that male trauma survivors face a "disconnection dilemma," an almost irresolvable conflict between their identity as men and their experiences of powerlessness and vulnerability associated with victimization.

Acknowledging fear and loss of control is tantamount to weakness and threatens men's identity as powerful and in control. Fallot and Bebout state that "developing a broader range of options for expressing emotions and for being in relationships is a key trauma recovery skill for men" (Fallot and Bebout 2012, p. 169). Reframing problematic behaviors, such as distrust, hypervigilance, and hair-trigger aggression, as understandable attempts to survive is another key element in recovery. Sharing power in a way that gives men maximum choice and voice in their recovery will lead to their demonstrating more openness with providers. *Motivational Interviewing (MI)* is among the primary ways in which choice and control become client priorities. (See Chapter 9 for a discussion of *MI*.)

David and Brannon (1976) identified four components of traditional masculine ideology: (1) that men should not be feminine ("no sissy stuff"); (2) that men should strive to be respected for successful achievements; (3) that men should never show weakness; and (4) that men should seek adventure and risk, even accepting violence if necessary. Levant and colleagues (2009) proposed that mild to moderate alexithymia ("without words for emotions") or a socialized pattern of restrictive emotionality reflects a sense of vulnerability and that one normative masculine role requirement is the restriction of emotional expression. They developed a psychoeducational program for alexithymia reduction treatment (ART).

Individuals Living with HIV/AIDS

With the introduction of combination antiretroviral therapy (ART), HIV was transformed from a fatal disease to one that was chronic, but manageable. Consequently, health-related quality of life (HRQL) and the management of comorbid chronic medical conditions have been moved to the forefront of overall health care for persons living with HIV. Research has shown that persons living with HIV are more likely than the general US population to have significant trauma histories (Cavanaugh, Hansen, and Sullivan 2010; Plotzker, Metzger, and Holmes 2007) and comorbid medical conditions (e.g., coronary artery disease, Hepatitis C) (Dong et al. 2004; Gander and Vonkanel 2006).

Nightingale and colleagues (2011) used path analysis to explore the relationships among prior trauma stressors, HIV diagnosis as a traumatic stressor, HIV-related trauma symptoms, comorbid chronic medical conditions, and health-related quality of life among patients living with HIV. Study participants were predominantly Black (89%) and men (73%) but represented all sexual orientations. Among them, 33 percent reported a history of severe traumatic stressors prior to learning HIV diagnosis and 31 percent reported experiencing their HIV status as a traumatic stressor. Thirty-nine percent had one comorbid condition, 11 percent had two, and 3 percent had three comorbid conditions. The authors recommend screening for trauma history and current trauma symptoms and offering additional support following an HIV diagnosis to attempt to prevent re-traumatization, ongoing risk behavior, and poor treatment adherence. The burden of chronic diseases in patients with HIV also needs further attention. Both trauma and anti-retroviral therapy are associated with the development of a number of chronic comorbid conditions, including coronary artery disease, diabetes and renal diseases, pulmonary disease, and chronic pain.

A broad literature describes factors associated with adherence to anti-retroviral therapy for HIV and consistently identifies the contributions of mental health disorders and substance use disorders to non-adherence. Recent studies have begun to focus on other psychosocial factors, such as traumatic events, as contributors to nonadherence (Lesserman et al. 2008). Mugavero and colleagues (2009) prospectively measured the influence of incident stressful and traumatic events on changes in self-reported antiretroviral therapy adherence and on virologic failure in the CHASE (Coping with HIV/AIDS in the SouthEast) cohort over 27 months of follow-up. The CHASE cohort consists of HIV-infected individuals receiving care at one of eight infectious disease clinics in five U.S. cities. Severe stressors included divorce/separation, death or illness of an immediate family member, major financial problems, more than a week in prison, and sexual and physical assault.

At baseline, patients reported a median of three types of traumatic events during their lifetimes. During the 27-month period following baseline, patients reported a median number of nine new stressful events, including three new severely stressful events, and 21 percent reported non-adherence to anti-retroviral therapy. Participants experiencing the median number of new stressful events (N = 9) had more than twice the predicted odds of nonadherence at follow-up compared with those as with no new stressful events (after controlling for relevant covariates). New stressful (but not traumatic) events were also associated with an increased risk of virologic failure over the follow-up period. The authors recommend that providers address histories of severe traumatic events, but also pay attention to less severe, but more frequent, stressful events that may occur while the patient is in care. In addition, they recommend that interventions teaching coping skills be implemented to maintain adherence to treatment and improve health outcomes.

Despite the availability of effective antiretroviral therapy, women face surprisingly high rates of HIV-related morbidity and mortality; trauma is increasingly recognized as an important factor in poor outcomes of HIV in women. Machtinger and colleagues have not only shown that women, and particularly women of color, living with HIV have high rates of trauma, but also that recent trauma was associated with antiretroviral failure. (See more detailed descriptions of these research findings in Chapter 10.)

The association between IPV and risk for HIV infection has been the focus of a growing body of research, which includes: (1) studies showing IPV as a risk factor for HIV infection among women and men; (2) studies showing both past and current violent victimization increasing HIV risk behaviors (e.g., substance abuse); (3) studies showing violence or fear of violence from an intimate partner as an impediment or as a consequence of HIV testing; (4) studies showing partner violence as a risk factor for sexually transmitted infections (STIs), which increase the rate of HIV infections; (5) studies showing the difficulties of negotiating safe sex behavior for abused partners; and (6) data suggesting that various adverse health effects related to IPV compromise women's immune systems in a way that increases their risk of HIV.

Children

Research has shown that childhood abuse or maltreatment are significant risk factors for later psychological disorders (e.g., depression), as well as physical problems (see discussion of ACE Study in Chapter 2). Co-occurring childhood adversities are common (Edwards et al. 2003; Dong et al. 2004). Trauma exposure in young children, during a sensitive developmental period, raises the risk of enduring changes in their stress-related systems and other brain centers. Research by Kisiel and colleagues (2009) suggests that early experience of chronic, interpersonal trauma leads to a cascade of neurobiological events, resulting in a range of trauma reactions, including affect dysregulation and decreased impulse control.

In a more recent study, Kisiel and colleagues (2014) examined patterns of trauma exposure and symptoms in more than 16,000 children in child welfare in Illinois. Children exposed to both interpersonal violence (physical and/or sexual abuse) and attachment-based ("non-violent") traumas (e.g., multiple out-of-home placements) had significantly higher levels of affective/physiological, attentional/behavioral, and self/relational dysregulation (in addition to posttraumatic stress symptoms) as compared to youth with either type of trauma alone or other types of trauma experiences. The authors state that these findings from a large-scale study "offer initial support for the utility of a developmental trauma framework as a construct for trauma-focused assessment and treatment planning"[1] (Kisiel et al. 2014, p. 11).

In the U.S., as reported by the Administration for Children and Families (ACF), 700,000 children per year are victims of trauma (ACF 2015). The estimated 20 percent of children who have serious emotional disturbance represent a public health crisis, since research has shown that 75 to 80 percent of these children do not receive services (Kataoka, Zhang, and Wells 2002). Using data from the national evaluation of the Comprehensive Community Mental Health Services program from 1997 to 2000, Whitson and Connell (2016) studied the effect of history of exposure to potentially traumatic experiences (PTEs) on trajectories in behavioral outcomes during a three-year period. The study sample included 9,198 children and their families. Caregivers' reports indicated that 59.8 percent of the children had exposure to PTEs (48.3% had witnessed DV; 25.5%, physical abuse; and 21%, sexual abuse). The need for a special focus on children who have experienced trauma is further discussed in Chapter 11.

In 2014, according to the Centers for Disease Control and Prevention (CDC) approximately 10,000 children and adolescents died as a result of traumatic injury (CDC 2015). More than 7.8 million were treated in emergency rooms/departments, and 166,000 of these were hospitalized (CDC 2016b). Each year 66,000 children have a new diagnosis of cancer, heart disease, or diabetes, or have organ transplantation (AHRQ 2007). These diagnoses and the treatments these children receive can be traumatic. (See discussion of the work of Kassam-Adams in Chapters 6 and 7.)

As will be further discussed in Chapter 11, many children served by the child welfare system have experienced at least one major traumatic event, and many have complex trauma histories (Taylor, Wilson & Igelman 2006). Abuse and neglect often occur in the home, with concurrent exposure to domestic violence, substance abuse, and community violence. As a consequence, these children also face removal from the home and multiple placements in out-of-home care, thus adding to their traumatic experiences. Although child welfare professionals may be aware of the traumatic experiences that brought the child to their attention, they may not be aware of the child's complete trauma history. For example, sexual abuse by an outsider (not within the home) is not typically assessed; most reports focus on the actions of the caregivers (Saar et al.).

Children of incarcerated parents are another group of children dealing with trauma. The incarceration rates in the U.S., particularly among poor and ethnic minority individuals, rose dramatically in the 1980s and 1990s, largely as a result of policies designed to "get tough" on drug offenders (Western and Wildeman 2009). In 2007, 1.7 million children had a parent in state or federal prison, an increase of 80 percent since 1991. Black children were 7.5 times more likely than white children to have an incarcerated parent (Glaze and Maruschak 2008). This experience (as is true with many of the ACE events) is traumatic for both the parents and the child. The Adoption and Safe Families Act (ASFA), enacted in 1997, mandates commencement of proceedings to terminate parental rights once a child has been in foster care for 15 out of the most recent 22 months (ASFA 1997). (See discussion of "time clocks" in Chapter 4.) The vast majority of children with incarcerated fathers live with their mothers during the incarceration period, while children with incarcerated mothers are more likely to live with grandparents, other family members, or in foster care (Glaze and Maruschak 2008; Poehlmann et al. 2010). It should also be noted that for young children, traumatic experiences are not necessarily linked to a specific event, but may result from the accumulation of adverse childhood events (e.g., parent incarcerated, loss of financial and emotional support from the incarcerated parent, etc.) and/or the physiological experience of fear associated with the failure of the caregiver to provide soothing, safety, and security.

Children are more likely to access mental health services through primary care and schools than through mental health clinics. Seventy-five percent of children under 12 see a pediatrician at least once per year, whereas only 4 percent see a mental health professional (Costello et al. 1998). The pediatric health care system provides the potential for continuing and ongoing relationships between providers and both children and families, which can serve as an inroad for identifying and initiating specialized care for traumatized children (Stuber et al. 2006). Concepts such as family-centered care and the growing move toward parent presence during emergency and critical procedures for children demonstrate the possible points of common ground/overlap between trauma-informed care and health care. By integrating trauma-informed care, providers can reduce the impact of difficult or frightening medical events and procedures, as well as helping children and families cope with their emotional reactions to illness and injury.

In 2010, Congress authorized the Maternal, Infant, and Early Childhood Home Visiting Program (HVP) to support evidence-based home visiting services for at-risk pregnant women and parents with young children up to kindergarten entry. Research reported by the Administration on Children and Family has shown that home visits by a nurse, social worker, or trained peer improves the lives of children and families by preventing child abuse and neglect, supporting positive parenting, improving maternal and child health, and promoting child development and school readiness (Sama-Miller et al. 2016). As of 2015, 17 models have met the criteria for evidence-based practices.

Understanding the role that toxic stress plays in mediating the lifelong consequences of childhood adversity highlights important opportunities for early intervention and prevention. Home visiting is one strategy for improving the capacity of caregivers and preventing some of the childhood adverse events. A number of home visiting programs are expanding their capacity to serve high-risk families by integrating a mental health provider into their programs. Since 2009, SAMHSA has funded a number of programs through its Project LAUNCH (Linking Actions for Unmet Needs in Children's Health) grant program; some grantees have developed models integrating mental health consultation into home visiting programs. Among the grantees funded between 2009 and 2011, eight are implementing early childhood mental health consultation within 12 home visiting programs.

In a randomized controlled study of *Child FIRST* (Child and Family Interagency, Resources, Support, and Training), a home-based, psychotherapeutic, parent-child intervention embedded in a system of care, Lowell and colleagues (2011) found that the *Child FIRST* intervention, a home-based intervention translating research into early childhood practice, had a strong effect on access to services at both six-month and 12-month assessments. *Child FIRST* families received a mean of 14.7 "wanted services" as opposed to Usual Care families, who received 5.1. *Child FIRST* families had significantly greater numbers of needs met in all domains then Usual Care. The *Child FIRST* intervention showed positive benefits in two key areas: children's language and socio-emotional/behavioral problems. *Child FIRST* was also successful in improving parenting outcomes, including parenting stress, mental health symptoms, and suspected child abuse and neglect. Another critical finding was that families in *Child FIRST* were significantly less likely to be involved with Child Protective Services three years after enrollment than were families in the "usual care" arm of the study.

The lifelong effects of early childhood adversity on physical and behavioral health underscore the need to move beyond risk factor identification to the critical task of developing and implementing more effective practices for reducing toxic stress and adverse childhood events and mitigating their impacts as early as possible. Shonkoff and colleagues (2012) present an ecobiodevelopmental framework that allows us to think about the biological mechanisms that underlie the link between early adversities and important adult health outcomes. Although genetic variability clearly plays a role in stress reactivity, early experiences and environmental influences also can have considerable impact. Both animal and human studies suggest that fetal exposure to maternal stress can influence later stress responsiveness. The most extensively studied physiological responses to stress involve the activation of the hypothalamic-pituitary-adrenocortical axis and the sympathetic-adrenomedullary system, which results in increased levels of stress hormones. Whereas transitory increases in these stress hormones are protective, excessively high levels or prolonged exposure can be quite harmful. This cumulative stress-induced burden on overall body functioning and the aggregated costs, both physiologic and psychological, required for coping and returning to homeostasis are referred to as allostatic load (McEwen 1998).

The National Scientific Council on the Developing Child (2014) proposed a taxonomy of three types of stress responses in young children—positive, tolerable, and toxic. Positive refers to a physiological state that is brief and mild to moderate in magnitude. Central to the concept of positive stress (e.g., getting an immunization) is the presence of a caring and responsive adult who helps the child cope with the stressor, thereby providing a protective effect. Tolerable stress refers to an exposure to nonnormative experiences that present a greater magnitude of threat (e.g., serious illness or injury to a family member). Whether this type of stress response is tolerable depends on the extent to which there is a protective adult available. Toxic stress results from strong, frequent, or prolonged activation of the body's stress response systems in the absence of the buffering protection of a supportive relationship (e.g., child abuse or neglect). The essential characteristic of this response is the disruption of brain circuitry and other systems during sensitive developmental periods. This disruption may result in anatomic changes (e.g., in brain structure) and/or physiologic dysregulations (hyperactivity in the amygdala) that are the precursors of later impairments in learning and behavior, as well as the roots of chronic, stress-related physical and mental illness.

A unified, trauma-informed, science-based approach to early childhood policy and practice across multiple sectors (including primary health care, child care and early education, child welfare, and mental health, among many others) could provide a framework for a new era in community-based programs. Enhanced collaboration between pediatricians and community-based agencies could be an important vehicle for new intervention strategies, rather than simply improved coordination between existing services. Interventions that strengthen the capacities of families and communities to protect young children from the disruptive effects of toxic stress are likely to promote healthier brain development and enhanced physical and mental well-being. Significant reductions in chronic disease could be achieved across the life course by decreasing the number and the severity of adverse experiences and by strengthening the protective relationships that help mitigate the harmful effects of toxic stress. Each system that touches the lives of children, as well as mothers before, during, and after pregnancy, offers an opportunity to leverage this rapidly growing knowledge base to strengthen the capacities that make lifelong healthy development possible. "To this end, science suggests that two areas are particularly ripe for fresh thinking: the child welfare system and the treatment of maternal depression" (Shonkoff et al. 2012, p. 241).

With regard to child welfare, Family Drug Treatment Courts (FDTCs) are designed to serve the multiple needs of families involved in the child welfare system who have substance abuse problems. There are more than 300 FDTCs currently operating in the U.S. Research results suggest that FDTCs are effective in improving treatment outcomes, increasing the likelihood of family reunification, and decreasing the time children spend in foster care. FDTCs were adapted from the adult drug court model and include frequent court hearings, drug testing, intensive judicial monitoring, provision of timely substance abuse treatment and wrap-around services, and rewards and sanctions based on service compliance (CSAT 2004). The team generally includes judicial, child welfare, substance abuse treatment representatives, and sometimes includes related systems such as mental health, children's treatment, domestic violence, and housing. The primary goal is to support parental sobriety and work toward family reunification, while maintaining child safety. For further discussion of child welfare and FDTCs, see Chapter 11.

Lesbian, Gay, Bisexual, and Transgender Clients[2]

The Institute of Medicine (2011) and the Office of Disease Prevention and Health Promotion (2010) identified health disparities and risk and protective factors among the lesbian, gay, and bisexual (LGB) population as one of the main gaps in current health research. Population and community-based studies have reported that a greater proportion of LGB adults experienced childhood sexual, physical, and emotional abuse than did heterosexual adults (Rothman, Exner, and Baughman 2011; Hughes et al. 2010; Austin et al. 2008). Data from the *National Epidemiologic Survey on Alcohol and Related Conditions* found lesbian and bisexual women to be three times as likely as heterosexual women to report childhood sexual abuse and gay men to be twice as likely as heterosexual men to report such abuse (Hughes et al. 2010).

Austin and colleagues (2016) evaluated the association of sexual orientation with health risks and chronic conditions in adulthood before and after adjustment for cumulative exposure to ACEs, using data from the *Behavioral Risk Factor Surveillance System (BRFSS)*. Health risks included current smoking, binge drinking, heavy drinking, obesity, and HIV risk behaviors. LGB individuals were significantly more likely than heterosexuals to report each ACE category. The greatest increase in odds were for sexual abuse, adult mental illness in household, and an incarcerated household member. Only one-fourth of LGB individuals reported no ACE item, as compared with 40 percent of heterosexuals; 15 percent of LGB individuals reported six or more ACEs.

In 2015, Flentje and colleagues (2015) identified differences in mental and physical health care needs between LGB and heterosexual individuals in substance abuse treatment.[3] The authors made the following recommendations for care: (1) assess for sexual orientation at intake in a manner that facilitates healthy and supportive provider-client dialogue; (2) train staff and counselors on the effects of stress on LGB individuals' health and treatment outcomes and the need to approach care with an LGB-affirmative stance, in order to minimize the likelihood of contributing to the stress; (3) create an inclusive and affirming treatment environment; and (4) coordinate physical and mental health care.

Recently, the CDC (2016a) released the first nationally representative data on the health risks of lesbian, gay, and bisexual high school students, based on data from the *2015 National Youth Risk Behavior Survey (YRBS)*. Findings show that LGB students experience physical and sexual violence and bullying at levels many times higher than that of their heterosexual peers, with very serious consequences. For example, LGB students are significantly more likely to report: being forced to have sex; sexual dating violence; physical dating violence; being bullied at school; and being bullied online. These experiences can lead to serious outcomes: More than 40 percent of LGB students seriously considered suicide, and 29 percent reported attempting suicide; LGB students were up to five times more likely to report using illegal drugs; more than one in ten LGB students have missed school during the past 30 days because of safety concerns.

Clements-Nolle and colleagues (2001) conducted interviews and HIV testing with male-to-female and female-to-male transgender persons. Estimates of HIV prevalence among male-to-female transgender individuals was higher than estimates from studies conducted with gay men and injection drug users of the same age as the transgender persons. Half of the transgender persons were HIV-positive and were not receiving HIV-related health care. The authors note that the study confirmed the fact that many transgender persons enter the medical system to obtain hormones. This gives health care providers an opportunity to: (1) screen for trauma and depression; (2) counsel and refer transgender clients in need of HIV, substance abuse, and mental health services; and (3) provide support groups.

In 2016, Miller and colleagues (2016) presented a set of preliminary practice observations intended to inform the development of a trauma-informed "transformative justice approach" specific to lesbian, gay, bisexual, queer, and transgender survivors of IPV. For LGBQT survivors the mandate to "Do No Harm" requires that providers understand the concept of sanctuary harm (Bloom and Farragher 2010). Organizations that work with LGBQT survivors need to operate from a place of understanding that perceived "challenges" may actually be creative "strengths." A trauma-informed approach aims to reframe coping strategies such as substance use, cutting, eating disorders, and disassociation as adaptive responses to intolerable situations (Elliot et al. 2005; SAMHSA 2014). These adaptive coping strategies have helped the victim survive, but then stand in the way of full healing. If providers are to truly be of service, a social justice and anti-oppression framework must become the cornerstone of their work. At a minimum, this principle requires cultural sensitivity across multiple aspects of identity. Transformative justice recognizes the profound harm and trauma that mainstream approaches have inflicted upon the LGBQT communities, particularly those who face multiple forms of oppression.

This chapter highlighted a number of populations at high risk for experiencing traumatic events and at high risk for re-traumatization in our systems of care. You may have already recognized some other high-risk populations that are in your system. In the next chapter, the focus is on why each of our systems (health care, mental health, and substance abuse treatment) should attend to trauma.

Notes

1 It should be noted that the diagnosis of PTSD does not adequately capture the varied effects of multiple interpersonal traumas, particularly among children. A proposed diagnosis of Developmental Trauma Disorder (DTD) was submitted for the Diagnostic and Statistic Manual (DSM-V), but was not accepted (Van der Kolk et al. 2009).
2 Each study may use different terminology for this population, depending on which of the subgroups (e.g., lesbian, gay, bisexual, transgender, etc.) are included.
3 While transgender individuals were not included in this study, Flentje, Heck, and Sorensen reported data on them in a separate study (2014).

References

Administration for Children and Families (ACF), Children's Bureau 2015, U.S. Department of Health and Human Services.

Adoptions and Safe Families Act of 1997 (H.R. 867), Public Law 105–89, December 1997.

Agency for Healthcare Research and Quality (AHRQ) 2007, *Care of Children and Adolescent in U.S. Hospitals*, Rockville, MD, U.S. Department of Health and Human Services.

Austin, A, Herrick, H, and Proescholdbell, S 2016, Adverse Childhood Experiences Related to Poor Adult Health Among Lesbian, Gay, and Bisexual Individuals, *American Journal of Public Health*, vol. 106, no. 2, pp. 314–320.

Austin, SB, Jun, HJ, Jackson, B et al. 2008, Disparities in Child Abuse Victimization in Lesbian, Bisexual, and Heterosexual Women in the Nurses' Health Study II, *Journal of Women's Health*, vol. 17, no. 4, pp. 597–606.

Bailham, D and Joseph, S 2003, Post-Traumatic Stress Following Childbirth: A Review of the Emerging Literature and Directions for Research and Practice, *Psychology, Health & Medicine*, vol. 8, no. 2, pp. 159–168.

Black, MC et al. 2011, *The National Intimate Partner and Sexual Violence Survey (NISVS) 2010 Summary Report*, Atlanta, GA, Centers for Disease Control and Prevention.

Bloom, SL and Farragher, B 2010, *Destroying Sanctuary: The Crisis in Human Service Delivery Systems*, New York, NY, Oxford University Press.

Brown, VB and Melchior, LA 2008, Women with Co-Occurring Disorders (COD): Treatment Settings and Service Needs, *Journal of Psychoactive Drugs*, SARC Supplement 5, pp. 365–376.

Cavanaugh, CE, Hansen, NB, and Sullivan, T 2010, HIV Sexual Risk Behavior Among Low-Income Women Experiencing Intimate Partner Violence: The Role of Posttraumatic Stress Disorder, *AIDS Behavior*, vol. 14, pp. 318–327.

Center for Substance Abuse Treatment (CSAT) 2004, *Family Dependency Treatment Courts: Addressing Child Abuse and Neglect Cases Using the Drug Court Model*, Washington, DC, Bureau of Justice Assistance, U.S. Department of Justice.

Centers for Disease Control and Prevention (CDC), National Center for Injury Prevention and Control 2015, *WISQARS Fatal Injury Report: 2014*.

Centers for Disease Control and Prevention (CDC) 2016a, *Morbidity and Mortality Weekly Report, August 11, 2016*, Atlanta, GA, CDC.

Centers for Disease Control and Prevention (CDC) 2016b, *Web-Based Injury Statistics Query and Reporting System*, Atlanta, GA, CDC.

Clements-Nolle, K, Marx, R, Guzman, R, and Katz, M 2001, HIV Prevalence, Risk Behaviors, Health Care Use, and Mental Health Status of Transgender Persons: Implications for Public Health Intervention, *American Journal of Public Health*, vol. 91, no. 6, pp. 915–919.

Costello, EJ, Pescosolido, BA, Angold, A, and Burns, BJ 1998, A Family Network-Based Model of Access to Child Mental Health Services, *Research in Community Mental Health*, vol. 9, pp. 165–190.

David, DS and Brannon, R 1976, *The Forty-Nine Percent Majority: The Male Sex Role*, Boston, MA, Addison-Wesley.

Declerq, E, Sakala, C, Corry, M, and Applebaum, S 2008, *New Mothers Speak Out: National Survey Results Highlight Women's Postpartum Experiences*, New York, NY, Childbirth Connection.

Devries, KM, Child, JC, Bacchus, LJ et al. 2014, Intimate Partner Violence Victimization and Alcohol Consumption in Women: A Systematic Review and Meta-Analysis, *Addiction*, vol. 109, pp. 379–391.

Dong, M, Giles, WH, Felitti, VJ et al. 2004, Insights into Causal Pathways for Ischemic Heart Disease: Adverse Childhood Experiences Study, *Circulation*, vol. 110, no. 13, pp. 1761–1766.

Dutton, MA, Green, BL, Kaltman, SI et al. 2006, Intimate Partner Violence, PTSD, and Adverse Health Outcomes, *Journal of Interpersonal Violence*, vol. 21, pp. 955–968.

Edwards, VJ, Holden, GW, Felitti, VJ, and Anda, RF 2003, Relationship Between Multiple Forms of Childhood Maltreatment and Adult Mental Health in Community Respondents: Results from the Adverse Childhood Experiences Study, *American Journal of Psychiatry*, vol. 160, pp. 1453–1460.

Elliot, DE, Bjelajac, P, Fallot, R et al. 2005, Trauma-Informed or Trauma-Denied: Principles and Implementation of Trauma-Informed Services for Women, *Journal of Community Psychology*, vol. 33, pp. 461–477.

Fallot, R and Bebout, R 2012, Acknowledging and Embracing "the Boy Inside the Man": Trauma-Informed Work with Men, in N Poole and L Greaves (eds.), *Becoming Trauma-Informed*, Toronto, Canada, Centre for Addiction and Mental Health, pp. 165–174.

Flentje, A, Heck, NC, and Sorensen, JL 2014, Characteristics of Transgender Individuals Entering Substance Abuse Treatment, *Addictive Behaviors*, vol. 39, no. 5, pp. 969–975.

Flentje, A, Livingston, NA, Roley, J, and Sorensen, J 2015, Mental and Physical Needs of Lesbian, Gay, and Bisexual Clients in Substance Abuse Treatment, *Journal of Substance Abuse Treatment*, vol. 58, pp. 78–83.

Gander, MI and Vonkanel, R 2006, Myocardial Infarction and Posttraumatic Stress Disorder: Frequency, Outcome, and Atherosclerotic Mechanisms, *European Journal of Cardiovascular Prevention and Rehabilitation*, vol. 13, pp. 165–172.

Ghandour, RM, Campbell, JC, and Lloyd, J 2015, Screening and Counseling for Intimate Partner Violence: A Vision of the Future, *Journal of Women's Health*, vol. 24, no. 1, pp. 57–61.

Gilbert, L, El-Bassel, N, Manuel, J et al. 2006, An Integrated Relapse Prevention and Relationship Safety Intervention for Women on Methadone: Testing Short-Term Effects on Intimate Partner Violence and Substance Abuse, *Violence and Victims*, vol. 21, pp. 657–672.

Glaze, L and Maruschak, L 2008, *Patients in Prison and Their Minor Children: Bureau of Justice Statistics Special Report, NCJ 22984*, Washington, DC, Bureau of Justice Statistics.

Hughes, T, McCabe, SE, Wilsnack, SC et al. 2010, Victimization and Substance Use Disorders in a National Sample of Heterosexual and Sexual Minority Women and Men, *Addiction*, vol. 105, no. 12, pp. 2130–2140.

The Institute of Medicine (IOM) 2011, *The Health of Lesbian, Gay, Bisexual, and Transgender People*, Washington, DC, National Academy of Science.

Kataoka, S, Zhang, L, and Wells, K 2002, Unmet Need for Mental Health Care Among U.S. Children: Variation by Ethnicity and Insurance Status, *American Journal of Psychiatry*, vol. 159, no. 9, pp. 1548–1555.

Kisiel, C, Fehrenbach, T, Small, L, and Lyons, JS 2009, Assessment of Complex Trauma Exposure, Responses, and Service Needs Among Children and Adolescents in Child Welfare, *Journal of Child and Adolescent Trauma*, vol. 2, pp. 143–160.

Kisiel, CL, Fehrenbach, TG, Torgersen, E et al. 2014, Constellations of Interpersonal Trauma and Symptoms in Child Welfare: Implications for a Developmental Trauma Framework, *Journal of Family Violence*, vol. 29, pp. 1–14.

Lesserman, J, Ironson, G, O'Cleirigh, C et al. 2008, Stressful Life Events and Adherence in HIV, *AIDS Patient Care and STDs*, vol. 22, pp. 403–411.

Levant, RF, Halter, MJ, Hayden, EW, and Williams, C 2009, The Efficacy of Alexithymia Reduction Treatment: A Pilot Study, *Journal of Men's Studies*, vol. 17, no. 1, pp. 75–84.

Lowell, DI, Carter, AS, Godoy, L et al. 2011, A Randomized Controlled Trial of Child FIRST: A Comprehensive Home-Based Intervention Translating Research into Early Childhood Practice, *Child Development*, vol. 82, no. 1, pp. 193–208.

McEwen, BS 1998, Stress, Adaptation, and Disease: Allostasis and Allostatic Load, *Annals of the NY Academy of Science*, vol. 840, pp. 33–44.

Miller, EC, Goodman, LA, Thomas, KA et al. 2016, *Trauma-Informed Approaches for LGBTQ Survivors of Intimate Partner Violence*, Washington DC, Family and Youth Services Bureau, DHHS.

Mojab, CG 2009, The Impact of Traumatic Childbirth on Health Through the Undermining of Breast Feeding, in VL Banyard, VJ Edwards, and KA Kendall-Tacket (eds.), *Trauma and Physical Health*, New York, NY, Routledge, pp. 65–90.

Moore, TM, Stuart, GL, Meehan, JC et al. 2008, Drug Abuse and Aggression Between Intimate Partners: A Meta-Analytic Review, *Clinical Psychology Review*, vol. 28, pp. 247–274.

Mugavero, MJ, Raper, JL, Reif, S et al. 2009, Overload: The Impact of Incident Stressful Events on Antiretroviral Medication Adherence and Virologic Failure in a Longitudinal, Multi-Site HIV Cohort Study, *Psychosomatic Medicine*, vol. 71, no. 9, pp. 920–926.

National Scientific Council on the Developing Child 2014, *Excessive Stress Disrupts the Architecture of the Developing Brain: Working Paper No. 3*, Updated Edition, www.developingchild.harvard. edu.

Nightingale, VR, Sher, YG, Mattson, M et al. 2011, The Effects of Traumatic Stressors and HIV-Related Trauma Symptoms on Health and Health Related Quality of Life, *AIDS Behavior*, vol. 15, no. 8, pp. 1870–1878.

Novac, S, Paradis, E, Brown, J, and Morton, H 2006, *A Visceral Grief: Young Homeless Mothers and Loss of Custody. Research Paper 206*, Toronto, Canada, Center for Urban and Community Studies.

Office of Disease Prevention and Health Promotion 2010, *Healthy People 2020*, *ODPHP Publication No. BO132*, Washington, DC, U.S. Department of Health and Human Services.

Olde, E, van der Hart, O, Kleber R, and Van Son, M 2006, Posttraumatic Stress Following Childbirth: A Review, *Clinical Psychology Review*, vol. 26, no. 1, pp. 1–16.

Plotzker, RE, Metzger, DS, and Holmes, WC 2007, Childhood Sexual and Physical Abuse Histories, PTSD, Depression, and HIV Risk Outcomes in Women Injection Drug Users: A Potential Mediating Pathway, *American Journal of Addictions*, vol. 16, pp. 431–428.

Poehlmann, J, Dallaire, D, Loper, AB, and Shear, LD 2010, Children's Contact with Their Incarcerated Parents, *American Psychologist*, vol. 65, no. 6, pp. 575–598.

Rothman, EF, Exner, D, and Baughman, A 2011, The Prevalence of Sexual Assault Against People Who Identify as Gay, Lesbian, or Bisexual in the United States: A Systematic Review, *Trauma, Violence & Abuse*, vol. 12, no. 2, pp. 55–66.

Saar, MS, Epstein, R, Rosenthal, L, and Vafa, Y (n.d.), *The Sexual Abuse to Prison Pipeline: The Girls' Story*, Washington, DC, Center on Poverty and Inequality, Georgetown University Law Center.

Sama-Miller, E, Akers, L, Mraz-Esposito, A et al. 2016, *Home Visiting Evidence of Effectiveness Review: Executive Summary*, Washington, DC, Office of Planning, Research and Evaluation, Administration for Children and Families, U.S. Department of Health and Human Services.

Shonkoff, JP, Garner, AS, and the Committee on Psychosocial Aspects of Child and Family Health, Committee on Early Childhood, Adoption and Dependent Care, and Section on Developmental and Behavioral Pediatrics et al. 2012, The Lifelong Effects of Early Childhood Adversity and Toxic Stress, *Pediatrics*, vol. 129, no. 1, pp. 232–246.

Stockman, JK, Hayashi, H, and Campbell, J 2015, Intimate Partner Violence and Its Health Impact on Disproportionately Affected Populations, Including Minorities and Impoverished Groups, *Journal of Women's Health*, vol. 24, no. 1, pp. 62–79.

Stuber, M, Shneider, S, Kassam-Adams, N et al. 2006, The Medical Traumatic Stress ToolKit, *CNS Spectrums*, vol. 11, pp. 137–142.

Substance Abuse and Mental Health Services Administration (SAMHSA) 2014, *Trauma-Informed Care in Behavioral Health Services: Treatment Improvement Protocol 57, HHS Publication No. (SMA) 14–4816*, Rockville, MD, SAMHSA.

Taylor, N, Wilson, C, and Igelman, R 2006, In Pursuit of a More Trauma-Informed Child Welfare System, *APSAC Advisor*, vol. 18, no. 2, pp. 4–9.

Van der Kolk, G et al. 2009, www.traumacenter.org/announcements/ DTC_papers_October_09.pdf.

Western, B and Wildeman, C 2009, The Black Family and Mass Incarceration, *The Annals of the American Academy of Political and Social Science*, vol. 621, pp. 221–242.

Whitson, ML and Connell, CM 2016, The Relation of Exposure to Traumatic Events and Longitudinal Mental Health Outcomes for Children Enrolled in Systems of Care: Results from a National System of Care Evaluation, *American Journal of Community Psychology*, vol. 57, pp. 380–390.

Chapter 4

The Impact of Trauma on Different Systems of Care

Why Attend to Trauma in Health Care

Our health care system has always been involved in trauma care in wartime and routinely addresses serious injuries and violent deaths in trauma centers and emergency rooms. Health care settings are among the first to see children, adolescents, adults, and older adults who have experienced traffic accidents, community violence, terrorist attacks, etc. However, recently more attention has been given to issues of domestic violence (DV) and intimate personal violence (IPV) in primary and emergency care and to child maltreatment in pediatric care.

Many traumatic events (e.g., sexual abuse, IPV, other forms of physical abuse, participation in and exposure to combat) involve violation of an individual's bodily integrity and a perceived threat to life and, therefore, profoundly influence attitudes and responses toward medical care. While trauma survivors may visit emergency rooms frequently, they often do not seek preventive care. As noted in Chapter 1, medical care and medical tests can be "triggering" for survivors, and medication adherence may be low because of distrust and difficulties with self-care. In addition, many patients with serious, life-threatening illnesses (e.g., cancer, HIV/AIDS) may be traumatized by their diagnoses and treatments and need special interventions in order to prevent these potentially traumatic experiences from leading to posttraumatic stress disorder (PTSD) and other problems. Painful and frightening medical experiences can be even more potentially traumatic for children and their families (e.g., those dealing with pediatric cancer and pediatric injuries). For these reasons, while all health care providers need not be specialists in trauma, they should be sufficiently trauma-informed to understand and identify trauma symptoms, know how to adapt some of their procedures for trauma survivors, and help traumatized individuals and families gain access to trauma specialists.

The patient-provider relationship is an important factor in increasing trust on the part of the patient and on the part of the provider. Trust is a two-way street; a patient with a trauma-filled history and recent trauma experiences will enter the medical encounter (or any other service encounter) with mistrust and may experience difficulty with disclosure and with adherence to any recommended treatment regimen. The provider, in expressing warmth, empathy, respect, and understanding, lends a form of social support that helps the patient feel heard, understood, and that the "burden of illness" is being shared. This trauma-informed approach increases trust and the motivation to follow treatment recommendations on the part of the patient. When the patient becomes more trusting and open to the provider's support and recommendations, the provider feels increased trust in the patient and will express more caring and support. The other important construct is social connectedness. Given the high rates of trauma experiences in our patients' histories and current lives, particularly those with person-related trauma (e.g., sexual abuse, physical abuse, emotional abuse, IPV, etc.), patients not only mistrust providers, but also others in their communities and in their lives. This leads to isolation and depression and can affect the ability to seek care and/or follow treatment recommendations. Trauma-informed care incorporates safety and collaboration in relationships, as well as rebuilding connectedness to others.

The health care system deals with a high prevalence of patients with trauma

Trauma survivors are over-represented in emergency room (ER) patient populations. They are there for many reasons, but include women who have experienced interpersonal violence, ethnic minority youth who have suffered gunshot wounds, and adolescents who have been in automobile accidents (CDC 2016). In 2014, the National Council of State Legislatures (NCSL 2014) reported that almost 700,000 youth, ages 10 to 24, are treated in ERs each year for injuries sustained from violent assaults.

However, providers also encounter a high prevalence of individuals with trauma in primary care settings. In a study by Alim and colleagues (2006), participants (96% of whom were African American) were surveyed for trauma exposure in the waiting rooms of four primary care offices. Of the patients with trauma exposure (65%), the mean number of "high-impact" traumatic events was 1.83; the most common trauma experiences participants reported were transportation accidents (42%), sudden unexpected death of a loved one (39%), physical assault (30%), assault with a weapon (25%), and sexual assault (24%). Sexual assault and unwanted sexual experiences were more common in females, while assault with a weapon, physical assault, and combat exposure were more common in males. Lifetime prevalence of PTSD in the trauma-exposed group was 51 percent. Forty-six percent of the lifetime PTSD cases had comorbid depression, and 52 percent had comorbid alcohol and other substance use disorders. The authors state that the high rate of PTSD in this sample of African Americans suggest that screening for traumatic experiences and PTSD may be as important as screening and intervention for depression in the primary care setting.

Weisberg and colleagues (2002) examined the relationship between PTSD, trauma, and self-reported nonpsychiatric medical conditions in a large sample of primary care patients. Of the patients who completed the *Structured Clinical Interview for DSM-IV (SCID)*, more than 33 percent met diagnostic criteria for one or more anxiety disorders, including PTSD. Of these, 17 percent reported no history of trauma, 46 percent reported a history of trauma, and 37 percent were diagnosed with PTSD. The most commonly reported trauma experiences were forced sexual contact or rape (45%), accident (38%), witnessing someone being injured or killed (37%), and an attack without a weapon (32%). The total number of medical problems was compared for the three groups. Participants who had a history of trauma reported a greater number of medical problems than those without trauma. Participants diagnosed with PTSD reported significantly more lifetime medical problems than either of the other two groups.

In 1998, I wrote a paper entitled, "Untreated Physical Health Problems Among Women Diagnosed with Severe Mental Illness" (Brown 1998). At that time, individuals diagnosed with severe mental illness had death rates approximately two-and-a-half times that of the general population, and up to 58 percent of their physical illnesses were undiagnosed by medical/psychiatric staff. In addition, more than 50 percent of women in psychiatric institutions had experienced sexual abuse, but they were rarely asked about histories of trauma. Failure to identify health issues and trauma histories often led to revictimization, inappropriate and inadequate treatment, and increased costs. Most of the women in our treatment program (PROTOTYPES) had used emergency rooms when they were seeking health care prior to entering treatment. I recommended that: "Rather than continuing to place the burden on the individual, it is time that systematic linkages are developed to integrate care" (Brown 1998, p. 160). I also recommended that our care systems: (1) include comprehensive screening and assessment of physical health, mental health, trauma histories, and substance abuse at all entry points into the system; (2) train providers on the comorbidities present in the population they are treating, on screening for trauma (including DV), and on strategies to prevent re-traumatization; (3) reorient from a focus on acute care to preventive health care (including dental care); and (4) promote continuity of primary care, mental health, and substance abuse treatment, as well as collaboration among providers.

Routine health care procedures can also be triggering

Many medical procedures and tests can be "triggers" for individuals who have been traumatized. These include pelvic exams, throat and mouth examinations, dentistry procedures, breast exams, rectal exams, and colonoscopy because they are invasive, as well as MRIs and CT scans because they restrict mobility and can be quite frightening. Furthermore, shame, depression, and isolation, prevalent among trauma survivors, make establishment of trust with health care providers uniquely challenging.

Trauma centers have been designed to treat major traumatic injuries, etc.

More than 41 million individuals each year present to acute care medical trauma centers and emergency departments for the treatment of traumatic physical injury (CDC 2014). However, less than 10 percent of trauma centers routinely provide post-injury screening or integrated care management targeting the cluster of PTSD and related comorbidities present in the injured population.

Few studies have evaluated interventions for injured patients with PTSD that can be feasibly implemented in surgical trauma centers. Zatzick and colleagues (2013) tested the effectiveness of a stepped collaborative care intervention at a Level I trauma center. The intervention, which included case management, evidence-based pharmacotherapy, motivational interviewing, and cognitive-behavioral therapy, lasted for 12 months and was delivered in both the hospital and outpatient clinics. Patients in the intervention group showed marked reductions in PTSD symptoms over the 12 months and significant improvements in physical functioning, as compared to patients in the control group. Patients with traumatic brain injury (TBI) responded as well to the intervention as those without TBI.

Zatzick and colleagues (2016) have designed an extensive study protocol to test the delivery of screening and intervention for PTSD and comorbidities across 24 Level I trauma centers in the U.S. The Trauma Survivors Outcomes and Support (TSOS) investigation employs a stepped wedge cluster randomized design in which sites are randomized sequentially to initiate the intervention. The protocol is being rolled out nationally and will be completed in 2019. Results will be presented at an American College of Surgeons' Policy Summit.

Staff may experience secondary traumatization/burnout

All providers, including first responders, need to be aware of the potential for secondary traumatization (sometimes called "vicarious victimization"), which involves intense emotional reactions on the part of providers when they hear stories of traumatic events and/or experience intense patient reactions. Providers may themselves be trauma survivors and, therefore, acutely sensitive to trauma issues of patients. This can lead to a sensitivity and empathic response to trauma survivors, but also can also lead to re-traumatization. Providers' feelings of powerlessness to help patients and family members can interact with and compound their personal identification with patients' situations (Stayer and Lockhart 2016).

Providers also need to be attentive to signs of "burnout" and how it is impacting the quality of care they are delivering. Burnout is particularly high among medical residents and those physicians, nurses, and medical assistants who have experienced trauma themselves. There are many factors that contribute to burnout, including high patient load, increased work hours, sleep deprivation, negative resident-supervisor interactions, and witnessing/committing major medical errors. West and colleagues (2011) studied quality of life, burnout, educational debt, and medical knowledge among internal medicine residents. Participants were 16,394 residents, representing 74.1 percent of all eligible U.S. internal medicine residents. Quality of life was rated "as bad as it can be" or "somewhat bad" by 14.8 percent of the residents. Overall burnout, high levels of exhaustion, and depersonalization were reported by 51.5 percent, 45.8 percent, and 28.9 percent of residents, respectively.

In a longitudinal study of the impact of trauma on female nurses and nursing personnel, Cavanaugh and colleagues (2014) conducted an analysis of secondary data from the Safe at Work Study. The nurses and nursing personnel who reported three or more different types of violence victimization at baseline (27.6%) had 2.15, 3.57, and 6.44 times greater odds of screening positive for depression, posttraumatic stress, or comorbid posttraumatic stress-depression, respectively, six months later than nurses who reported no trauma at baseline. Threats or physical workplace violence was the most common type of victimization reported. Given the high rates of childhood abuse, intimate partner violence, and workplace violence in this population, the implementation of trauma training, including issues of secondary traumatization and self-care, is imperative for female nurses and nursing personnel.

In a recent *Medscape* report on bias and burnout, Peckham (2016) reported on the top causes of burnout mentioned by more than 15,800 physicians from 25 specialties. These included: too many bureaucratic tasks; spending too many hours at work; increased computerization of practice; feeling just like a cog in a wheel; impact of the Affordable Care Act; too many difficult patients; too many patient appointments in a day; and an inability to provide patients with the quality of care they need. When asked which patient characteristics "trigger bias," the physicians reported: emotional problems, weight, intelligence, language differences, age, income level, race, level of attractiveness, and gender.

Treatment burdens of health care for trauma survivors are quite high

As discussed in Chapter 1, complex treatment regimens, a large number of medications, and short visits (15 minutes) make it extremely difficult for patients with trauma histories and current trauma to follow through, particularly if there is also some cognitive impairment (e.g., among battered woman or combat veteran who have traumatic brain injury). In addition, patients with comorbidities have multiple needs and often require the assistance of multiple providers, who may or may not effectively communicate and coordinate.

Why Attend to Trauma in Mental Health

Historically, there have been two major populations that have led providers in mental health to advocate for the integration of trauma into treatment; viz., veterans of war and women. (Veterans are discussed in Chapter 11.) Trauma has not been a central focus of the mental health field until the increased acknowledgement of re-traumatization in psychiatric inpatient hospitals fueled awareness of the need for trauma-informed care (Pritchard 1995; Jennings 1995; Jennings 1998). Coercive approaches involving forced medications and seclusion and restraint were reported by patients/consumers as "violence" and "harming" to them; they expressed fear of violence, as well as disrespect and humiliation from staff (Bloom and Farragher 2010). In 1994 SAMHSA/CMHS held the *Dare to Vision* Conference, bringing together mental health providers, researchers, policy makers, and consumer advocates to begin a dialogue about changing mental health treatment. In her address at this conference, Ann Jennings (Jennings 1995, p. 17) shared the experiences that her daughter encountered and that many consumer/survivors have found in psychiatric institutions:

> "Just as her childhood abuser had tied her up and held her down and bound her arms and hands, she was, in the system, repeatedly subjected to take-downs, restraints, and the shackling of her arms and legs to a bed. As her abuser had stripped her when she was a child, pulling her T-shirt over her head, she was, in the system, forcibly stripped of her clothing when secluded or restrained, often by or in the presence of male attendants. As her childhood abuser had pulled off her pants leaving her with 'nothing on below,' so, in the system, her underpants were pulled down, often by male attendants, in order to forcibly inject her with medications. As the abuser had blindfolded her with her little T-shirt, towels or sheets were thrown over her face if she spat or screamed while tied down with four-point restraints in mental hospitals. As her childhood abuser had opened her legs, so also, in four-point restraints, her legs were forced open and tied down in spread-eagle position. As her childhood abuser had examined and 'put things into her that hurt,' so also institutional staff continually and painfully injected medication into her body against her will."

One of the important products of the *Dare to Vision* conference was the *Report and Recommendations of the Massachusetts Department of Mental Health Task Force on the Restraint and Seclusion of Persons Who Have Been Physically or Sexually Abused* (Carmen et al. 1996) (See *Commonwealth of Massachusetts Department of Mental Health De-Escalation Form for DMH Facilities/Vendors* in Appendix B.)

There has been re-traumatization in the mental health system

It has been shown that the mental health system can re-traumatize survivors through coercion and control in inpatient psychiatric units, i.e., through seclusion and restraint procedures and forcible medication (Bloom and Farragher 2010). While the re-traumatization may be unintentional and unanticipated, mental health providers need to acknowledge the prevalence of trauma in their patient population and the impact of coercive procedures on survivors of trauma. Staff may also be traumatized when they are required to perform coercive procedures, rather than other procedures that might be more helpful. If the provider has also experienced trauma, then the impact of this traumatizing behavior is even more intense (Esaki and Larkin 2013).

Patients with severe mental illness, who may already feel unsafe in their daily lives because of their illness and histories of trauma, may also feel unsafe in inpatient psychiatric settings, particularly because of seclusion and restraint procedures, forced medications, other patient's aggressive behaviors, etc. These procedures are triggering. While much has been done to reduce the extent of seclusion and restraint, more attention to patients' safety issues is needed. In addition, patients who have experienced trauma may not adhere to medications because the medications can trigger feelings of being out of control.[1]

There is a high prevalence of patients with trauma in the mental health system

In 1987, the Epidemiological Catchment Area (ECA) Study (Robin and Regier 1991) was implemented under the National Institute of Mental Health to identify baseline rates of mental disorders within treated and untreated populations in the U.S. It was the first non-institutionalized population survey of PTSD prevalence. The study sampled 18,000 community residents and 2,290 institutional residents in five sites (New Haven, Connecticut; Baltimore, Maryland; St. Louis, Missouri; Durham, North Carolina; and Los Angeles, California). The study found that approximately 20 percent of the women and men interviewed had a mental disorder within the past 12 months. The median age of onset was 16 years, while 90 percent of the sample experienced initial symptoms by age 38. Helzer and colleagues (1987) estimated the lifetime prevalence of PTSD to be 0.5 percent among men and 1.3 percent among women. Vietnam veterans who were wounded had the highest prevalence of PTSD (20%). Results also underscored important gender differences in the rates of specific mental disorders; women showed higher rates of affective and anxiety disorders, while men had significantly higher rates of alcohol abuse/dependence, drug abuse/dependence, and antisocial personality disorders.

The National Comorbidity Study (NCS) incorporated DSM-III-R diagnoses, and examined risk factors more extensively on a national sample of 8,000 non-institutionalized individuals. Results showed that 29.5 percent had a diagnosable alcohol, drug abuse, or mental disorder. Approximately 5 percent experienced both a mental and substance abuse disorder within the past year, and approximately 14 percent had both disorders in their lifetime. Data collected from both the ECA and NCS confirmed that approximately 60 percent of people with diagnosable disorders did not receive treatment (Kessler et al. 1994).

Research has demonstrated that persons in the mental health system have experienced higher rates of interpersonal violence than the general population. A systematic review of the literature estimated that approximately half of the persons in mental health agencies experienced physical abuse (ranging from 25% to 72%) and more than one-third had experienced sexual abuse (ranging from 24% to 49%) in childhood and/or adulthood (Mauritz et al. 2013).

Other research (Khalifeh et al. 2015) has found that people with severe mental illness are more likely to have experienced domestic and sexual violence in the previous year compared to the general population (27 percent of women and 13 percent of men with severe mental illness had experienced domestic violence compared to 9 percent and 5 percent, respectively, of the general population; 10 percent of women with severe mental illness had experienced sexual violence compared to 2 percent of the general population). The prevalence of child sexual abuse among female inpatients ranges from 36 percent to 85 percent. In addition, research over the past decade has increasingly supported the notion that childhood trauma is linked to adult psychosis (Bentail et al. 2014; Kessler et al. 2010; Varese et al. 2012).

The mental health system has not done well with comorbidities

For many years the mental health system has not included substance use disorders as a significant part of its work. Patients with co-occurring disorders often were sent away from mental health settings to other providers, i.e., drug treatment or alcohol treatment providers. Needless to say, many of these clients never made it to treatment, and many have overdosed. Now, with the influx of large numbers of active duty military personnel and veterans into mental health systems (e.g., VA hospitals) for PTSD, substance abuse, depression, and traumatic brain injury, the mental health system needs to change/expand its understanding of comorbidities and its scope of treatments.

In the face of the prevalence of child maltreatment, mental health needs to expand its prevention strategies, as well as its trauma-informed and trauma-specific interventions

Trauma diagnoses (PTSD and others) are mental health diagnoses, and many trauma-specific interventions are practiced in mental health systems by mental health specialists. Many traumatic events (e.g., sexual abuse, physical abuse, exposure to combat, extreme neglect of children) involve perceived threat to life, and, therefore, have influence on a patient's attitudes toward seeking mental health treatment. Effective, trauma-specific children's mental health approaches are important for reducing child maltreatment and preventing PTSD. (See discussion of prevention in Chapter 8.)

Mental health providers are at risk of secondary traumatization or re-traumatization and consequent burnout

Mental health staff may themselves be trauma survivors and, therefore, acutely sensitive to trauma issues of patients. This can lead to a sensitivity and empathic response to trauma survivors, but also could lead to re-traumatization.

If trauma is not addressed in mental health treatment, then treatment of patients is considered inadequate

In the past, neither trauma nor substance use problems, both of which are key risk factors complicating mental health recovery, were routinely identified and addressed in mental health treatment. This has begun to change. Several states and the VA are now requiring that questions about physical and sexual abuse, as well as other traumatic events, be asked. All of these questions should be asked with the clear message and understanding that the client may choose not to answer them (Brown 2012).

In a recent study by Williams and colleagues (2016), 1,008 patients meeting DSM-IV criteria for major depressive disorder (MDD) were randomly assigned to eight weeks of treatment with escitalopram, sertraline or venlafaxine, and matched with 336 healthy controls from the iSPOT-D multi-site clinical trial. Exposure to 18 traumatic events (e.g., abuse/personal violation, family breakup, family health/ death, etc.) before the age of 18 was assessed. Results showed that participants with MDD had been exposed to significantly more early-life trauma than the healthy controls; 62.5 percent of MDD participants reported more than two traumatic events compared with 28.4 percent of controls. MDD participants had a four-fold or higher rate of exposure to abuse than controls. The greater the exposure to trauma, the less likely the patients were to achieve remission of their MDD symptoms following treatment with one of the three antidepressants. The results also show that remission rates may be especially low when abuse occurs between 4 and 7 years of age, and following treatment with sertraline. One of the important messages of these findings is that screening for childhood trauma in the clinical management of depression is advised to identify those patients that may not benefit from first-line antidepressants and may require psychotherapy to deal with the impact of trauma. Since primary care physicians prescribe about two-thirds of antidepressants, trauma screening is important in primary care.

Treatment burdens of the mental health system are quite high

As noted earlier, for the patient with traumatic experiences in her history, psychiatric medications can be quite frightening. They take away control from the patient, they may have unpleasant side effects, and they often require considerable changes in dosages in order for the patient to reach stability. Young clients often report that the psychiatric medications make them "feel different" from their peers without mental health problems, as well as making them feel worse than street drugs do, and this leads to nonadherence. In addition, mental health systems have not only been slow in providing appropriate treatment for substance use disorders and trauma, but also have been slow in providing gender-sensitive treatment and peer recovery interventions. This adds to the burden of treatment for many clients.

In a report by Smith and colleagues (2013), individuals with serious mental illness and providers were interviewed regarding reasons for disengagement from mental health services. Findings indicated that individuals with serious mental illness and the providers working with them can have markedly different perspectives regarding the reasons for engagement and disengagement. The reason most commonly (30%) reported by the individuals with serious mental illness was that services were not meeting their needs. "I just got aggravated, because it didn't seem like the issues I was having, anyone was really addressing them" (Smith et al. 2013, p. 772).

Twenty-nine percent of them described experiences with providers whom they perceived as critical or negative, while 21 percent reported they had no mental health problems requiring treatment and 20 percent noted lack of continuity with providers. In contrast, among the providers, 76 percent described stigma as an important impediment to treatment; in addition, 68 percent noted lack of awareness of illness, 64 percent identified family and cultural barriers to accepting services, and 84 percent noted transportation barriers.

When asked about strategies to increase engagement, 27 percent of the individuals with serious mental illness mentioned providers who foster engagement by being caring and non-critical, and 21 percent endorsed a recovery and strengths-based approach. Sixty percent of the providers also reported that clinicians with caring, non-critical attitudes were more likely to engage clients, while 52 percent described approaches that included psychoeducation and 48 percent endorsed more client choice. Both the clients (23%) and providers (68%) mentioned transportation assistance as helpful in promoting engagement, and 68 percent of providers emphasized flexibility of scheduling (extended clinic hours, unscheduled appointments, and meetings between clients and staff members in the community). Ninety-two percent of providers mentioned the need to work with families or provide culturally sensitive therapy. It should be noted that none of the individuals with serious mental illness endorsed family interventions.

In the 1940s, some of the mental health inpatient facilities began to reorganize into therapeutic milieus or therapeutic communities (Jones 1953; Wilmer 1958). These environments rested on several assumptions: (1) the total organization is seen as affecting the therapeutic outcome (therapeutic milieu); (2) patients should be responsible for much of their treatment; (3) the running of the unit should be more democratic than authoritarian; (4) patients are capable of helping one another; (5) restraint should be kept to a minimum; and (6) psychological methods are preferable to physical methods of control. Thus began the movement toward trauma-informed care, both in mental health and substance abuse treatment systems.

Why Attend to Trauma in Substance Abuse Treatment System

The ACE Study (see Chapter 2) allowed us to look at trauma experiences, without PTSD, and their effects on health, mental health, and substance use. When the study's authors (Dube et al. 2003) looked at the relationship between ACE scores and addiction, they found that injecting illicit drugs showed a similar dose-response pattern to health and mental health issues; i.e., the likelihood of injection drug use increases strongly and in a graded fashion as ACE scores increase. In addition, Population Attributable Risk (PAR) analysis showed that 78 percent of drug injection by women can be attributable to ACEs. For men and women combined, the PAR is 67 percent. Moreover, this PAR has been constant in four age cohorts whose birthdates span a century.

The substance abuse treatment system deals with high prevalence of clients with trauma

Many individuals entering the substance use disorders treatment system have been survivors of trauma from childhood through adulthood; i.e., many have experienced childhood traumatic events (scores very high on ACE events), but also have experienced additional trauma as they participated in the drug culture (e.g., women forced into sex work, who experienced trauma as a result of that; men and women in jail and/or prison who experienced significant traumatic events in those settings; clients witnessing the death of "running buddies" caused by overdose or bad drug deals; and clients diagnosed with HIV).

Kessler and colleagues (1995) showed, using the National Comorbidity Survey (NCS) data, that PTSD was significantly associated with a diagnosis of drug abuse or dependence. In addition, they found that PTSD was more often the primary or first diagnosis. The NCS generated a lifetime PTSD prevalence estimate of 5 percent among men and 10.4 percent among women, and yielded far higher estimates of lifetime prevalence of trauma exposure and of the risk of developing PTSD. Lifetime prevalence of trauma exposure was estimated to be 60.7 percent among men and 51.2 percent among women. The majority of those who reported any trauma experience reported multiple traumas. The risk of developing PTSD conditional on trauma experiences was estimated to be 8.1 percent among men and 20.4 percent among women. Combat was most frequently associated with PTSD in men; sexual assault was most frequently associated with PTSD in women. Among both men and women, the relative odds of experiencing either an alcohol disorder or a drug disorder among those who experienced PTSD compared to those who did not were statistically significant. Among men, the odds ratio for alcohol disorder was 2.06, and the odds ratio for drug disorder was 2.97. Among women, the odds ratio for alcohol and drug disorder was 2.48 and 4.46, respectively. Kessler also estimated upper and lower bounds for the proportion of comorbid PTSD and SUDs in which PTSD occurred first. Among men, estimates ranged from 52.7 percent to 65.3 percent; among women, 65.1 percent to 84.3 percent. These results suggested that PTSD predated substance use disorders in the majority of individuals who experienced both. Since trauma experiences predated PTSD and PTSD predated substance abuse, if we do a good job of screening and treating trauma, we should be able to prevent both PTSD and substance use disorders in a sizable group of individuals.

Anda and colleagues (2002) examined how growing up with alcoholic parents and having adverse childhood events (ACEs) were related to risk of alcoholism and depression in adulthood. Parental (mostly father-only) alcohol abuse was reported by 20.3 percent of respondents. Those respondents who had grown up with at least one alcohol-abusing parent were: two to three times as likely to report ACEs (39% had an ACE score of 4 or more); two to five times as likely to have lived with a household member who used illicit drugs, had mental illness, attempted suicide, or had been incarcerated; and three to eight times as likely to have had a battered mother as those with no history of parental alcohol abuse. Respondents with higher ACE scores were more likely to have a personal history of alcoholism. Another important finding was that depressive disorders among adult children of alcoholics appeared to be largely due to the likelihood of having adverse childhood experiences at home with their parents. It is important that screening for childhood trauma is implemented in substance abuse treatment programs in order to address these issues.

Some substance abuse treatment procedures are triggering

Intense, aggressive confrontation in old-style therapeutic communities can trigger negative responses (e.g., depression, a sense of hopelessness, and re-traumatization) in clients with trauma histories, and clients will leave treatment early and relapse. Many other routine treatment procedures can be triggers as well, such as body searches, urine testing, night check-ins by counselors in residential treatment, co-ed programming, and reporting to courts and/or child welfare. With regard to urine testing, the need to have someone (e.g., a counselor or nurse) observing the testing can be quite "triggering" for survivors. It is important to explain that we are mandated to do observed testing, and that may feel uncomfortable for the client. We need to ask, "What can I do to make you feel more comfortable?" In relapse prevention, clients may identify situations and emotions related to past trauma that can be triggering and may put them at risk for using substances. Teaching grounding skills and self-soothing strategies can be empowering.

Coping deficits associated with substance use disorder-PTSD lead to poorer treatment outcomes

Coping deficits have been associated with substance use disorder (SUD-PTSD) in a number of studies. Ouimette and colleagues (1997) found that problems from substance use at a one-year follow-up were partially explained by SUD-PTSD patients' greater use of emotional discharge coping (e.g., risk-taking, yelling) and decreased expectations of benefits from abstinence. In a subsequent study (Ouimette, Finney, and Moos 1999), emotional discharge and cognitive avoidance coping (e.g., trying to forget about the trauma) both partially explained poorer two-year substance use outcomes. In a third study, Brown and colleagues (2003) found that individuals with unremitted PTSD had poorer substance use outcomes and poorer coping than those whose PTSD symptoms had remitted or those who had never been diagnosed with PTSD. The study also provided support for the critical role of coping in PTSD-SUD. The authors recommend that clinicians focus on helping these patients decrease their maladaptive coping strategies and learn more adaptive coping approaches. Two trauma-specific interventions that have a strong emphasis on coping skills for SUD-PTSD are *Seeking Safety* (see Chapters 2, 5, and 7) and *Transcend* (Donovan and Padin-Rivera 1999).

Higher treatment burden leads to poor retention

Higher levels of burden, including those resulting from experiences of trauma, are related to lower levels of retention in treatment programs. For clients who have experienced trauma, it takes time to see reductions in the anxiety, fear, and mistrust that the clients bring with them into treatment. It also takes time for these clients to feel a positive connection to providers and to other clients in the program. Although the treatment program offers a safe and supportive environment, clients with trauma histories may feel overwhelmed by the need to participate with others, to behave in a structured way, and to comply with program rules and procedures. If clients have been cognitively impaired by domestic violence (mostly women), they may not be able to understand program rules or follow them. A mother who has experienced domestic violence and who has to come into residential treatment without her children will be fearful of what is happening to the children when she is not there protecting them; this can interfere with the woman's participation in treatment and recovery. This is why residential treatment programs for mothers and children are important for both.

Substance abuse treatment providers are at risk of secondary traumatization or re-traumatization and consequent burnout

Staff may themselves be trauma survivors and, therefore, acutely sensitive to trauma issues of clients. This can lead to a sensitivity and empathic response to trauma survivors, but also can lead to re-traumatization, especially if the staff member has not dealt with his/her trauma experiences.

History

Historically, the substance abuse treatment system has had two main tracks, other than hospitalizations, into recovery: Alcoholics Anonymous (AA) for alcohol problems, and therapeutic communities (TCs) for drug use problems. Alcoholics Anonymous (AA) was founded in 1935 by two recovering alcoholics, Bill Wilson (Bill W) and Dr. Bob Smith (Bob S) (Wilson 1957). The 12 Steps and the 12 Traditions of AA are the principles that guide the individual in his/her recovery process. These emphasize admission of one's loss of control over the substance and a surrender to one's "higher power," self-examination, seeking help from one's higher power to change, making amends to others, and helping others to engage in a similar process. The power in AA and other 12-step programs (AA, NA, CA, etc.) is that they provide structure, support, and new ways of coping 24/7; they are also free and can be lifelong. It is also important to note that 12-step programs do not require people to be abstinent before we engage with them. The only requirement for membership is a desire to stop using. There have been many adaptations of the AA formula to address the needs of individuals addicted to drugs; these include Narcotics Anonymous, Cocaine Anonymous, and Dual Recovery.

Therapeutic communities (TCs) first appeared in psychiatric hospitals, pioneered by Jones and others (Wilmer 1958) about 15 years before therapeutic communities were developed for individuals with addictions (Yablonsky 1965; DeLeon, Skodol, and Rosenthal 1973; Deitch 1973). The essential components of TCs for addictions first evolved in Synanon, which was founded in 1958 in California. The critical components in the Synanon TC included the residential setting of the TC, its organizational structure, profiles of the clients, goals, and orientation. The clients in the TC included opioid addicts and substance abusers of all kinds; most clients had a history of criminal activity or legal problems. In the TC, the power of change primarily resided within the individual and was activated through his/her full participation in the peer community (DeLeon 2000). The groups in TCs were marked by intense mutual confrontation designed to expose and weaken defenses against personal honesty and to encourage the expression of authentic feelings.

In the TC, learning responsibility, consistency, and accountability reflected complex individual growth and recovery. The TC provided opportunities for developing a positive identity, including being a role model for others, advancing in the work structure, and progressing through the stages of the program. The entering client could navigate the occupational ladder (from service crew or kitchen crew to chief expediter or coordinator), moving through the resident job functions to staff-in-training. Thus, work was both a goal and a means of recovery.

Long-term TCs typically had a treatment duration of 18 to 24 months. The power of a 24/7 structured living environment for up to two years wrapped the client in a consistent and supportive environment. Most of our other services do not do this. For individuals with complex disorders, it is important that they have this type of program available. Funding pressures have led to shorter treatment durations; however, it is not economical to cut these programs. They save millions of dollars in costs of stolen property and other crimes, jail and prison time, and disease caused by needle use (HIV/AIDS, Hepatitis C) and sex work (HIV/AIDS, STDs, etc.), utilization of ERs for any health concerns, etc.

However, there have been some problems with the TC model and its dependence on aggressive confrontation. These included the fact that many of the women, if they entered a TC at all, never were able to discuss their childhood sexual and physical abuse, their later DV/IPV, their sexual abuse in sex work and then again in prison, and some of the coercive aspects of the TC and its male leadership. In addition, the intense confrontation style only added to the anxiety and hyperarousal symptoms of men and women with trauma experiences. There were high rates of drop-out of women in the TCs early in treatment. The emphasis on harsh confrontation was particularly problematic for populations (both men and women) with a high frequency of traumatic experiences and/or with serious mental illness.

The TC has continued to evolve. A more recent variation is the Modified TC for clients with co-occurring disorders and for women with their children (Brown et al. 1996). Women and children's residential TC programs are important for a number of reasons: (1) they protect women and their children from DV; (2) they protect the children from other traumatic experiences in the addiction environment; (3) they protect homeless women from violence in the streets; and (4) they allow women the opportunity to learn parenting skills in a supportive environment. With the modifications for women and their children, trauma was also taken into account. When trauma and other serious mental health disorders are integrated into the TC, intense confrontation is eliminated, and other trauma-informed strategies are incorporated. These modifications were also important for many of the men who were sexually and/or physically abused as children, sexually abused in prison, and were veterans of war (Sacks, Sacks, and DeLeon 1999).

Other important modalities in the drug abuse treatment system include: methadone maintenance, and other medically assisted treatments (buprenorphine, vivitrol, etc.); detoxification; intensive outpatient services; and continuing care. One of the problems regarding substance use disorder treatment is that substance abuse/dependence is a chronic disease, but has been treated episodically, as an acute illness.

The recovery movement has now focused upon the use of American Society of Addictive Medicine (ASAM) criteria for appropriate placement and continuing care, using peer recovery coaches to provide ongoing, supportive care to those individuals who exit treatment with positive outcomes. The recovery coach is a person who helps remove personal and environmental obstacles to recovery, links the newly recovering person to the recovery community, and serves as a personal guide and mentor (White and Kurtz 2006). The recovery coach is different than a 12-step program sponsor, who works within the beliefs and practices of a particular recovery fellowship. Recovery coaches also monitor and implement recovery checkups.

In 1992, the Center for Substance Abuse Treatment (CSAT) of SAMHSA asked a group of programs to develop guidelines for a comprehensive treatment model for women. The group identified 17 issues, one of which was interpersonal violence, including incest, rape, battering, and other abuse (CSAT 1994). In the same year, SAMHSA funded residential substance abuse treatment grants for women and their children. Eleven projects were funded in October 1992, under CSAT's Women and Children's Branch. A unique feature of these grants was that treatment could be up to 18 to 20 months and was to be family-centered, holistic, and comprehensive.

In 1997 to 1998, PROTOTYPES undertook a qualitative study (Brown 2000) focused upon the provision of mental health, trauma, and HIV/AIDS services, in addition to the substance abuse treatment services, in these 11 CSAT-funded projects. Ten projects participated in the interviews. In addition to the interviews, the projects sent PROTOTYPES other program data, evaluations, and published papers. Seven of the ten programs had been providing substance abuse treatment services before the new CSAT funding. A number of these were based on the therapeutic community (TC) model and moved toward a more comprehensive, integrated, and family-centered model as a result of the funding. All the programs served a significant percentage of women with trauma histories, as well as current domestic violence (60% to 100%). The programs reported 1,168 admissions of women and 1,113 children. Crack cocaine was reported as the primary drug of use at admission (64.2%). Alcohol was the next, at 11.7 percent. Of the women, 79 percent had previously been in substance abuse treatment. Among the women, 64.1 percent were African American, 24.9 percent were Caucasian, and 9.2 percent were Latina.

Most of the programs reported that they were surprised by the extent of trauma in the lives of the children they were serving. They also reported that they changed from believing that "if we treat the mother, the child will be healthy" (prevention model for the children) to recognizing the need for treatment services for the children as well as their mothers. Most of the program staff also reported that the women talked more about protecting their children than about nurturing them. When staff addressed this issue, the women were able to admit that they were unable to keep themselves and their children safe and that these difficulties arose because of their own experience with physical and sexual abuse. Having the women and their children together in treatment presented a unique opportunity to facilitate the emotional growth of the mothers, increase their bonding/nurturing/parenting skills, and keep the children safe. For all ten programs, safety was a recurrent theme: for the women; for the children; in the residential community; in the outside community; in housing; and in the broadest context. Staff members related that their programs were not comfortable with clients who were angry and expressed rage, with women who self-injured, and especially with mothers who physically punished their children.

In terms of treatment results, those women who remained in treatment for more than six months were significantly more likely to be drug free and employed and less likely to be incarcerated at six and 12 months post treatment. The two most reported "effective components" of treatment were more integrated services (60%) and parenting skills training (60%). What "didn't work" were: sending women to outside providers (e.g., mental health providers); traditional AOD treatment; not dealing with children intensively; and fighting time limits under the Adoption and Safe Family Act (ASFA 1997) and child welfare system. Young and Gardiner (1998) have termed this the "four clocks problem": (1) the child welfare system has a timetable of six months for reviews of a parent's progress, which the federal legislation accelerates to a requirement for a permanency hearing at 12 months; (2) the timetable for AOD treatment and recovery, which often takes longer than AOD-based funding allows and which is often incompatible with child welfare deadlines; (3) the timetable now imposed for TANF clients, who must find work in 24 months; (4) the developmental timetable that affects the children as they achieve bonding and attachment or fail to pass through the period of the first 18 months to three years.

For individuals with substance use disorders and trauma histories and/or PTSD, the harm reduction model of drug treatment would appear to be appropriate. Harm reduction is any program that is designed to reduce drug-related harm without requiring abstinence. It involves tapering and reducing the use of harmful substances and is most useful/effective for certain populations, such as clients with co-occurring disorders (substance use disorder, mental health disorders, and trauma histories) and pregnant women. For example, using methadone is a safer alternative than heroin for a pregnant woman and reduces the risks of harm to both mother and fetus. However, the substance abuse treatment system has developed as an "abstinence" model. This model expects the client to be "clean and sober" early in treatment, which is burdensome for these clients. This is despite the fact that 12-step programs like Alcoholics Anonymous do not expect people to be abstinent before they are engaged in the fellowship. The substance abuse treatment system is moving toward integrating harm reduction with recovery support services, but slowly. Harm reduction also means understanding the need for clients with trauma histories/PTSD and other co-occurring disorders (e.g., depressive disorders) to receive psychiatric medications, if needed and wanted.

Another treatment burden is that substance abuse treatment continues to get shorter because of funding considerations, while clients with substance use disorders and trauma histories/PTSD and/or other comorbid conditions need longer-term treatment. It takes more than 90 days for clients who have substance use disorders, mental health disorders, and histories of trauma to trust providers, experience reductions in anxiety and depression, adjust to treatment structure and rules, and fully participate in treatment.

Blakey and Bowers (2014) studied the barriers to integrating trauma into substance abuse treatment. Twenty substance abuse treatment providers participated in the study; these included 11 counselors (four of whom were also supervisors or administrators), five technicians, and four parenting professions. These staff members were all from a women's treatment program. The barriers to integration were four major beliefs on the part of the staff:

- Belief that it takes more time to deal with trauma than they have;
- Belief that the trauma was secondary to the substance use problems;
- Belief that clients should get clean and sober the same way the staff/counselors got clean and sober (which was often through confrontation); and
- Belief that focusing on trauma means that women would not take responsibility for their drug use.

As can be seen above, our systems of health care, mental health, and substance abuse treatment have many reasons to integrate trauma screening/assessment, trauma-specific interventions, and trauma training, as well as to incorporate a trauma-informed approach, in order to enhance services and service delivery. A trauma-informed approach fits perfectly with family-centered care, patient-centered care, collaborative care, and health/medical homes.[2] It adds an important missing component to these—attention to all the individuals we serve who have experienced traumatic events. In the next chapter, trauma-informed practice is described in detail.

Notes

1 In a study from Australia, Carol Muskett (2014) summarized the literature from 2000 to 2011 in order to identify practices and clinical activities that have been implemented to provide trauma-informed care in inpatient mental health settings. Many of the studies identified attention to the physical environment as a significant strategy. The refurbishment of units to provide a welcoming and more supportive environment included the use of "home-like" furniture, warm colors, calming auditory stimulation (soft music), and a special space for "time-out options." Studies also highlighted the nature of the nurse-patient relationship as critical for clients and the need for staff that are seen as caring, supportive, respectful, and empowering. Many practices and procedures used traditionally in inpatient psychiatric settings—such as ward rounds, search procedures, locked doors, mixed-sex patient populations, and seclusion and restraint—are experienced by patients/consumers as retraumatizing, emotionally unsafe, and disempowering.

2 In March 2007, the American Academy of Family Physicians (AAFP), American Academy of Pediatrics (AAP), American College of Physicians (ACP), and American Osteopathic Association (AOA) published *Joint Principles of the Patient-Centered Medical Home*. These principles define the patient-centered medical home "as a transition away from a model of symptom and illness based episodic care to a system of comprehensive coordinated primary care for children, youth and adults. Patient centeredness refers to an ongoing, active partnership with a personal primary care physician who leads a team of professionals dedicated to providing proactive, preventive and chronic care management through all stages of life. These personal physicians are responsible for the patient's coordination of care across all health care systems, facilitated by registries, information technology, health information exchanges, and other means to ensure patients receive care when and where they need it. With a commitment to continuous quality improvement, care teams utilize evidence-based medicine and clinical decision support tools that guide decision making as well as ensure that patients and their families have the education and support to actively participate in their own care. Payment appropriately recognizes and incorporates the value of the care teams, non-direct patient care, and quality improvement provided in a patient-centered medical home."

References

Adoptions and Safe Families Act of 1997 (H.R. 867), Public Law 105–89, December 1997.
Alim, N, Graves, E, Mellman, TA et al. 2006, Trauma Exposure, Posttraumatic Stress Disorder and Depression in an African American Primary Care Population, *Journal of the National Medical Association*, vol. 98, no. 10, pp. 1620–1636.

Anda, RF, Whitfield, CL, Felitti, VJ et al. 2002, Alcohol-Impaired Parents and Adverse Childhood Experiences: The Risk of Depression and Alcoholism During Adulthood, *Journal of Psychiatric Services*, vol. 53, pp. 1001–1009.

Bentail, R, deSousa, P, Varese, F et al. 2014, From Adversity to Psychosis: Pathways and Mechanisms from Specific Adversities to Specific Symptoms, *Social Psychiatry and Psychiatric Epidemiology*, vol. 49, pp. 1011–1022.

Blakey, BM and Bowers, PH 2014, Barriers to Integrated Treatment of Substance Abuse and Trauma Among Women, *Journal of Social Work Practice in the Addictions*, vol. 14, no 3, pp. 250–272.

Bloom, SL and Farragher, B 2010, *Destroying Sanctuary: The Crisis in Human Service Delivery Systems*, New York, NY, Oxford University Press.

Brown, PJ, Read, JP, and Kahler, CW 2003, Comorbid Posttraumatic Stress Disorder and Substance Use Disorders: Treatment Outcomes and the Role of Coping, in P Ouimette and PJ Brown (eds.), *Trauma and Substance Abuse*, Washington, DC: American Psychological Association, pp. 171–188.

Brown, VB 1998, Untreated Physical Health Problems Among Women Diagnosed with Severe Mental Illness, *Journal of the American Medical Women's Association*, vol. 53, no. 4, pp. 159–161.

Brown, VB 2000, *Changing and Improving Services for Women and Children: Strategies Used and Lessons Learned*, Culver City, CA, PROTOTYPES System Change Center.

Brown, VB 2012, Integrated Screening, Assessment and Training as Critical Components of Trauma-Informed Care, in N Poole and L Graves (eds.), *Becoming Trauma-Informed*, Vancouver, Canada, Centre for Addiction and Mental Health, pp. 319–327.

Brown, VB, Sanchez, S, Zweben, JE, and Aly, T 1996, Challenges in Moving from a Traditional Therapeutic Community to a Women and Children's TC Model, *Journal of Psychoactive Drugs*, vol. 28, no. 1, pp. 39–46.

Carmen, E, Crane, W, Dunnicliff, M et al. 1996, *Task Force on the Restraint and Seclusion of Persons Who Have Been Physically or Sexually Abused: Report and Recommendations*, Boston, MA, Massachusetts Department of Mental Health.

Cavanaugh, C, Campbell, J, and Messing, JT 2014, A Longitudinal Study of the Impact of Cumulative Violence Victimization on Comorbid Posttraumatic Stress and Depression Among Female Nurses and Nursing Personnel, *Workplace Health and Safety*, vol. 62, no. 6, pp. 224–232.

Center for Substance Abuse Treatment (CSAT) 1994, *Practical Approaches in the Treatment of Women Who Abuse Alcohol and Other Drugs*, Washington, DC, U.S. Government Printing Office.

Centers for Disease Control and Prevention (CDC), National Center for Injury Prevention and Control 2014, *Web-Based Injury Statistics Query and Reporting System*, Atlanta, GA, CDC.

Centers for Disease Control and Prevention (CDC), National Center for Injury Prevention and Control 2016, *Web-Based Injury Statistics Query and Reporting System*, Atlanta, GA, CDC.

Deitch, DA 1973, The Treatment of Drug Abuse in the Therapeutic Community: Historical Influences, Current Considerations, Future Outlook, in *Drug Use in America, Volume 4*, Rockville, MD, National Commission on Marijuana and Drug Abuse, pp. 158–175.

DeLeon, G 2000, *The Therapeutic Community*, New York, NY, Springer Publishing Co., Inc.

DeLeon, G, Skodol, A, and Rosenthal, MS 1973, The Phoenix House Therapeutic Community for Drug Addicts: Changes in Psychopathological Signs, *Archives of General Psychiatry*, vol. 28, pp. 131–135.

Donovan, BS and Padin-Rivera, E 1999, Transcend: A Program for Treating PTSD and Substance Abuse in Vietnam Combat Veterans, *National Center for PTSD Clinical Quarterly*, vol. 8, pp. 51–53.

Dube, SR, Felitti, VJ, Dong, M et al. 2003, Childhood Abuse, Neglect, and Household Dysfunction and the Risk of Illicit Drug Use: The Adverse Childhood Experiences Study, *Pediatrics*, vol. 111, pp. 564–572.

Esaki, N and Larkin, H 2013, Prevalence of Adverse Childhood Experiences (ACEs) Among Child Service Providers, *Families in Society: The Journal of Contemporary Social Services*, vol. 94, no. 1, pp. 31–37.

Helzer, J, Robins, L, and McEvoy, L 1987, Posttraumatic Stress Disorder in the General Population: Findings of the Epidemiologic Catchment Area Survey, *New England Journal of Medicine*, vol. 317, no. 26, pp. 1630–1634.

Jennings, A 1995, Retraumatizing Victims of Sexual Abuse, in M Pritchard (ed.), *Dare to Vision: Shaping the National Agenda for Women, Abuse, and Mental Health Services*, Holyoke, MA, Human Resource Association of the Northeast, pp. 16–18.

Jennings, A 1998, On Being Invisible in the Mental Health System, in BL Levin, AK Blanch, and A Jennings (eds.), *Women's Mental Health Services*, Thousand Oaks, CA, SAGE Publications, pp. 326–347.

Jones, M 1953, *The Therapeutic Community: A New Treatment Method in Psychiatry*, New York, NY, Basic Books.

Kessler, RC, McGonagle, KA, Zhao, S et al. 1994, Lifetime and 12-month Prevalence of DSM-III-R Psychiatric Disorders in the United States, *Archives of General Psychiatry*, vol. 51, pp. 8–19.

Kessler, RC, McLaughlin, KA, Green, JG et al. 2010, Childhood Adversities and Adult Psychopathology in the WHO World Mental Health Surveys, *British Journal of Psychiatry*, vol. 197, pp. 378–385.

Kessler, RC, Sonnega, A, Bromet, E, Hughes, M, and Nelson, CB 1995, Posttraumatic Stress Disorder in the National Comorbidity Survey, *Archives of General Psychiatry*, vol. 52, pp. 1048–1060.

Khalifeh, H, Moran, P, Borschmann, R et al. 2015, Domestic and Sexual Violence Against Patients with Severe Mental Illness, *Psychological Medicine*, vol. 45, no. 4, pp. 875–886.

Mauritz, M, Goossens, P, Draijer, N, and and van Achterberg, T 2013, Prevalence of Interpersonal Trauma Exposure and Trauma-Related Disorders in Severe Mental Illness, *European Journal of Psychotraumatology*, vol. 4, pp. 1–15.

Muskett, C 2014, Trauma-Informed Care in Inpatient Mental Health Settings: A Review of the Literature, *International Journal of Mental Health Nursing*, vol. 23, pp. 51–59.

National Council of State Legislatures (NCSL) 2014, *Reducing Youth Violence Through Community-Level Strategies*, www.ncsl.org/research/health/reducing-youth-violence-through-community-level-strategies.aspx.

Ouimette, PC, Ahrens, C, Moos, RH, and Finney, JW 1997, Posttraumatic Stress Disorder in Substance Abuse Patients: Relationship to 1-year Posttreatment Outcomes, *Psychology of Addictive Behaviors*, vol. 11, pp. 34–47.

Ouimette, PC, Finney, JW, and Moos, RH 1999, Two-Year Posttreatment Functioning and Coping of Substance Abuse Patients with Posttraumatic Stress Disorder, *Psychology of Addictive Behaviors*, vol. 13, pp. 105–114.

Peckham, C, Jan 13, 2016, *Medscape Lifestyle Report 2016: Bias and Burnout*.

Pritchard, M (ed.) 1995, *Dare to Vision: Shaping the National Agenda for Women, Abuse, and Mental Health Services*, Holyoke, MA, Human Resource Association of the Northeast.

Robin, LN and Regier, DA 1991, *Psychiatric Disorders in America: The Epidemiological Catchment Area Study*, New York, NY, The Free Press.

Sacks, S, Sacks, JY, and DeLeon, G 1999, Treatment for MICAs: Design and Implementation of the Modified TC, *Journal of Psychoactive Drugs*, vol. 32, pp. 19–30.

Smith, TE, Easter, A, Pollock, M et al. 2013, Disengagement from Care: Perspectives of Individuals with Serious Mental Illness and of Service Providers, *Psychiatric Services*, vol. 64, no. 8, pp. 770–775.

Stayer, D and Lockhart, JS 2016, Living with Dying in the Pediatric Intensive Care Unit, *American Journal of Critical Care*, vol. 25, no. 4, pp. 350–356.

Varese, F, Smeets, F, Drukker, M et al. 2012, Childhood Adversities Increase the Risk of Psychosis: A Meta-Analysis of Patient-Control, Prospective and Cross-Sectional Cohort Studies, *Schizophrenia Bulletin*, vol. 38, pp. 661–667.

Weisberg, RB, Bruce, SE, Machan, JT et al. 2002, Nonpsychiatric Illness Among Primary Care Patients with Trauma Histories and Posttraumatic Stress Disorder, *Psychiatric Services*, vol. 53, no. 7, pp. 848–854.

West, CP, Shanafelt, TD, and Kolars, JC 2011, Quality of Life, Burnout, Educational Debt, and Medical Knowledge Among Internal Medicine Residents, *Journal of the American Medical Association*, vol. 306, no. 9, pp. 952–960.

White, W and Kurtz, E 2006, *Linking Addiction Treatment and Communities of Recovery: A Primer for Addiction Counselors and Recovery Coaches*, Pittsburgh, PA, IRETA/NeATTC.

Williams, LM, Debattista, C, Duchemin, AM et al. 2016, Childhood Trauma Predicts Antidepressant Response in Adults with Major Depression: Data from the Randomized International Study to Predict Optimized Treatment for Depression, *Translational Psychiatry*, vol. 6, e799, pp. 1–7.

Wilmer, H 1958, Toward a Definition of the Therapeutic Community, *American Journal of Psychiatry*, vol. 114, pp. 824–837.

Wilson, B 1957, *Alcoholics Anonymous Comes of Age: A Brief History of AA*, New York, NY, Alcoholics Anonymous World Services.

Yablonsky, L 1965, *Synanon: The Tunnel Back*, New York, NY, Macmillan.

Young, NK, Gardner, SL, and Dennis, K 1998, *Responding to Alcohol and Other Drug Problems in Child Welfare: Weaving Together Practice and Policy*, Washington, DC, CWLA Press.

Zatzick, D, Jurkovich, G, Rivera, FP et al. 2013, A Randomized Stepped Care Intervention Targeting Posttraumatic Stress Disorder for Surgically Hospitalized Injury Survivors, *Annals of Surgery*, vol. 257, no. 3, pp. 390–399.

Zatzick, DF, Russo, J, Darnell, D et al. 2016, An Effectiveness-Implementation Hybrid Trial Study Protocol Targeting Posttraumatic Stress Disorder and Comorbidity, *Implementation Science*, vol. 11, no. 58.

Chapter 5

Trauma-Informed Practice

In a trauma-informed practice all staff members understand the prevalence and impact of trauma on their patient population, integrate knowledge about trauma into policies and procedures, avoid re-traumatizing those who are seeking help, and provide trauma-specific interventions either directly or through collaborative partners. Harris and Fallot (2001) defined the five core values or principles of a trauma-informed approach, viz., safety, trustworthiness, collaboration, empowerment, and choice.

- Safety. Patients/clients, family members, and staff feel physically, psychologically, and culturally safe. This means that the physical environment is safe and nurturing, that interactions between staff and client promote a sense of safety and respect, and that all procedures feel culturally safe to the patient. It is also important to be aware of the importance of language. We need to use terms that are not stigmatizing ("addicts," "borderlines"), are anti-oppressive, and are inclusive. Safe relationships are consistent, predictable, respectful, nonviolent, non-shaming, and non-blaming.
- Trustworthiness. Procedures are conducted with transparency; each step of the organization's processes from intake/admissions through treatment and after-care is explained in appropriate language, and patients are given enough time and respect to ask questions and receive appropriate answers; confidentiality is explained and honored; all procedures are predictable; and incentives and consequences are consistently given.
- Collaboration. There is sharing of power in decision-making between staff and clients, as well as collaboration between all providers in the system and the broader community network. Optimizing and improving patient processes across organizational boundaries is an important goal.
- Empowerment. The patient's strengths are recognized and validated, and the learning of new coping skills is provided in a respectful way. In addition, we normalize responses typically defined as "symptoms"; instead they are seen as "adaptations." Survivors are not seen as manipulative, attention-seeking, or destructive, but as trying, instead, to cope using any means available to them. Also, it is important to assist in enhancing the client's resources and support networks. Recovery from trauma and other comorbid conditions involves developing skills not only for managing intense feelings and situations, but for living a life that minimizes exposure to trauma triggers.

- Choice. The patient is given choices in as many ways as possible, e.g., choices about how they will be contacted, which treatments they will be given, how the treatments will be given, which problem she/he would like to start with, "what matters the most," etc. Choice also includes the client working at his/her own pace.

In addition to these core values, there are additional principles that are important for a trauma-informed practice. These include sensitivity to cultural issues and the inclusion of peer support.

What Does a Trauma-Informed Program Look Like?

One of the consistent questions agencies ask when they participate in trauma trainings is: "What does a trauma-informed program look like?" Because of the high prevalence of trauma within the populations entering their systems, organizations that work with children, youth, adults, and families should expect that the clients they serve have experienced some form of traumatic event. Once again, "trauma is the expectation, not the exception." The client may appear anxious, withdrawn, or unable to speak, or she/he may be hostile, defiant, mistrustful; providers must remember that these may, in fact, be "fight, flight, freeze" responses.

Physiologically, trauma can lead to perception of threat of life to hyperarousal. In a hyperarousal state, the individual can respond to benign stimuli as if they were life-threatening. For example, a veteran may hear a car backfire and drop to the ground, afraid he is about to be attacked as he was in combat. This prepares the individual to respond with "fight, flight, or freeze" responses; you may observe outbursts of anger (fight), clients leaving treatment early (flight), or a client with an appearance like "a deer in the headlights" (freeze). The last response is often seen in children who cannot, as easily as adults, fight or flee.

With regard to psychological responses, there are two sets: (1) denial and emotional numbing, which represent efforts to avoid painful thoughts, images, and feelings; and (2) intrusions and re-experiencing of the trauma, which represent efforts to confront the trauma. We have pathologized denial and numbing; however, it is important to remember that they serve an adaptive purpose. Denial enables the survivor to face the realities of "what happened" in a more gradual and manageable way. These responses were seen in victims of the atomic bombings in Hiroshima and of the Holocaust. Talking about the event ("bearing witness") plays an adaptive role in coping. Treatment and social support provide the survivor with a holding environment in which to do the necessary cognitive-emotional work of healing. Rape victims, cancer patients, and veterans know that others in their support groups understand experientially what they have gone through and can speak openly about fears and concerns, as well as ways to cope.

It should also be noted that, following traumatic events, survivors may also avoid "people, places, and things" associated with the event. This coping strategy is typically not available for victims of repeated child and intimate partner abuse, who are forced to continue to be engaged with the perpetrators of the abuse. Many survivors use drugs and/or alcohol to modulate their arousal. For substance abuse treatment providers, this raises the issue of "triggers" that can increase the substance use. Triggers are quite relevant to trauma work, as well as to substance abuse treatment. Treatment providers also need to be very aware that relapse prevention, in which the discussion of people, places, and things occur, can trigger trauma responses in those clients who have been traumatized.

Trauma-informed practices are different than trauma-specific interventions. Trauma-specific interventions help the client deal specifically with their traumatic experiences and teach coping skills to facilitate healing. These interventions include both individual and group treatment. Trauma-informed practices are approaches that incorporate a thorough understanding of the prevalence and impact of trauma, and are designed to avoid re-traumatizing those who seek care/help. SAMHSA has defined a trauma-informed approach as:

> A program, organization, or system that is trauma-informed realizes the widespread impact of trauma and understands potential paths for recovery; recognizes the signs and symptoms of trauma in clients, families, staff, and others involved with the system; and responds by fully integrating knowledge about trauma into policies, procedures, practices, and seeks to actively resist re-traumatization (SAMHSA 2014, p. 9).

Such practices/approaches demonstrate an understanding that the impacts of trauma are often seen in life domains not obviously related to the experiences of trauma and victimization (e.g., health concerns, incarceration, poor educational achievement). Trauma-informed practice expands the range of trauma sequelae; it goes beyond a focus upon PTSD, because we want to be able to prevent PTSD in patients who have already experienced trauma. It recognizes the strengths that survivors have used in dealing with interpersonal violence, i.e., that the specific symptoms such as substance abuse and/or hostility have helped the victim survive and manage the emotional and physical distress. In her inpatient psychiatric milieu, Bloom (1994) proposed a shift in perspective on the part of all staff (nurses, doctors, support personnel), patients, and families. She suggested that they begin to base their understanding and practice "on an injury-based model." As Bloom stated, we all know something about comforting injured people—we can identify with them—but it is far more difficult for us to identify with "sickness" (e.g., serious mental illness) or "badness" (e.g., in incarcerated populations who we are punishing). The goal of this change in perspective was to move the fundamental question that we pose when we confront a troubled or troubling person from "What's wrong with you?" to "What's happened to you?" and "How can we help?"[1,2]

An important part of being a trauma-informed provider organization is an awareness that providers (doctors, nurses, therapists, case managers, counselors, and other helpers) may also have experienced trauma. Even if they have not, working with people who have survived traumatic experiences and listening to their stories can take an emotional toll and lead to secondary trauma. (See Chapter 3.) Secondary trauma is also referred to as vicarious traumatization. Secondary symptoms may include an increase in arousal and/or avoidance reactions, re-experiencing personal trauma, sleeplessness, fearfulness, or anger.

In order to move toward trauma-informed practice, there are a number of recommended organizational culture shifts:

- An administrative commitment to the change process is important for moving knowledge about trauma and violence/victimization into a central place in service delivery practices. Supportive leaders allocate their own time to reflect the importance of trauma-informed modifications by attending and/or leading trauma trainings for staff, establishing a "trauma initiative" group, monitoring progress toward goals, and ensuring funding, space, and staff time for the initiative.

- Universal screening for trauma should be implemented in all health, mental health, and substance abuse treatment systems. Often problems related to trauma are not identified and, in the case of children, parents may not volunteer concerns without prompting. If the provider does not identify trauma, the provider may misdiagnose and inadequately treat. Not only does trauma screening help us identify clients' issues and needs, but it conveys to the clients that trauma/violence is an important issue to discuss. It also assists us in identifying clients who may be in immediate danger and in developing a comprehensive treatment plan. Screening/assessment should be conducted in a manner that is sensitive to a history of possible physical, sexual, and domestic violence. Clients should be told that if they do not want to answer a question, all they have to do is state that they do not want to answer. This should be documented in the clients' charts.

- Workforce development, including training on trauma and trauma-informed practice, trauma-informed supervision, and strategies to address secondary trauma in staff and to promote self-care is needed to begin transformation. Training should include all staff, including administrators, direct care staff, and support staff (e.g., receptionists, cooks, maintenance, security guards, etc.). Training should be multi-leveled, so that everyone receives basic trauma training, clinical staff receive additional training including trauma-specific interventions, and supervisors receive training in responsive supervision. Trauma training should also occur at college and graduate levels for students planning to enter the helping professions. (See Appendix E for health care trainings.)

- Supervision can provide a physically and emotionally safe place for the practitioner to examine his/her work with an experienced, supportive mentor. Ongoing supervision in trauma-informed care is recognized as a major protective factor in buffering against vicarious trauma. Consistent with the principles of trauma-informed practice, this relationship must be built on trust, which is based on the supervisor establishing clear boundaries and expectations, listening without judgment, assisting supervisees to reflect on their practice, and giving feedback about their work in a noncritical fashion. One other role of the supervisor is to educate supervisees about vicarious/secondary trauma and guide them in managing workload and self-care (Berger and Quiros 2014; Pearlman and Sackvitne 1995).

- There should be an understanding at all levels of the organization that many of the symptoms and behaviors (e.g., substance use) of trauma survivors are adaptations to the trauma; that these have helped the victim survive. This adaptation model helps providers and survivors to focus on the resiliency to trauma (strengths), rather than defining the symptoms and behaviors as "weakness" and "failures."

- Program policies and procedures need to be reexamined and revised to incorporate trauma-informed practices (e.g., reduction of seclusion and restraint; prevention of re-traumatization).

- Stage-Oriented Treatment ("Do No Harm") should be considered. In 1992, Herman proposed a three-stage model for trauma treatments (Herman 1992). The first stage is "safety"; the second is "remembrance and mourning"; and the third is "reconnection." A number of the trauma-specific group curricula that have been developed focus on Stage 1; these include: *Seeking Safety*, *TREM*, *Beyond Trauma*, *Risking Connection*, and *Atrium*. In this first stage, the patient is supported and helped to learn the connection between trauma and his/her symptoms, as well as to learn new coping strategies and methods of symptom containment. In the later stages, treatment is individualized, based on the patient's strengths, vulnerabilities, and cultural factors, and focuses more on the narrative of the survivor's trauma story.
- While anger expressed by clients may be uncomfortable for providers, it is important to recognize the centrality of anger as a response to abuse and victimization. When providers can allow the expression of anger and help survivors feel they are accepted, even when they are angry, then the anger can be integrated and clients can be helped to modulate their rage.

Kluft and colleagues (2000) have discussed several principles that can guide a trauma-informed approach, as well as trauma-specific interventions, namely: (1) as trauma involves the breaking of boundaries, a trauma-informed approach will present firm and consistent boundaries so that the patient can feel safe; (2) as trauma imposes loss of control and helplessness, a trauma-informed approach will focus upon the patient having control over aspects of the treatment and being a full partner in treatment decisions; (3) as trauma overwhelms a patient's resources, treatment must be paced to minimize the possibility of the patient being overwhelmed and to maximize the building of strength and new coping skills; and (4) as trauma usually induces shame, the provider must take an active, warm stance that emphasizes connectedness to the patient.

Building on the work of Harris and Fallot (2001) and the Trauma Committee of the Women with Co-Occurring Disorders and Violence Study (WCDVS), Elliott and colleagues (Elliott et al. 2005) reported on ten principles that define a trauma-informed approach.

1. Trauma-informed services recognize the impact of violence and victimization on development and coping;
2. Trauma-informed services identify recovery from trauma as a primary goal;
3. Trauma-informed services employ an empowerment model;
4. Trauma-informed services strive to maximize a woman's choices and control over her recovery;
5. Trauma-informed services are based in a relational collaboration;
6. Trauma-informed services create an atmosphere that is respectful of survivors' need for safety, respect, and acceptance;
7. Trauma-informed services emphasize women's strengths, highlighting adaptations over symptoms and resilience over pathology;
8. The goal of trauma-informed services is to minimize the possibilities of re-traumatization;
9. Trauma-informed services strive to be culturally competent and to understand each woman in the context of her life experiences and cultural background; and

10. Trauma-informed agencies solicit consumer input and involve consumers in designing and evaluating services.

It should be noted that, while WCDVS focused upon women, these principles apply to men as well.

Trauma-informed self-assessments are available to help organizations identify steps for modifications in their structures, environment, and procedures (e.g., Creating Cultures for Trauma-Informed Care, Walk-Through Assessment). (See Appendix D.)

No Wrong Door

Many individuals with comorbidity, including trauma, find it difficult to navigate our complicated and fragmented service systems. When we began to develop principles that should guide systems of care for people with co-occurring disorders, one of the main principles was "no wrong door," i.e., that, wherever a person seeking care enters the system, s/he must be accepted and actively assisted in getting the treatment s/he wants and needs. This might mean a screening and referral or acceptance into the program the individual entered, as opposed to sending her/him from one agency to another.

In a publication on outreach to injection drug using (IDU) women, Gross and Brown (1993) investigated the results of outreach by 63 research projects funded by the National Institute on Drug Abuse. The goal of the projects was to outreach to these individuals and to attempt to engage them in HIV/AIDS risk reduction interventions, including drug abuse treatment. Almost 6,000 injection drug using women and more than 18,000 IDU men were studied. The hypothesis tested by Gross and Brown was that the population recruited through non-institutional forms of outreach contained only a small fraction of "invisible" women and that most of the women recruited would have been exposed to one or more public institutions in the six months prior to their recruitment. The results indicated that almost 75 percent of the women were, at the time of the recruitment interview, dependent upon social welfare, had had some contact with a public institution (e.g., emergency room or prenatal clinic, or had been in jail or prison) during the prior six months. Approximately 65 percent of the men were seen in social welfare or the criminal justice system during this same period. One of the conclusions to be drawn from these results is that there is a notable deficit in existing institutions; i.e., while they were well positioned to link these at-risk individuals to relevant services, they did not do so. The authors recommended that more resources be devoted to "inreach," i.e., training all human services staff in screening/assessment, Motivational Interviewing (see Chapter 9), and techniques for referring clients to any needed treatment.

The patient/client pathway to services is extremely important in trauma-informed practice. When a patient begins her/his journey can make a difference in whether or not s/he will relapse, experience increased symptoms, or be revictimized, and can provide an opportunity for prevention. By improving access to services and reducing waiting times and cumbersome procedures, we enhance the patient/client experience; by providing trauma-informed care, we improve the chances that s/he will follow through with treatment, feel safe and heard, and be satisfied with the care delivered.

Screening

Because of the high prevalence of traumatic experience across all diagnostic categories and because of the very low spontaneous disclosure rate, it is recommended that trauma screening be implemented in all three systems, i.e., health, mental health, and substance abuse. The best time would be during an intake appointment, when other issues, such as smoking, drug/alcohol use, IPV, and depression, are being assessed. The Affordable Care Act (ACA) created a federal definition of "screening" and mandated screening for the presence of depression, tobacco use, and substance abuse in health settings. These screens can be very short, e.g., the PHQ-2 or PHQ-9 for depression.[3] Under the ACA, screening is the foundation of preventative medicine. Most screening, which is reimbursable by insurance (albeit at a very low rate), can be performed by a nurse, medical assistant, or counselor.

Identification of a trauma history is critical if a provider/program is to be able to effectively respond to an individual. The provider/program needs to: (1) determine imminent danger (as in the case of domestic or interpersonal violence); (2) communicate that the provider/program believes trauma and violence are significant events; (3) communicate openness to a discussion of painful events; (4) determine the most appropriate follow-up; and (5) open the possibility of later disclosure if the client is not ready at this time. Screenings are only beneficial if there are follow-up procedures in place and resources available for handling positive screens.

Survivors of childhood maltreatment and/or adult abuse and other traumatic experiences are often reluctant to talk about those experiences. In fact, the average time before disclosure has been reported to be between nine and 16 years, and some survivors never reveal their victimization to providers. If you have experienced trauma at the hands of another person, particularly someone who has been important to you and who you believed to be protective of you (e.g., parents, older siblings, teachers, coaches, clergymen), then you do not trust people—especially when they try to assure you that they want to help you and that you should trust them.

In an exploratory study on the practices of, attitudes toward, and perceived barriers to screening adult patients for childhood sexual and physical abuse, Weinreb and colleagues (2010) surveyed members of the Massachusetts Academy of Family Physicians. Less than one-third of providers who responded "usually or always" screened for childhood trauma and correctly estimated childhood abuse prevalence rates; 25 percent reported that they "rarely or never" screened patients for trauma. Five questions were asked about physicians' own exposure to childhood sexual abuse or physical abuse, adult interpersonal violence, and the witnessing of parental violence.

More than one-fourth of physicians reported that they usually or always screened female patients; 12.2 percent usually or always screened men. Among 12 possible barriers to screening, most physicians saw three as major barriers: not enough time to evaluate or counsel childhood abuse victims, not enough time to ask about childhood abuse history, and competing primary care recommendations. Among the 95 percent of physicians responding to the questions about personal trauma, 33.6 percent acknowledged a history of personal abuse (physical or sexual) or personal trauma, including witnessing abuse between parents. Nearly a third reported physical or sexual abuse (as adults or children). The study authors recommended training programs on screening for physicians. It seems important to also include nurses and medical assistants in the training to help ensure that all patients are screened.[4] In addition, it is important to include training on secondary traumatization and self-care for providers.

Facilitators for screening on trauma include:

1. Adding a few screening items on trauma to screening already being done. (Most providers are already screening on the issues that are related to their specialty. For example: Health providers screen for substance use including tobacco, interpersonal violence or domestic violence, and depression; mental health providers screen for depression, anxiety, and substance use; and substance abuse treatment providers screen for past and current drug and alcohol use, as well as depression, anxiety and other mental health issues.);[5]
2. Training providers on when and how to ask about trauma and how to respond to the answers given by patients/clients;
3. Identifying the person(s) on the treatment team who are best equipped to do the screening (e.g., intake person, admission clerk, nurse, medical assistant, peer);
4. Keeping the screening questions short; and
5. Giving the patient/client the option not to answer the screening questions.

The reason for asking about trauma at the initial assessment is that if the questions are not asked then, they tend not to be asked at all. If the patient is too distressed at that point, then delaying the questions is appropriate. In those cases, it should be clearly recorded that the questions were not asked and the patient's file flagged for trauma screening at a later point. A trauma-informed introduction to screening might be, "I'm going to ask you some sensitive questions. If you don't want to answer, please tell me that. It's fine if you prefer not to answer."

There are two important points about that introduction. First, it prepares the patient that there are some sensitive questions coming and that they have some importance to the provider. Second, if the patient states s/he does not want to answer a question about interpersonal violence, for example, this signals to the provider that the client probably has some problem with abuse and may have important reasons for not answering the questions at this time. Reasons for not answering may be that: the abuser is sitting in the waiting room and the patient is afraid to speak about the abuse; s/he is afraid you will alert the authorities, that the abuser may then be punished, and that this will make him/her even more abusive; s/he is afraid you will alert the authorities and have the children taken away; the client simply doesn't trust any providers yet.

Questions should be about specific behaviors, e.g., in the ACE questionnaire, the patient is asked, "Did anyone ever act in a way that made you afraid that you might be physically hurt?" It is also important to ask about present abuse and to ensure a safety plan is in place if there is any danger to the patient and/or children. When using a structured questionnaire, the provider should discuss the patient's responses immediately after. Drs. Felitti and Anda described asking the following question after the ACE questionnaire was completed. "I see that you have _____. Tell me how that has affected you later in life" (Felitti and Anda 2010, p. 85).

With regard to responding, validation of the patient's experience(s) and of their reaction to disclosure will communicate that you understand the importance of what has happened to them, that you care about what happened, and that you are non-judgmental. Some recommendations include: affirming that it was a good thing for the patient to tell you; offering support; checking the patient's emotional state at the end of the session; and offering follow-up. The need to offer support means that the provider must become familiar with abuse-related services in their own agency and in the broader community.

In the Women with Co-Occurring Disorders and Violence Study, the consumer/survivor/recovering staff or "persons with lived experience" told us numerous times how no one had asked them about their abuse experiences. If they themselves had brought up their abuse, they were told that they were mentally ill or "schizophrenic" and that's why they "thought" they were abused. These women believed that if someone (particularly a psychiatrist) had believed them, they would not have been given so many diagnoses. They also told us many times that they were revictimized/retraumatized in inpatient psychiatric facilities, particularly by the use of seclusion and restraint.

A study examining screening and intervention for comorbid substance disorders, PTSD, depression, and suicide at trauma centers was conducted by Love & Zatzick (2014). Respondents at all level I and level II trauma centers in the U.S. were asked to complete a survey describing screening and intervention procedures for alcohol and drug use problems, suicidality, depression, and PTSD. Overall, the study found that more than 80 percent of level I and II trauma centers routinely screen for alcohol and drug problems; 49 percent screen for suicidality; 23 percent screen for depression; and only 7 percent screen for PTSD. The authors recommended adopting population-based, automated screening procedures for PTSD, which would make it possible to reach more people and have a greater impact on the trauma center population. Given that a history of traumatic experiences has been linked to mental health disorders, substance use disorders, and physical disease, and that the prevalence of PTSD diagnosis is much lower than accumulation of severe trauma experiences, I recommend that trauma center staff be trained to screen for childhood and adult trauma experiences.

Screening and brief intervention to address alcohol use has been recommended in national practice guidelines, but is infrequently implemented in health care settings. *SBIRT (Screening, Brief Intervention, and Referral to Treatment)* fits the alcohol and brief counseling performance measure developed and approved by the American Medical Association's Physician Consortium for Performance Improvement, the Affordable Care Act's Provision for substance use services, and Medicare reimbursement codes for *SBIRT* (Ghitza and Tai 2014). The most common barriers to *SBIRT* delivery in primary care are limited physician time and competing priorities (Agley et al. 2014). Non-physician implementation of *SBIRT* can be a viable approach toward overcoming these barriers. Mertens and colleagues (2015) found that: (1) medical assistants screened at higher rates than physicians; and (2) clinical health educators, behavioral medicine specialists, and registered nurses delivered brief interventions and referral to treatment. Medical assistants are important additions to the process, since it is consistent with their role of collecting and recording vital signs. The authors concluded that a model of medical assistant screening and physician intervention may have the highest odds of implementation in primary care.

I had the opportunity, as a member of the Co-Occurring Joint Action Committee (COJAC) for the State of California and Co-Chair of its Screening/Assessment Sub-Committee, to develop a short screening instrument for co-occurring disorders (mental health, substance use disorders, and trauma), known as the *COJAC Screener* (Brown 2012). The original nine questions (three for mental health, three for substance use, and three for trauma) were later enhanced, in order to qualify for *SBIRT*. The *Revised COJAC Screener* (see Appendix G) was pilot-tested at two large facilities, PROTOTYPES and Tarzana Treatment Centers. Results showed that: (1) medical assistants, behavioral health specialists (psychologists, social workers), and recovering staff members all were able to administer the screener easily; (2) clients were amenable to answering the questions and able to do so without difficulty; (3) the results of the screening showed high rates of all three issues. Referrals to treatment were significant, since both treatment centers could admit the clients needing treatment. (See Appendix B for screening instruments.)

Trauma-Specific Interventions

As part of a trauma-informed organization/system, trauma-specific interventions need to be available, either on-site or by referral. These interventions directly address the effects of trauma on the client's life and facilitate trauma recovery by: helping the client understand the connections between the trauma and subsequent feelings and behaviors; and teaching coping skills to help the client gain a sense of control, build more positive and safe relationships, and adopt safer behaviors. Trauma-specific interventions include both trauma-specific individual therapy and group interventions. If your organization does not provide trauma-specific interventions, it is important that you are knowledgeable about other agencies that do. (See Appendix C for a list of interventions.)

Trauma-specific group interventions[6] include two of the key components/principles of trauma recovery—empowerment and reconnection with others. The groups provide participants with opportunities to break down the isolating barrier of shame and to rebuild trust in others. As noted earlier in this chapter, staged treatment is central to doing this group work (Herman 1992). The most frequently used trauma-specific interventions for adults are Stage 1 groups: *Seeking Safety, Trauma Recovery and Empowerment (TREM), Beyond Trauma*, and *Helping Men Recover*. (See Appendix C.) It is recommended that these groups have two co-facilitators, one of whom can be an abuse survivor or peer. This ensures that, if a participant needs to leave the group because of becoming triggered, one facilitator can go with him/her. The groups also provide the learning of coping skills such as "grounding," which helps survivors calm themselves down when they are triggered by trauma memories. The secrecy and shame associated with a history of abuse may be more alleviated in a group setting than in individual treatment.

Peer Support Services

Our care systems (health, mental health, and substance use) have many barriers imposed by protocols, attitudes, and approaches. The outreach worker/community health worker/peer recovery specialist can provide not only linkages, but also support and sustained contact, effectively motivating clients to make the move to enter treatment, stay in treatment, and continue healing/recovery in aftercare/continuing care. The peer who "has been there" can empathize with a client's resistances and fears; they are able to recognize and confront denial, as well as educate the client on what to expect and how to continue changing her/his life.

The concept of peers helping peers is not new. In 1935 Alcoholics Anonymous, the oldest of the peer programs, came into being. It was viewed as a response to the limited effectiveness of traditional services and was intended to draw on the power of individuals to offer mutual support, solace, and learning. The achievements of self-help groups such as Alcoholics Anonymous were based on the principle that people who share a disease or disability have "something to offer each other that professionals can't provide."

Self-help groups for persons with mental illness emerged in the 1950s. These included: Schizophrenics Anonymous, the National Depressive and Manic-Depressive Association, and Recovery, Inc. Fountain House is another important example; founded in the 1950s in New York City by individuals with mental illnesses who created a supportive community of peers, it gave birth to a clubhouse movement in which consumers play active roles in the management and operation of the program. There are now many more consumer-run programs available to individuals with mental illness.

In 1965, Reiff and Reissman (1965) described the use of "indigenous nonprofessionals" as "bridgemen," who bridged the social distance between those who need services (patients) and those providing services, i.e., the server and the served. They described the worker as a "peer of the client (who) shares a common background, language, ethnic origin, style, and group of interests" (Reiff and Reissman 1965, p. 81). In the 1970s, a number of programs pioneered the use of formerly addicted drug abusers to locate and bring into treatment heroin users from the streets, emergency rooms, and criminal justice system (Hughes and Crawford 1972; Inciardi et al. 1979; Toborg et al. 1976). In the late 1980s and 1990s, during the early years of the AIDS epidemic, the National AIDS Demonstration Research (NADR) Project, funded by the National Institute on Drug Abuse, made use of these strategies for reaching injecting drug users and their sexual partners to reduce risk-taking associated with needle-using and sexual behaviors (Brown and Beschner 1993). Community health outreach workers in programs throughout the U.S. brought AIDS education to the streets and taught many thousands of individuals how to reduce their risk of acquiring and transmitting HIV through the use of clean needles, condoms, and other harm reduction strategies.

At the same time, the consumer movement in mental health was becoming stronger. The theme, "nothing about us, without us," was an important step in raising awareness of the needs and preferences of clients with diagnoses of severe mental illness. As the peer support movement in mental health expanded, it became more political and took on a human rights stance. Consumers banded together around their negative experiences in mental health treatment, including seclusion, restraint, over-medication, and rights violations (e.g., forced medication), and demanded changes.

In 2002, PROTOTYPES produced a monograph (Brown & Worth 2002) to help programs integrate consumer staff into their programs. The monograph was based on our experience with the Women's Initiative for HIV Care and Reduction of Perinatal HIV Transmission (which was funded by the Health Resources and Services Administration from 1998 to 2003), as well as our 15 years (at the time of the monograph's publication) of experience with the employment of consumer staff. The monograph includes consumer staff members' voices, as well as the voices of other program staff who may or may not be consumers. Among the benefits they saw to having consumer staff were the following:

- One consumer staff member said that she and her health benefitted "by learning about new medications." This, she said, led to her taking her medications regularly and to encouraging other consumers to take their medicines.
- "When the populations we serve are truly represented on staff, we are modeling 'de-stigmatization' of the problems/diseases we treat—we are the people we serve. The culture of us/them is changed."
- "It brings a realism, when you are dealing with families. They reach out to someone who shares the same language they do."
- "The message in trainings that 'we are all consumers' is important. Being able to demonstrate in trainings that we all participate in some type of 'care' services" (mental health, AOD, health care, etc.) sensitizes all staff to client/patient needs.
- "It keeps programming very real when consumers are actually part of the planning process, giving daily input to the program; it makes the program much more effective."
- "Women are encouraged to go to school, have a career, move ahead."

The importance of peers in the implementation of trauma-informed approaches to care is also discussed in Chapters 7 and 9.

Trauma Prevention

Caplan, often thought to be the father of crisis intervention, stated that a crisis is provoked when "a person faces an obstacle to important life goals that are for a time insurmountable through the utilization of customary methods of problem solving" (Caplan 1961, p. 18). In crisis theory, the term "crisis" means a "turning point," i.e., the period of transition from one level of functioning to another, in which there may be a danger. At the same time, there is an opportunity for change and growth. The major elements of crisis theory have been summarized and expanded by a number of writers, including Parad, Jacobson, and Brown (Parad 1965; Jacobson 1980; Brown 1990), each of which built on the pioneering work of Lindemann (1944) and Caplan (1961). Various investigators (Jacobson, Strickler, and Morley 1968) have observed that, during a crisis, memories of old problems that are linked symbolically to the present ones are triggered and can be dealt with by relatively brief therapeutic intervention.

In this model of crisis intervention, the meaning given to the hazardous event or stressful life event determines whether it triggers a crisis. Crisis intervention is an important strategy if a patient has just suffered a traumatic experience. Establishing a safe environment for the client requires the mobilization of supports for her/him and the development of a safety plan for the future. An individual may resolve a crisis in one of three ways: by functioning at the same level as pre-crisis; at a higher level; or at a lower level. Crisis intervention allows us to push the odds toward better post-crisis functioning. Rapid entry is essential to crisis intervention if we are to take advantage of the client's heightened motivation for help. The first session involves the "detective work," i.e., "Why now?," "What brought you to get help at this time?," "What happened to you?," "Has this ever happened to you before?," and "How did you cope with it at that time?"

Crisis theory also leads us into the area of prevention (Caplan 1964). If we can identify and define stressful life events and describe typical processes of coping with these events, then we should be able to implement effective programs to prevent crises, including child maltreatment. Researchers and clinicians have studied the crises of childbirth and premature births, separation and divorce, bereavement, rape/sexual assault, and serious physical illness. Generic crisis intervention can be practiced by persons without formal psychotherapeutic training. The interventionist (e.g., rape center advocate, community health worker) working on this level needs a thorough knowledge of the specific kinds of crises and the kinds of approaches typically effective in resolving them. Individually tailored crisis intervention should be carried out only by mental health professionals trained in crisis intervention. The interventionist at this level relies not only on her/his knowledge about the characteristics of particular crises, but also upon knowledge about the meaning of the crisis to the client, the client's history, and the client's strengths and weaknesses.

Another important concept in crisis work is the "crisis matrix." The crisis matrix defines a period, extending over several months to several years, during which time the individual is likely to experience a series of crises (e.g., separation/divorce). These crises are clustered in accordance with a common guiding principle, but they have separate and unique characteristics. In 1990, I (Brown 1990) described a crisis matrix involving HIV/AIDS, extending from: (1) the individual's first showing symptoms or finding out that the lover/partner has tested positive for HIV to, (2) the individual's testing positive to, (3) receiving a diagnosis of AIDS to, (4) telling family members (particularly when he/she may also have to tell family he/she is gay or a drug user) to, (5) receiving treatment with antiretroviral therapy to, (6) dealing with test results or reaching an undetectable viral load. Each of these crisis points will be resolved in a separate and unique way and will have an impact on how the individual responds to the next crisis point(s).

With prevention efforts, it is important to work both with individuals at risk and key persons in their lives, including family members and caregivers. Three-quarters of behavioral health disorders start by the age of 24 (Kessler et al. 2005), with the first symptoms typically occurring two to three years before diagnosis. This time window gives us an opportunity for preventive interventions. Risk factors that could be altered include family dysfunction, untreated parental mental illness and/or substance abuse, and the experiencing of traumatic events. Home-visiting programs to encourage infant-mother bonding, social and emotional skills training for children in school, parenting skills training in all of our systems (health, mental health, and substance abuse treatment), and prevention programs for depression, substance abuse, and risky sexual behaviors have been shown to be successful throughout our systems.

Using the ACE risks to define priority populations for prevention, we would focus attention on children of incarcerated parents, children in the child welfare system, children in domestic violence situations, children who have lost a parent through death, and children experiencing community violence. Prevention of trauma/PTSD is at the cross section of our primary care/pediatrics, mental health, and substance abuse treatment systems. Preventive education classes or groups can help individuals "not feel alone," to understand what normal reactions to particular situations are, what actions might help them, and what new coping skills they might need.

The Children's Hospital of Philadelphia's (CHOP) trauma-informed Center for Pediatric Traumatic Stress (CPTS) is an excellent example of a prevention program. (See Chapter 6; CPTS was one of the programs I visited.) The concept of "potentially traumatic events" (PTEs) guides their trauma-informed responses. The immediate time period around a traumatic event often includes multiple PTEs; e.g., learning one's child has cancer, early days of medical workups and treatment initiation, and waiting for the results of initial diagnostic workups. During treatment, PTEs include side effects and complications of treatment, pain, death of other children from cancer, concerns regarding relapse, and relapse/recurrence.

In a recent *Harvard Business Review*, Berry and colleagues (2015) discuss an ongoing study being conducted for the Institute for Healthcare Improvement on how to improve the service journey that adult cancer patients and their families take from diagnosis through treatment to recovery, and in some cases to end-of-life care. Cancer care was chosen because, as the authors state, few services involve more intense emotions. They interviewed cancer patients, family members, oncologists, and other health care staff at ten cancer centers in nine U.S. states (one of which is Bellin Health Systems in Wisconsin, where one of the study authors, Jody Wilmet, is Vice-President for Oncology).

Bellin Health Systems follow four guidelines to prevent crises:

1. Identify emotional triggers. Example: When breast cancer survivors were asked how they would design the cancer center if money were no object, the majority said that it should not be inside the flagship hospital, which they perceived as "a complex, scary, and inconvenient place." So Bellin designed a free-standing facility a few miles from the hospital, offering a calming experience through easy parking, serene design using soft colors and natural light, and a garden visible from the infusion room.
2. Prepare patients for what to expect and respond early to intense emotions. Not knowing what lies ahead is a major source of anxiety for patients and their families. Consequently, attending to the patient's needs in a timely and thorough manner is crucial to moderating their emotional responses and intensity. Intermountain Healthcare offers a comprehensive set of medical appointments over the course of one day, typically within a week of diagnosis. Patients and family members sit in one room during their "multidisciplinary clinic" day, and the members of the care team (e.g., surgeon, medical oncologist, radiation oncologist, social worker, nurse, etc.) individually come to them. At the end of the day, patients receive a written care plan that includes scheduled appointments. Since the beginning of every stage of a long-term treatment can heighten client's emotions, it is important to explain what to expect from/at each stage. For example, the North Shore-Long Island Jewish Cancer Institute in New York gives radiation patients and family members tours of the treatment rooms in advance.

Another critical phase for patients is the end of treatment, which can generate a mixture of relief and anxiety, including the fear of recurrence and the impending loss of their medical support network. In 2015, a formal survivorship program became an accreditation standard for cancer hospitals. At Bellin, patients meet with their nurse practitioner at the end of treatment. Patients and their primary care physicians receive take-home information summarizing their treatments, symptoms of recurrence, when to seek medical help, and ways to manage physical changes.

It is also important to understand that body language, choice of words, tone of voice, and appearance of staff members can have a big impact on anxious patients. "Communicate with care" is an important lesson for staff.

3. Provide a direct contact and mobile technology for patients. Many cancer centers employ patient navigators to help patients and family members overcome barriers to care. In addition, mobile technology can reduce anxiety by providing patients with real-time information and access to assistance.

4. Hire the right people and prepare them for the role. Staff must be able to effectively cope with stress, respectfully communicate with patients and family members, and strengthen patients' coping skills.

Systems Change

Along with changes within specific agencies, changes need to occur within systems and across collaborations (with other agencies in the service networks, counties, states). Cross-training of staff and managers on trauma and trauma-informed practice helps them learn a common language, understand the need for trauma-informed services, acquire and practice new skills, and increase their willingness to work together.

On a policy level, barriers such as separate documentation requirements need to be addressed. It is important that clients do not have to answer the same or similar assessment questions to receive services from multiple agencies in a service network. A uniform assessment across substance abuse, mental health, and health would be less burdensome and time consuming for clients and would dispel the notion that "no-one is listening; they keep asking the same questions." A core assessment process could be implemented with the help of attorneys who understand the legal requirements for sharing information across siloed service systems, particularly when public funding is involved.

Ongoing system change management meetings with all partners in the collaboration can help keep the focus on trauma-informed changes. This coordinating group should include all key stakeholders, including persons with lived experience (peers). Including county and state administrators can do much to move system-wide changes forward. The group can promote system change by developing a common vision statement, reviewing existing community services and identifying strengths and gaps, and overseeing change implementation. Creating safety for dissenting viewpoints and opinions helps sustain creative problem-solving.

In the next chapter, you will be introduced to a number of organizations that have successfully transitioned to using a trauma-informed approach to care or that were designed around such an approach. The following chapters will tell you more about why they became part of this transformative movement in health care, mental health treatment, and substance abuse treatment, how they did it, how they measure their success, and how you, too, can embrace this movement and bring about transformation in your practice/organization.

Notes

1 Dr. Bloom has credited Joseph Foderaro with this shift.
2 It is interesting to note that in 1973 Foucault, in *The Birth of the Clinic*, stated that this new structure, the clinic, was indicated by the "minute but decisive change, whereby the question: 'What is the matter with you?' with which the eighteenth century dialogue between doctor and patient began ... was replaced by that other question 'Where does it hurt?' in which we recognize the operation of the clinic and the principle of its entire discourse" (Foucault 1973, p. xviii).
3 The *PHQ-9* incorporates DSM-IV diagnostic criteria for depression with other leading depressive symptoms into a brief self-report (nine questions) that is an excellent screener. The *PHQ-2* was developed using two of the questions from the *PHQ-9*.
4 In an earlier study (Read, Hammersley, and Rudegeair 2007), providers identified these barriers to asking about trauma: other, more immediate needs and concerns; concerns about offending or distressing clients; fear of inducing "false memories"; clients' being male; clients' being more than 60 years old; fear of having to report the abuse; clients' having a diagnosis of psychosis; and a lack of training in how to ask and how to respond to the answers.
5 It is important to note that the ACE questions (when asked in person) take five minutes on average.
6 One of the most widely read publications from the WCDVS (Finkelstein et al. 2004) reviews features of the trauma-specific groups used in the study and discusses the steps agencies may want to take in selecting a group intervention.

References

Agley, J, Gassman, RA, Vannerson, J, and Crabb, D 2014, Assessing the Relationship Between Medical Residents' Perceived Barriers to *SBIRT* Implementation and Their Documentation of *SBIRT* in Clinical Practice, *Public Health*, vol. 128, no. 8, pp. 755–758.

Berger, R and Quiros, L 2014, Supervision for Trauma-Informed Practice, *Traumatology*, vol. 20, no. 4, pp. 296–301.

Berry, LL, Davis, SW, and Wilmet, J October 2015, When the Customer Is Stressed, *Harvard Business Review*, pp. 86–94.

Bloom, SL 1994, The Sanctuary Model: Developing Generic Inpatient Programs for the Treatment of Psychological Trauma, in MB Williams and JF Sommer (eds.), *Handbook of Post-Traumatic Therapy: A Practical Guide to Intervention, Treatment, and Research*, New York, NY, Greenwood Publishing, pp. 474–491.

Brown, BS and Beschner, GM 1993, *At Risk for AIDS—Injection Drug Users and Their Sexual Partners*, Westport, CT, Greenwood Press.

Brown, VB 1990, The AIDS Crisis: Intervention and Prevention, in HL Pruett and VB Brown (eds.), *Crisis Intervention and Prevention. New Directions for Student Services. No. 49*, San Francisco, CA, Jossey-Bass, pp. 67–74.

Brown, VB 2012, Integrated Screening, Assessment and Training as Critical Components of Trauma-Informed Care, in N Poole and L Graves (eds.), *Becoming Trauma-Informed*, Vancouver, Canada, Centre for Addiction and Mental Health, pp. 319–327.

Brown, VB and Worth, D 2002, *Recruiting, Training, and Maintaining Consumer Staff: Strategies Used and Lessons Learned*, Culver City, CA, PROTOTYPES System Change Center.

Caplan, G 1961, *An Approach to Community Mental Health*, New York, NY, Grune and Stratton.

Caplan, G 1964, *Principles of Preventive Psychiatry*, New York, NY, Basic Books.

Elliot, DE, Bjelajac, P, Fallot, R et al. 2005, Trauma-Informed or Trauma-Denied: Principles and Implementation of Trauma-Informed Services for Women, *Journal of Community Psychology*, vol. 33, pp. 461–477.

Felitti, VJ and Anda, RF 2010, The Relationship of Adverse Childhood Experiences to Adult Medical Disease, Psychiatric Disorders, and Sexual Behavior: Implications for Healthcare, in RA Lanius, E Vermetten, and C Pain (eds.), *The Impact of Early Life Trauma on Health and Disease: The Hidden Epidemic*, Cambridge, England, Cambridge University Press, pp. 77–88.

Finkelstein, N, VanDeMark, N, Fallot, R et al. 2004, *Enhancing Substance Abuse Recovery Through Integrated Trauma Treatment*, Sarasota, FL, National Trauma Consortium.

Foucault, M 1973, *The Birth of the Clinic*, New York, NY, Vintage Books.

Ghitza, UE and Tai, B 2014, Challenges and Opportunities for Integrating Preventive Substance-Use-Care Services in Primary Care Through the Affordable Care Act, *Journal of Health Care for the Poor and Underserved*, vol. 25, no. 1 supplement, pp. 36–45.

Gross, M and Brown, V 1993, Outreach to Injection Drug Using Women, in BS Brown and GM Beschner (eds.), *At Risk for AIDS—Injection Drug Users and Their Sexual Partners*, Westport, CT, Greenwood Press, pp. 445–463.

Harris, M and Fallot, R (eds.) 2001, *Using Trauma Theory to Design Service Systems*, San Francisco, CA, Jossey-Bass.

Herman, JL 1992, *Trauma and Recovery*, New York, NY, Basic Books.

Hughes, P and Crawford, GA 1972, A Contagious Disease Model for Researching and Intervening in Heroin Epidemics, *Archives of General Psychiatry*, vol. 27, pp. 149–155.

Inciardi, JA, Russe, BR, Pottieger, AE et al. 1979, *Acute Drug Reactions in a Hospital Emergency Room*, Rockville, MD, National Institute on Drug Abuse.

Jacobson, GF (ed.) 1980, *Crisis Intervention in the 1980s. New Directions for Mental Health Services, No. 6*, San Francisco, CA, Jossey-Bass.

Jacobson, GF, Strickler, M, and Morley, WE 1968, Generic and Individual Approaches to Crisis Intervention, *American Journal of Public Health*, vol. 58, no. 2, pp. 338–343.

Kessler, RC, Berglund, P, Demler, O et al. 2005, Lifetime Prevalence and Age-of-Onset Distributions of DSM-IV Disorders in the National Comorbidity Survey Replication, *Archives of General Psychiatry*, vol. 62, no. 6, pp. 593–602.

Kluft, RP, Bloom, SL, and Kinzie, JD 2000, Treating Traumatized Patients and Victims of Violence, in Bell, CC (ed.), *Psychiatric Aspects of Violence: Issues in Prevention and Treatment, New Directions for Mental Health Services, No. 86*, San Francisco, CA, Jossey-Bass, pp. 79–102.

Lindemann, E 1944, Symptomatology and Management of Acute Grief, *American Journal of Psychiatry*, vol. 101, pp. 141–148.

Love, J and Zatzick, D 2014, Screening and Intervention for Comorbid Substance Disorders, PTSD, Depression, and Suicide: A Trauma Center Survey, *Psychiatric Services*, vol. 65, no. 7, pp. 918–923.

Mertens, JR, Chi, FW, Weisner, CM et al. 2015, Physician Versus Non-Physician Delivery of Alcohol Screening, Brief Intervention and Referral to Treatment in Adult Primary Care: The ADVISe Cluster Randomized Controlled Implementation Trial, *Addiction Science & Clinical Practice*, vol. 10, no. 1, p. 26.

Parad, HJ (ed.) 1965, *Crisis Intervention: Selected Readings*, New York, NY, Family Service Association of America.

Pearlman, L and Sackvitne, K 1995, *Trauma and the Therapist: Countertransference and Vicarious Traumatization in Psychotherapy with Incest Survivors*, New York, NY: W.W. Norton and Co.

Read, J, Hammersley, P, and Rudegeair, T 2007, Why, When, and How to Ask About Childhood Abuse, *Advances in Psychiatric Treatment*, vol. 13, pp. 101–110.

Reiff, P and Reissman, F 1965, *The Indigenous Non-Professional: A Strategy for Change in Community Action and Mental Health Programs. Community Mental Health Journal Monograph Series, No. 1*, New York, NY, Behavioral Publications.

Substance Abuse and Mental Health Services Administration (SAMHSA) 2014, *SAMHSA's Concept of Trauma and Guidance for a Trauma-Informed Approach, HHS Publication No (SMA) 14–4884*, Rockville, MD, Substance Abuse and Mental Health Services Administration.

Toborg, MA, Levin, R, Milkman, RH, and Center, LJ 1976, *Treatment Alternatives to Street Crime (TASC) Projects*, Washington, DC, Law Enforcement Assistance Administration.

Weinreb, L, Savageau, JA, Candib, LM et al. 2010, Screening for Childhood Trauma in Adult Primary Care Patients: A Cross-Sectional Survey, *Primary Care Companion to the Journal of Clinical Psychiatry*, vol. 12, no. 6, pp. 1–10.

Part II

Chapter 6

Program Descriptions

This book utilizes an approach to enhancing quality of care that identifies innovative strategies from "positive deviants" in health care and behavioral health, i.e., those organizations and their leaders that have demonstrated ways of effectively integrating trauma-informed care into their practice. The central premises of a positive deviant approach (Marsh et al. 2004) are that: (1) solutions to problems facing a community or system often exist within that community/system; and (2) certain members of organizations possess knowledge and experience that can be generalized to improve the performance of other organizations. The positive deviance approach has two primary goals: (1) to identify (usually using qualitative research methods) common methods and practices among the positive deviants that enable them (and their organizations) to achieve high performance; and (2) to promote the uptake of these best practices by working in partnership with key stakeholders, including potential adopters, on dissemination.[1]

The positive deviance approach allows us to look at real-life implementation by identifying not only the practices and processes that are present in the organization, but also the context (e.g., concepts of organizational culture, leadership, norms of behavior, inter-group relations) in which they exist. This context is often missing in randomized controlled trials and is difficult to measure in quantitative studies. In addition, this approach to identification and dissemination of best practices employs some of the key features thought to speed diffusion, or spread. Rogers (2003) suggested that innovations diffuse more rapidly if: they are perceived to provide advantage relative to the status quo; they are compatible with current practices; they are relatively simple to understand and implement; and they generate observable improvements. He also noted that mass media and journal articles are important at the awareness-knowledge stage. However, Rogers and Kincaid (1981) postulated that interpersonal communication with peers is necessary to persuade most individuals to "adopt" a new idea or practice. Kotter and Cohen (2003) also believe that one key ingredient for implementing change in organizations is providing case studies of successful implementation to bolster confidence that change is both possible and beneficial.

My interest in identifying and studying programs doing innovative work in the area of trauma-informed practice began almost two decades ago with my participation in the Women with Co-Occurring Disorders and Violence Study (WCDVS) and continued in the years since then as I attended and presented at a great many conferences about trauma-informed practice around the country. When selecting organizational case studies for this book, I originally identified a list of 25 programs in the fields of health, mental health, and substance abuse treatment. I then under-took a literature search for more information about these programs and the research that had been done on them. Following that, I narrowed the list to seven programs and contacted them. These seven programs were selected based on a number of factors: (1) these organizations and their leaders have integrated, trauma-informed approaches (which include trauma-specific interventions) to the delivery of health, mental health, and substance abuse treatment/prevention services; (2) they have implemented research studies on the effectiveness of their practices; and (3) they represent diversity in size, geographical location, and populations served.

The directors of five of these programs consented to have me conduct in-depth examinations of their organizations, including: review of the organizations' archival documents; review of the research generated by the organizations' leadership; and in-depth, in-person interviews[2] and site visits with the leaders of the organizations focused around their trauma-informed practices.

The interviews and site visits allowed for insights into organization features, such as collaborative relationships with community groups, leadership, and culture, that are important components of transformation and systems change. Using a positive deviance approach also allowed me to study real-life implementation issuers, viz., what was most difficult and easiest to implement and what adaptations in practice had to be made within the organizations to implement trauma-informed care.

This chapter describes these five organizations and their leaders. The other two programs I chose were unavailable for visits and interviews; however, I have included descriptions of these programs at the end of the chapter because of their importance to the field of trauma-informed practice.

Community Connections

Maxine Harris, Ph.D., CEO and Roger Fallot, Ph.D., Trauma Consultant Washington, DC

Maxine Harris and Helen Bergman[3] founded Community Connections in 1984 with the intent of providing comprehensive mental health services to men and women diagnosed with major mental health disorders who were re-entering the community and needed help to regain skills lost after years of institutional care. Community Connections quickly discovered that most of the individuals they wel-comed to the agency also struggled with substance abuse and trauma and began expanding services to meet the growing needs. Over the last 30 years, Community Connections has grown from serving a few dozen adults to now serving more than 3,000 men, women, children, and families annually.

During the early 1980s in Washington, D.C., the use of crack cocaine reached epidemic proportions. Many of Community Connections' consumers' experiences of trauma, combined with their mental health and addiction issues, led to strug-gles with homelessness. The District did not have shelter options readily available to meet the need of Community Connections' consumers. Recognizing this, the agency created outreach and residential programs specifically designed to care for homeless and dually diagnosed adults. Community Connections also adjusted its clinical programming to include a full range of residential and outpatient services for dually diagnosed individuals.

Throughout its continued work, the staff at Community Connections heard stories of violence and victimization, sexual and physical abuse that began in childhood and continued into consumers' present lives. The prevalence rates for childhood and adult victimization approached 100 percent. The very symptoms Community Connection was originally treating as being solely the product of mental illness, substance addiction, or homelessness, turned out, in fact, frequently to be the long-term after effects of abuse. Because of this, the agency began to provide trauma-specific services directly to address trauma and its impact. An increasing number of promising and evidence-based practices address PTSD and other consequences of trauma, especially for people who often bring other complicating vulnerabilities (e.g., substance use, severe mental health problems, homelessness, contact with the criminal justice system) to the service setting. In the 1990s, Community Connections developed the *Trauma Recovery and Empowerment Model (TREM)* group intervention led by Dr. Maxine Harris. In the years since then, more than 1,500 clinicians in more than 20 states have been trained in this model, which is based in both clinical experience and the research literature.

In 2002 Community Connections developed services for children affected by serious mental illness. What began as a pilot, with three children of three mothers with serious emotional disturbances and mental health diagnoses, has grown into the Center for Families and Children, the second largest children's program in the District. Within this program, Community Connections has implemented three trauma-informed evidenced-based practices; the *Girl's Trauma Recovery Empowerment Model (G-TREM), the Strengthening Families Coping Resources (SFCR), Multi-Family Recovery Intervention*, and the *Trauma-Focused Cognitive Behavioral Therapy (TF-CBT)* model. In addition, one other trauma-specific intervention was developed, *M-TREM* for men. (See Appendix C.)

With the assistance of grants and donations, Community Connections has evolved over the years to meet the needs of its consumers and has grown and enhanced its programs. In 1988, it began its Youth in Transition Program in Montgomery County, MD; in the 1990s, its Day Services program; in 2009, Assertive Community Treatment teams (ACT); in 2015, an Outpatient Behavioral Health Clinic (OBHC); in 2014, Outpatient Addictions Services; in 2016, Health Homes; and in 2015, in partnership with Genoa, a pharmacy within the waiting room.

Stanley Street Treatment and Resources, Inc. (SSTAR)

Nancy Paull, M.S., Director Fall River, Massachusetts

Stanley Street Treatment and Resources, Inc. was incorporated as a not-for profit-organization in 1977 as the Fall River/New Bedford Center for Alcohol Problems Inc. The agency was started by a group of concerned citizens who were concerned that the New Bedford Detoxification closure due to mismanagement would negatively affect the citizens of Southeastern Massachusetts. Under the direction of Frederica Alpert, Edwin Jaffe, Dr. Frank Lepreau, and others, an organization was formed to run an alcohol detoxification program, as well as outpatient alcohol counseling and a driver alcohol education program. SSTAR's mission is to provide a quality continuum of care and support to all people, especially those affected by addiction, by responding to their physical, mental, emotional, and spiritual needs.

The agency officially opened in June of 1977. Shortly after its inception, staff noticed that the ratio of men to women accessing services was about ten to one. A group was formed internally to look at the reasons women were not accessing services and to develop programs and policies which would encourage their participation. A pilot day treatment program for women with children was implemented, and, based on the success of that program, SSTAR developed several specialized services and treatments for women. SSTAR became a Women's Minority Business Enterprise in the Commonwealth of Massachusetts.

In accordance with SSTAR's philosophy of treating the total individual, it employs a comprehensive approach, one that is sensitive to the social, cultural, familial, gender, physical, psychological, and economic issues affecting the population it serves. In 1982, the agency became a licensed mental health center and developed the Women's Center, funded by the Massachusetts Departments of Social Services, Public Health, and Mental Health. It also began to address the needs of survivors of domestic violence. In 1986, SSTAR opened its ambulatory building for the provision of outpatient services and opiate detoxification services using a clonidine protocol. After HIV became apparent in its drug-addicted clients beginning in 1986, SSTAR applied for and received the first counseling and testing grant (Project Aware) awarded to a drug treatment facility in the Commonwealth of Massachusetts. Project Aware became a model for other programs in the state and, to meet the needs of the clients it serves, has expanded its services to include: counseling and testing; client support services; case management services; outreach to commercial sex workers and injection drug users; a consumer consortium group; and outreach to physicians who treat HIV infected pregnant women. In 1992, SSTAR opened a residential drug treatment program for women and their children.

In 1996, SSTAR's leadership made the decision to begin offering health care services and opened a 330 Federally Qualified Health Care Center (FQHC). In 1998, SSTAR became involved in the Women with Co-Occurring Disorders and Violence Study and took important steps toward enhancing its trauma-informed approach to service delivery. In March 2012, SSTAR opened a second health center and soon after was awarded a Primary and Behavioral Health Care Integration (PBHCI) grant from the Substance Abuse and Mental Health Services Administration (SAMHSA).

In an effort to enhance the delivery of scientifically based treatments to drug abuse patients, in 2003 the National Institute on Drug Abuse established the National Drug Abuse Treatment Clinical Trials Network. Early in the development of this network, SSTAR was invited to partner with McLean Hospital of Harvard University and four other community treatment programs across New England to form what is known as the Northern New England Node. SSTAR participated in two clinical trials, which not only afforded its staff members the professional and intellectual fulfillment of working with the nation's best academic researchers, but also allowed the agency to provide no-cost, cutting edge treatment to its patients. Also in 2003, SSTAR's Acute Treatment Services (detoxification) received accreditation from the Joint Commission (JCAHO).

SSTAR is part of a number of other networks. In 2004, SSTAR was awarded membership in the Network for the Improvement of Addiction Treatment (NIATx), funded by the Robert Wood Johnson Foundation. The network's work on process improvement and rapid change cycles is particularly relevant to SSTAR's role as a "resource center"; the program has been able to teach its partners how to use the NIATx strategies within their own agencies and systems. In 2005, SSTAR became one of 20 founding members of United Nations Treatment, an international network of drug dependence treatment and rehabilitation resource centers. SSTAR's experience with the training of staff from Armenia, Georgia, and Russia has led to a productive exchange of ideas.

In 2009, SSTAR began operating Lifeline Methadone Treatment Center at St. Anne's Hospital in Fall River and, in 2012, opened the first integrated Methadone, Primary Health, and Behavioral Health Clinic in Massachusetts. SSTAR's South End Services opened a new satellite site to serve residents of the south end of Fall River. This site integrates behavioral health, substance abuse, and primary medical care services under one roof; HIV counseling and testing, Hepatitis C testing, and case management for chronic illness are also available at the site. The Lifeline Methadone Center has also relocated to this site and includes a confidential area for methadone treatment and substance abuse counseling.

SSTAR's Open Access model (Open House) was implemented in 2014. Open House includes outpatient, inpatient, and methadone medication services, delivered in a way that is flexible enough to meet clients' individual treatment needs. No appointment is necessary to access these services. Clients can just walk in and get an assessment and treatment plan on the spot. New clients receive a one-on-one evaluation with a Master's trained and licensed clinician lasting 30 minutes to two hours, depending on the type(s) of services that are indicated. Open House is open from 7:30 AM to 11:30 AM Monday through Friday. In June 2016, hours for the Open Access program were extended through the establishment of an Opioid Urgent Care Center.

SSTAR admits more than 5,000 individuals per year for behavioral health services and provides 50,000 primary health care visits per year.

PROTOTYPES: Centers for Innovation in Health, Mental Health and Social Services

Vivian B. Brown, Ph.D., Founder and (retired) Chief Executive Officer[4] Southern California

PROTOTYPES: Centers for Innovation in Health, Mental Health, and Social Services (PROTOTYPES) is a nonprofit 501(c)(3) public benefit corporation dedicated to meeting the needs of women, men, their children, their families, and their communities in Southern California. Established in 1986, PROTOTYPES remains on the cutting edge of designing and implementing innovative prevention and treatment programs that meet the critical needs of communities (including integrated services for co-occurring disorders). PROTOTYPES has a 30 year history of providing: substance abuse treatment and recovery services for women, children, and men; mental health services for women, children, and men; services for the criminal justice population; HIV/AIDS services for women and children; services for women and men with co-occurring disorders; services for women and men with histories of trauma and/or current trauma; and trauma-informed services for adolescents and transition-age-youth.

PROTOTYPES' philosophy includes empowering its staff and the communities it serves. PROTOTYPES' goals are: (1) to meet emerging community needs through the development of innovative models of service delivery; (2) to test, refine, and disseminate those models; (3) to promote the health and psychological wellbeing of individuals and families through the provision of health, mental health, and alcohol and other drug abuse services; and (4) to enhance the effectiveness of other social service and health agencies through the provision of training and technical assistance. The agency provides services in five major divisions:

- Division of Substance Abuse: substance abuse prevention and treatment programs for women, children, and men, including residential, day treatment, and outpatient programs in Los Angeles, Ventura County, and Orange County;
- Division of Mental Health: mental health treatment for children, adults, transition-age youth, and older adults, with a specialized focus on co-occurring disorders;
- Division of AIDS Prevention and HIV/AIDS Services: HIV/AIDS prevention programs for women and families, including outreach, prevention, and education to high-risk women, and comprehensive health and mental health services for women (and their families) living with HIV/AIDS;
- Division of Trauma and Domestic Violence Services; violence prevention programs; research on violence and victimization; domestic violence programs for women with co-occurring disorders (including a shelter); and comprehensive, trauma-informed co-occurring disorders treatment services; and
- Division of Training, Consultation, and Technical Assistance.

Design of Innovative Service Delivery Models

PROTOTYPES Women's Center—Pomona, a comprehensive residential facility located in Pomona, California, is nationally recognized as a model for integrated treatment for women with co-occurring disorders (mental health, substance abuse, HIV, and trauma) and their children. This comprehensive treatment center includes a 200-bed residential program, day treatment for more than 150 women and men, and outpatient services for women and men. It also includes a specialized treatment program that was one of the first California Prisoner Mother Programs—CPMP—funded by the California Department of Corrections. This program allows incarcerated women with children less than 6 years of age to serve out their sentences with their children in residential substance abuse treatment. In 2006, PROTOTYPES added housing to its services by building a 32-unit affordable housing complex on its Pomona campus. This allowed women and children to live together in a beautiful setting with immediate assistance and supportive services available 24/7. Later, the model of residential treatment for women and children was also implemented by PROTOTYPES in Ventura County and Orange County, California.

In 1987, PROTOTYPES implemented a five-site research and demonstration project, WARN, designed to test a multicultural AIDS prevention/intervention program for female sex partners of injecting drug users. The project was implemented in: Juarez, Mexico; San Diego, California; Los Angeles, California; San Juan, Puerto Rico; and Boston, Massachusetts. Approximately 3,000 women were recruited, enrolled, provided with services, and evaluated by the project. This was one of the first U.S. programs to develop outreach and engagement services designed for women at risk for HIV/AIDS, provided culturally sensitive and language-sensitive outreach services that proved effective in reducing HIV/AIDS risk behaviors. The program was committed to community empowerment, and its services were proactively responsive to the needs of women. Women were recruited from the streets, community centers, public health clinics, and hospitals.

PROTOTYPES WomensLink opened in 1994 to provide an integrated outpatient program for women living with HIV/AIDS. The program used a traditional settlement house model in which the women and their children could drop into the center and access a wide variety of services, including substance abuse and mental health treatment. Of the women enrolled in WomensLink, 29.8 percent met the criterion for triple diagnosis, and, of this triply diagnosed group, 83.7 percent were women of color.

There are numerous benefits of integrated care for multiply diagnosed women with HIV/AIDS. By setting aside beds exclusively for women with HIV/AIDS in its residential drug treatment program, PROTOTYPES became one of the first programs in Los Angeles County to provide integrated care for dually and multiply diagnosed women. In the facility, women receive medical, mental health, trauma, and addiction treatment in one location.

The PROTOTYPES Josette Mondanaro Women's Resource Center, located on the Pomona campus, provides cross-training and technical assistance to service providers and community groups on key issues in substance abuse, mental health, health, trauma, and violence. The PROTOTYPES Cross-Training Project was an innovative substance abuse and HIV/AIDS training project designed to provide training on HIV/AIDS prevention and treatment issues to drug and alcohol treatment and prevention providers, as well as to train HIV/AIDS service providers about chemical dependency. Each group was given training to enhance their skills in working with specific populations, including women, individuals with mental illness, gay and lesbian people, and individuals with trauma histories.

PROTOTYPES Community Assessment Center (CASC) provides assessment services for substance abuse, mental health, and domestic violence for Service Planning Area (SPA 3) of Los Angeles County (SPA 3 includes approximately 3 million people). The Assessment Center provides more than 8,000 assessments per year.

Experience in Trauma-Integrated Services

PROTOTYPES was one of nine sites funded by the Substance Abuse and Mental Health Services Administration (SAMHSA) to implement a trauma-integrated treatment program (WCDVS) for women with co-occurring disorders and histories of violence. PROTOTYPES was also one of four sites that implemented a children's subset study. (See Chapter 2 for a complete description.) While trauma had already been an important focus of PROTOTYPES' work, after completion of WCDVS, PROTOTYPES implemented trauma-integrated services in all of its divisions. Since 1986, PROTOTYPES has provided outreach and supportive services to domestic violence survivors, and in 1999 the agency established a domestic violence shelter program, STAR House, for women with co-occurring disorders and current domestic violence experience. In addition, PROTOTYPES served as the administrative agency for the National Trauma Consortium, which had contracts with the Center for Mental Health Services, the Center for Substance Abuse Treatment, and the HHS Office of Women's Health, and has published a number of monographs on trauma-informed practice.

The Center for Pediatric Traumatic Stress

Nancy Kassam-Adams, Ph.D., Director Philadelphia, Pennsylvania

The purpose and mission of the Center for Pediatric Traumatic Stress (CPTS) at Children's Hospital of Philadelphia (CHOP) is to ensure that our nation's pediatric health care system is trauma-informed and to expand access to evidence-based prevention, intervention, and integrated care for children and families affected by medical trauma. CPTS, which was established in 2002, has a multidisciplinary leadership team bringing together colleagues from psychology, critical care medicine, emergency medicine, nursing, oncology, pediatrics, and surgery. CPTS addresses traumatic stress and other psychosocial sequelae in children and families affected by a wide range of medical experiences, including cancer, asthma, sickle cell disease, organ transplantation, diabetes, as well as intensive care and emergency treatment. The Center promotes a trauma-informed health care system in which providers are knowledgeable and skilled in addressing both the potentially traumatic impact of medical events and the impact of other (non-medical) trauma exposures, such as injuries, which their pediatric patients and their families have experienced.

As a partner in the federally funded National Child Traumatic Stress Network since 2002, CPTS is a national and international leader in promoting trauma-informed pediatric care, providing training resources, and developing tools to help health care providers effectively prevent or address traumatic stress in their pediatric patients. From 2002 through 2016, CPTS consulted with or trained more than 20,000 service providers at more than 75 healthcare institutions; it has reached nearly 200,000 with its information and resource website, www. HealthCareToolbox.org.

The CPTS mission is to reduce child and family medical traumatic stress by: (1) promoting trauma-informed health care practice; (2) integrating practical evidence-based tools for screening, secondary prevention, and treatment into pediatric medical care; (3) ensuring that health care providers are knowledgeable and skilled in this area; and (4) significantly expanding the empirical knowledge base regarding effective interventions for traumatic stress related to pediatric illness and injury and the successful implementation of those interventions.

To accomplish this mission, CPTS develops and evaluates: empirically-based interventions for ill and injured children and their families; tools to facilitate delivery of trauma-informed pediatric health care; and training and curricular materials for health and mental health professionals.

CPTS provides training for health and mental health professionals regarding trauma-informed pediatric care and screening and preventive interventions with ill and injured children and their families. It also disseminates state-of-the-art information on pediatric traumatic stress to professionals and the public and provides expertise and consultation, tailored to the needs of health care providers and health service systems regarding: child trauma exposure and its impact; and the design and implementation of trauma-informed services, screening, and secondary preventive interventions.

As it works with providers to have them consider ways of preventing and addressing traumatic stress in ill or injured children, CPTS has them consider three things: distress, emotional support, and family (the "DEFs"). Under the category of "distress (D)," providers are encouraged to: assess and manage pain; ask about fears and worries; and consider grief and loss. Under "emotional support (E)," providers should look at what the patient needs now and what barriers exist to mobilizing existing supports. Finally, under "Family (F)," it is important for providers to: assess the distress of parents, siblings, and others close to the child; gauge family stressors and resources; and address other needs (beyond medical).

Current CPTS products and services include:

- The HealthCareToolbox.org website, a one-stop, comprehensive resource for information tools, training, and regular updates on trauma-informed pediatric care. More than 80,000 visitors per year use the website, downloading patient education materials, taking online courses, and learning how to help children and families facing medical traumatic stress. The website also has an active social media presence on Facebook, Twitter, and Pinterest.
- DEF protocol (see above), with resources including reminder cards, users' guide, nursing assessment forms, and online training.
- Training for health care professionals in skills for trauma-informed pediatric health care, including: a growing library of free online continuing education (CE) courses for nurses; in-person training for health care professionals and other staff in health care settings; seminars, webinars, Grand Rounds lectures, ongoing focused training services for departments or practice groups; and focused training on implementation of the *Psychosocial Assessment Tool (PAT)* and *Surviving Cancer Competently Intervention Program (SCCIP)*.
- Training for mental health professionals related to pediatric health and medical trauma.
- Free, downloadable materials including a comprehensive Resource Guide for Mental Health Professionals.
- Online CE courses for child welfare professionals and for social workers (under development).
- Resources for parents and children, in English and Spanish, to promote resilient adaptation to potentially traumatic medical events. Materials are based in the latest research and are designed to be warm, engaging, and developmentally appropriate.
- Consultation services for health care practices and providers regarding medical traumatic stress.

Women's HIV Program (WHP) at the University of California San Francisco (UCSF)

Edward Machtinger, M.D., Director San Francisco, California

For the last 20 years, the UCSF Women's HIV Program (WHP) has provided comprehensive health and social services to women, girls, and their families living with HIV/AIDS in the San Francisco Bay Area. It was one the first programs in the country specifically designed to care for women with HIV, most of whom are low-income women of color. The program strives to provide the most innovative and effective care possible; its research is focused on identifying ways to effectively address the root causes of the health and social challenges faced by its patients. WHP's principle area of research is understanding and responding to the impact of trauma on health.

The program's focus on trauma began tragically. In 2010, a woman's body was found floating in a suitcase in San Francisco Bay. Rose (not her real name) was a patient at WHP. Before she died, Rose had been receiving regular medical care and took her HIV medications faithfully. Unfortunately, she lived in a tragically abusive relationship and, despite WHP's best efforts, she was murdered by her husband. After Rose's death, WHP convened a series of meetings with more than 30 medical and psychosocial workers from clinics and social service organizations throughout the Bay Area who had worked with and loved Rose. The goal of these meetings was to learn as many lessons as possible from her death. It quickly became clear that Rose's situation was tragic, but by no means unique. The group determined that primary-care clinics like WHP's were not designed to offer women like Rose a trauma-informed approach to promote healing from lifelong abuse and prevent re-victimization. WHP concluded that for the large number of patients who have experienced trauma, there is a fundamental mismatch between the treatment offered in primary care and the healing that is actually needed.

WHP has performed studies that found that unaddressed childhood and adult trauma leads to most of the illness and death among its patients, even among those effectively treated for HIV. This research, coupled with the experience of losing patients to preventable illnesses, inspired WHP staff to rethink the standard of care for this vulnerable population. Trauma is defined broadly to include: childhood and adult physical, sexual, and emotional abuse; neglect; loss; community violence; and structural violence such as racism, homophobia, and transphobia. WHP has dedicated itself to understanding the scale of trauma's impact on women living with HIV and to transitioning its clinic to a culture and practice of healing, instead of simply treating people with medications and procedures.

WHP's published research identified three crucial findings, the most important of which is that it is possible to heal from the lifelong impacts of trauma:

- Trauma and PTSD are strikingly common among women living with HIV; more than half have experienced intimate partner violence, 60 percent have experienced sexual abuse, and 30 percent have current symptoms of PTSD;
- Unaddressed recent and lifelong trauma are the key factors underlying HIV medication failure, illness, and death among our patients; and
- It is possible to heal from lifelong abuse and prevent victimization through practical interventions that help patients reduce isolation, safely disclose their

HIV status and histories of trauma, and receive individual and/or group trauma-informed therapy.

WHP formed a partnership with the Positive Women's Network-USA, the largest national membership body of women living with HIV, and co-convened with them a national strategy group composed of key stakeholders from the government, military, academia, community organizations, clinics, and women living with HIV. The group designed a new approach to the primary care of HIV-positive women and girls, trauma-informed primary care (TIPC), and published a paper on TIPC in *Women's Health Issues*. The paper described the four key components of trauma-informed care. The first of these components is creating a trauma-informed environment designed to reduce trauma-related triggers and promote healing. All staff members and providers receive training about the impact of trauma on health; available trauma-specific services; and trauma-informed practices for use with both patients and one another. The physical space provides opportunities for privacy, confidentiality, and community. Providers work as an interdisciplinary team to ensure that existing services are trauma-informed and that the social aspects of illness and health are fully integrated into care. Outreach is offered to encourage access and connection to trauma-informed services. Power differentials among staff and between patients and providers are acknowledged and minimized. The environment also supports providers, many of whom may have experienced trauma themselves or may experience vicarious trauma working with affected patients.

In working with clients, WHP staff recognize that a patient's disclosure of recent or past abuse is, in itself, potentially therapeutic. Provider responses to trauma disclosures are empathetic and supportive. They are trained to validate individuals' experiences, choices, and autonomy, as well as to build upon patient strengths.

WHP has begun a novel study to implement and evaluate the impact of TIPC on the health and wellbeing of women and girls living with HIV. The model is flexible and not HIV- or women-specific. As such, it can be replicated in a variety of clinics caring for many other populations experiencing high rates of trauma. WHP has been recognized by the Robert Wood Johnson Foundation as a national demonstration site for this model of care. Ultimately, the goal is to fundamentally improve primary care for women and girls living with HIV, as well as for the many other men and women throughout the country who are affected by trauma. In order to accomplish that, WHP plans to broadly disseminate the study findings.

Other Programs (Not Interviewed)

The Sanctuary Network Sandra Bloom, M.D., Director

The birth of the "therapeutic community" took place in the 1940s in England and the U.S. (Jones 1953; Main 1946). The community was designed to create "living-learning" opportunities for patients and staff: learning how to trust self and others; learning how to protect oneself and one's boundaries in more adaptive ways; learning how to manage one's intense affect and sooth oneself without resorting to self-destructive or other destructive behaviors (e.g., self-mutilation, bingeing/purging, using drugs and/or alcohol, risk-taking, violent acting-out); learning to identify what are one's external and internal triggers and how one can ground oneself; and learning to express anger and resolve conflicts in healthy ways. The rationale for the therapeutic community was that, since all human development occurs within a social context and interpersonal trauma experiences have also occurred within a relational context, then providing survivors with a corrective emotional and relational experience should also occur within a group context.

The Sanctuary Model was originally developed in a short-term acute inpatient psychiatric setting for adults who had been traumatized as children. In the Sanctuary Model, a trauma-therapeutic community model of psychiatric treatment, described by Bloom (2000), "Safety with oneself and each other was considered paramount," and "the community was designed to provide multiple opportunities for all participants to have new experiences in learning how to trust self and others.... The concept of 'sanctuary' refers to the important emphasis we place on the active and conscious development of a sense of safety within the context of a therapeutic milieu" (Bloom 2000, p. 74). Bloom discussed four levels of safety—physical, psychological, social, and moral.

With Bloom's creation of the Sanctuary Model (Bloom 1994; Bloom 1997), trauma-informed care and the therapeutic community model of treatment were merged. The Sanctuary Model arose out of concern that individuals who had experienced trauma came into treatment seeking healing and were, instead, further hurt by a system that they perceived did not understand them and treated them in a way that re-victimized them (e.g., seclusion and restraint, etc.). The concept of "sanctuary" refers to the emphasis on the development of a sense of safety. It was designed to be a truly therapeutic community, one in which patients share in the development and implementation of a non-violent, non-abusive environment, i.e., a health-promoting environment. Key principles of the TC included self-responsibility, joint-decision making, open communication, and the belief that all community members—staff and patients alike—are active agents in healing. SAGE is an acronym for the four important aspects of recovery under the Sanctuary Model: safety, affect management, grief, and emancipation (social reconnection, finding meaning, and establishing a survivor mission) (Foderaro and Ryan 2000).

The Sanctuary Model is now being used as a trauma-informed method for changing an organizational culture in residential treatment centers, schools, domestic violence shelters, and other human service organizations. The aim is to guide an organization in the development of a culture with seven dominant characteristics: non-violence; emotional management; social learning; shared governance; open communication; social responsibility; and growth and change.

Bloom (2010) believes that organizations, like individuals, are vulnerable to the effects of chronic stress and traumatic experiences. In discussing the mental health system, she states that staff members are frequently caught between the demands of the organization and the demands of the clients. Sources of stress include: excessive paperwork, increased demands for productivity, inadequate time for supervision, staff turnover, client suicides, and staff injuries. These are what I call "treatment burdens on staff." (See Chapter 1.)

Organizations committed to working with traumatized clients face stresses such as financial, regulatory, and political environments, which limit funding and length of treatment. These stresses may lead to traumatized organizations, which can become reactive, change-resistant, coercive, punitive, and mistrustful of others. As agencies across the country began to use the Sanctuary Model, Dr. Bloom formed the Sanctuary Network to train agencies on the model and then bring those agencies together to share their experiences and provide ongoing, long-term support to each other. Reported improvements after adoption of the Sanctuary Model include: reduced use of physical restraints; a decrease in aggression; improved staff morale; lower staff turnover; fewer injuries to staff and clients; and improved clinical outcomes.

SELF is an updated conceptual tool, replacing SAGE, that is a fundamental component of the Sanctuary Model as it is being implemented today around the U.S. It stands for: safety, emotional management, loss, and future. It provides both a structure for organizations using the Sanctuary Model and a framework for an intervention, the *SAFE Psychoeducational Group* (available at www.sanctuaryweb.com). The group intervention is designed to provide clients and staff with an easy-to-use cognitive framework for trauma work.

Healing Hurt People

John Rich, M.D., M.P.H., Director; Theodore Corbin, M.D., Co-Director, and Sandra Bloom, M.D., Coordinator Center for Nonviolence and Social Justice, Drexel University School of Public Health Philadelphia, Pennsylvania

The hospital emergency department is a key setting for violence intervention. Patients who present to the emergency room (ER) with an intentional injury are often hypervigilant and hyper-aroused. Their behavioral response to feeling unsafe may be to obtain a weapon or assemble friends to retaliate. A prospective study (Fein 2002) conducted at two urban emergency departments suggested that acute stress symptoms assessed in the "immediate aftermath of traumatic injury are useful indicators of risk for later post-traumatic stress" (Fein 2002, p. 836). A trauma-informed approach to violence recognizes that "trauma feeds the cycle of violence" (Corbin et al. 2011, p. 515).

Healing Hurt People is a trauma-informed program, housed in the ER of Hahnemann University Hospital in Philadelphia, Pennsylvania, that emphasizes a restorative process to help African American youth understand the effects of trauma and gain positive coping skills to manage difficult emotions (Corbin et al. 2011). It is a collaboration between the hospital and the Drexel University College of Medicine and School of Public Health. The organizational framework of the program is the Sanctuary Model. The team includes an emergency medicine physician, a psychiatrist, a primary care physician, a clinical psychologist, social workers, a community intervention specialist, and a representative from the Philadelphia Department of Human Services.

The work of Healing Hurt People is divided into five primary components: assessment; navigation and case management; mentoring; *SELF* psychoeducational groups; and case review. A priority of assessment is to evaluate whether the patient is safe and whether he is actively planning to retaliate. The social worker also orients the youth and family about the likely symptoms of traumatic stress. The community intervention specialist follows up with the client through phone calls and scheduled home visits after discharge, serving as the navigator to various support services and as a mentor. Staff members have been trained in Motivational Interviewing. The *SELF* group involves ten weekly sessions with a trained facilitator. Clients who exhibit more severe traumatic symptoms are referred to appropriate providers for trauma-specific treatment. The program has created a comprehensive database and is collecting data on all participants (including: type of injury; mental health; substance abuse, legal, and trauma histories; ACE screen; PTSD screen; and history with the child welfare system).

In a 2005 study, Rich and Grey (2005) interviewed Black male victims of gunshots and community violence to understand their experience of violence. Qualitative analysis of their narratives revealed how their struggle to reestablish safety shaped their response to injury. The authors used a framework from the work of Elijah Anderson (1999), who described a "code of the street" based on his ethnographic work in inner-city Philadelphia. Rich and Grey identified three main aspects of the code that related to safety after violent injury:

- "Being a sucker" (loss of respect). "Respect, defined as receiving the deference that one deserves, is a central part of how young urban men make their way through the dangerous world in which they live" (p. 818). The code of the street dictates that when someone disrespects you, you must respond aggressively to regain your respect. If you do not retaliate, you are a "sucker" and tolerate victimization and are vulnerable.
- "The last people I call" (lack of faith in the police). The police are most often viewed as representing the dominant white culture and not caring to protect inner-city residents. The youth reported that they do not rely on the police if threatened, but instead feel they must handle the threat themselves.
- "Feeling shook" (trauma-related symptoms). Sixty-five percent of the youth met criteria for PTSD. Respondents reported nightmares, intrusive thoughts, emotional numbing, and a heightened sense of awareness or "jumpiness."

Two of the ways in which the youth try to address their fear are self-protection and substance use. Twenty-seven percent acknowledged sometimes carrying a weapon or thinking about acquiring a weapon. Sixty-seven percent of the youth reported that they smoke marijuana on a regular basis; however, some of them had increased their use of marijuana in an attempt to allay their symptoms of trauma.

With regard to trauma and organizations, Rich and colleagues (2000) authored a monogram entitled, *Healing the Hurt: Trauma-Informed Approaches to the Health of Boys and Young Men of Color* for The California Endowment. They state: "Just as the lives of people exposed to repetitive and chronic trauma, abuse, and maltreatment become organized around traumatic experiences, so too can entire systems become organized around the recurrent and severe stresses that accompany services and clients" (Rich et al. 2000, p. 21). The authors recommend: (1) support for and expansion of community-based efforts that are consistent with a trauma-informed approach; (2) a focus on trauma-informed prevention activities (for boys and young men); and (3) infusing health and human service systems with trauma-informed practices to promote healing from trauma and adversity at the individual, family, and community levels.

Notes

1   The positive deviance approach has been shown to be an effective way of addressing health issues around the world; for example, it has been used to enhance childhood nutrition. In 1991, for example, more than 65 percent of all children in rural Vietnam villages were suffering from malnourishment. Researchers (Sternin, Sternin, and Marsh 1999) identified a group of women in these villages as "positive deviants" because their children were thriving despite high rates of childhood malnutrition. It was found that these women were including in their cooking tiny shrimp and crabs and sweet potato greens, all of which were found in large quantities in the rice paddies, but not normally fed to young children. In addition, these mothers fed their children three to four times a day, rather than twice a day, as was usual in the villages. The randomized controlled trial showed significant improvements in the health outcomes of children fed in this way. After the two years of the project, childhood malnutrition in these villages was reduced by 85 percent. Over the next several years, the positive deviance intervention became a national program.
2   The interview protocol can be found in Appendix F.
3   Helen Bergman died in the summer of 2011. Community Connections strives to carry on her mission.
4   I was interviewed for this book by Michael Gross, Ph.D., a researcher in the fields of substance abuse and HIV.

References

Anderson, E 1999, *Code of the Street: Decency, Violence and the Moral Life of the Inner City*, New York, NY, W.W. Norton and Co.

Bloom, SL 1994, The Sanctuary Model: Developing Generic Inpatient Programs for the Treatment of Psychological Trauma, in MB Williams and JF Sommer (eds.), *Handbook of Post-Traumatic Therapy: A Practical Guide to Intervention, Treatment, and Research*, New York, NY, Greenwood Publishing, pp. 474–491.

Bloom, SL 1997, *Creating Sanctuary: Towards the Evolution of Sane Communities*, New York, NY, Routledge Press.

Bloom, SL 2000, Creating Sanctuary: Healing from Systemic Abuses of Power, *The International Journal for Therapeutic and Supportive Organizations*, vol. 21, no. 2, pp. 67–91.

Bloom, SL 2010, Organizational Stress as a Barrier to Trauma-Informed Service Delivery, in M Becker and B Levin (eds.), *A Public Health Perspective of Women's Mental Health*, New York, NY, Springer, pp. 295–311.

Corbin, TJ, Rich, JA, Bloom, SL et al. 2011, Developing a Trauma-Informed Emergency Department-Based Intervention for Victims of Urban Violence, *Journal of Trauma & Dissociation*, vol. 12, pp. 510–525.

Fein, JA, Kassam-Adams, N, Gavin, M et. al. 2002, Persistence of Posttraumatic Stress in Violently Injured Youth Seen in Emergency Department, *Archives of Pediatrics and Adolescent Medicine*, vol. 156, no. 8, pp. 836–840.

Foderaro, JF and Ryan, RA 2000, SAGE: Mapping the Course of Recovery, *The International Journal for Therapeutic and Supportive Organizations*, vol. 21, no. 2, pp. 93–104.

Jones, M 1953, *The Therapeutic Community: A New Treatment Method in Psychiatry*, New York, NY, Basic Books.

Kotter, J and Cohen, D 2003, Creative Ways to Empower Action to Change the Organization: Cases in point, *Journal of Organizational Excellence*, vol. 22, no. 2, pp. 101–110.

Main, TF 1946, The Hospital as a Therapeutic Institution, *Bulletin of the Menninger Clinic*, vol. 10, no. 3, pp. 66–70.

Marsh, DR, Schroeder, DC, Dearden, KA et al. 2004, The Power of Positive Deviance, *British Medical Journal*, vol. 329, pp. 1177–1179.

Rich, J, Corbin, T, Bloom, S et al. 2000, *Healing the Hurt: Trauma-Informed Approaches to the Health of Boys and Young Men of Color*, Los Angeles, CA, The California Endowment.

Rich, J and Grey, CM 2005, Pathways to Recurrent Trauma Among Young Black Men: Traumatic Stress, Substance Use, and the "Code of the Street," *American Journal of Public Health*, vol. 95, no. 5, pp. 816–824.

Rogers, EM 2003, *Diffusion of Innovations (5th Edition)*, New York, Free Press.

Rogers, EM and Kincaid, DL 1981, *Communication Networks: A New Paradigm for Research*, New York, Free Press.

Sternin, M, Sternin, J, and Marsh, D 1999, Scaling Up Poverty Alleviation and Nutrition Program in Vietnam, in T Marchione (ed.), *Scaling Up, Scaling Down*, Philadelphia, PA, Gordon and Breach Publishers, pp. 97–117.

Chapter 7

Core Components of Trauma-Informed Practice

A Passionate and Committed Leader

In the interviews I conducted for this book, I was stuck by how the leaders of the programs I selected all expressed their strong commitment to incorporating trauma into their programs and their vision of constant change toward better treatment, service, and prevention. They are what I like to call "change champions." Once they integrated two or more issues (e.g., substance abuse and mental health, or substance abuse and HIV/AIDS) in their practices/organizations, they saw the need to focus on others, as well, and integrated them into their programs. In addition, they shared a focus upon collaborations across boundaries. They also exhibited "person-centeredness," another one of the high-impact leadership behaviors defined by the Institute for Healthcare Improvement (IHI) (Swenson et al. 2013). A leader demonstrates person-centeredness by: routinely participating in rounds to talk with patients and families; consistently inviting and supporting patient and family participation; discussing results in terms of persons and communities (not only in terms of diseases and dollars); and declaring harm prevention as a personal and organizational priority (Swenson et al. 2013). Interviewees also described finding ways around funding issues/barriers; i.e., most of them pursued many different funding streams in order to create the kinds of programs they envisioned. Finally, they all embraced the utilization of peers in their programs. It was clear to me that these leaders saw what was happening to their clients, what was happening in their communities, and what gaps there were in their systems of care.

Here are these leaders' own words on how they embraced person-centered, trauma-informed care.

> *Paull:* "Instead of having a shelter, we set up a series of safe homes where local community people would take in the women. And the women and kids could stay with them until we found appropriate housing.... I personally housed people and I thought it was a great experience for my family and my children."
>
> "Our Women's Center has stayed and grown. We help around 450 to 500 women each year, and we go to court with them, and we scrounge places for them to live, we scrounge money for them, and we give them trauma treatment. I think from day one we recognized trauma and we tried to deal with it in our own way. And then we were part of the Women with Co-Occurring Disorders and Violence Study and the Children's Subset Study,

which was wonderful because it provided a lot of training for the entire staff. And that led us to using evidence-based practices and understanding trauma even more and spreading it more."

Harris: "As one of the two people who founded the organization in 1984, its mission was certainly not to be trauma-informed and it was certainly not to deliver trauma services. It took a while for that to become part of what we did, but it did become an important part."

"Our commitment to trauma-informed services exists alongside the commitment to providing concrete residential services for homeless people, diversion from incarceration for mentally ill people who have picked up charges, reunification of mothers with their children. Those are content areas, some of which we have been able to successfully make trauma-informed, and others of which, when we are dealing with outside systems like the courts or Child and Family Services, it is more difficult."

Machtinger: "I think most of us come from backgrounds that have led us, drawn us toward working with individuals who have experienced trauma or who are marginalized by their HIV status, by their race, by their gender identity, by their sexual identity or their sexual orientation, because we relate to it. And we feel like working with this population in a healing way will resonate with us, will feel meaningful and will ultimately be healing for us too."

"I come from a background that is very different from most of my patients. I'm white, I'm male, I didn't grow up poor, I went to Harvard Medical School. So the assumption would be that I do not come from a background of trauma. But in fact I really do. My father came here from Poland when he was 8 years old, just with his brother and his mother. His father was already here. Soon after they left there was a massive pogrom in the village and the entire family was killed. So, my father was raised by his parents who were devastated emotionally.... My grandfather was morbidly depressed, he ended up going through shock therapy in the 1950s. He was a really broken person.

"My father really was emotionally and severely traumatized by all of this. I didn't have a normal conversation with either of my parents until I was about 30. I was raised with plenty of material substance, but without really any connections. Really no connections to my parents. No mentorship, no conversations. I felt very much alone."

"And then the AIDS crisis hit. I was active in the AIDS movement, in the gay men's health crisis, and in ACT-UP. I've been moved towards dealing with violence against people, animals, and the environment since I was very young. I was really moved by AIDS because AIDS brought together so many issues that were so relevant: sexuality, discrimination, drug use, politics, fear. I keyed in that this was a really historical epidemic. People were really dealing with it quite poorly, the federal government was absent in a way that was profoundly negligent."

"I got into Harvard Medical School ... and I made some very good friends there, many of whom came out with me here to UCSF. I think more concretely my goal was to run a really creative HIV program for populations who were neglected or marginalized. And so that is what I ended up doing. I got a job right after my residency working here on the faculty at UCSF. So, I started at the university, and then there was a job opening in the women's HIV program. I interviewed, and it never occurred to me until then that I would work with women."

"The program was founded in 1993 by Ruth Greenblatt and Susan Shea, and it was among one of the first programs that was specifically designed for women living with HIV. Susan Shea was a nurse practitioner, and Ruth Greenblatt is a very well-known infectious disease specialist. Up until that time, the women were being seen in the men's program. They really weren't faring very well. The men's program was designed for gay men, and the women were very different. They were all types of women, but they were typically women of color and typically poor, and they would come into these programs and there would be all these beefcake guy posters on the wall."

"I could build onto what they had created in a way that felt very personal and very organic. And I could begin to hire my own people to work with, because it's very different to have people that you have hired and recruited and that you know you can work with rather than inheriting people to work with. Most of the people now working here I have hired. So that has allowed for a really cohesive team because it's people that I work with and like and love and we take care of each other."

"For my first six years at the program I mainly focused on figuring out how to make the program financially sustainable. Because I inherited a program that really wasn't financially sustainable, it was sustained only by a single funding source, which was Ryan White federal grants. It had no other funding streams whatsoever. Through increasingly large foundation grants and increasingly successful philanthropy, we were able to stabilize the program financially, stabilize my job financially, so that I could be here instead of being all over the place."

"An understanding of the role of trauma in the lives of women living with HIV in our program came after many years of practice. Many people for many years have studied and understood the impact of trauma on many populations. I am far from the first person who has had the epiphany that trauma underlies most illness, death, and disability in the country. That epiphany—that it's trauma that is leading to most of the HIV cases that come to our program and that trauma is leading to most of the poor outcomes and deaths in our program—came to me about five or six years ago."

"In our program we take really good care of people in terms of their HIV, much better than people across the country. We have 85 percent of our patients on HIV drugs; 85 percent of them are undetectable in their virus in their blood and that is the principle medical outcome in HIV, having undetectable virus in your blood. That means you will not die from HIV and you will not transmit the virus to your partner. The average across the country is 30 percent undetectable, but, in our program, it's approximately 85 percent. We're working with particularly marginalized people, and to have that rate of undetectability is very successful; we were widely recognized as a very successful HIV program. But it really felt like the bar in HIV care, really all of primary care, was far too low. In HIV care we are expected to achieve an undetectable viral load. And that is it! That is how we are evaluated. There is something called the "Getting to Zero" campaign. And the Getting to Zero campaign is about zero new HIV infections, zero new AIDS-related deaths, and zero AIDS-related discrimination. And most people will interpret that to mean zero new infections and zero AIDS-related deaths. They don't determine that to mean zero preventable deaths in people living with HIV. Which is a very different thing."

"Many HIV programs/providers didn't seem to care or be aware or feel it was in their domain to deal with the actual causes of death in the people entrusted in their care. And the actual causes of death were violence including murders and inter-partner violence, substance use, and depression in particular. There was no recognition that, in order to help somebody with substance use and depression, you had to deal with their trauma."

"A couple of things happened that really allowed us to understand that addressing trauma was a crucial missing ingredient of our care model and that not addressing trauma was undermining the quality of care we were providing. So, we looked at what existed in the literature around the evidence on effective interventions and came up with a framework of what are the core components of trauma-informed primary care. So that someone like me, a clinic director who is really interested in embracing trauma-informed care and dealing with trauma in my patients would know where to begin. Because I think when I first started I really, really had no idea, or even what the definition of trauma was. What was the scope of trauma? What can you do for trauma? How do you help people heal from trauma?"

Brown: "While I was working at the Didi Hirsch Community Mental Health Center (DHCMHC) in Los Angeles, I designed one of the first residential substance abuse treatment programs for women and children in the U.S. That was in 1971. We collected data and did research on the program and, as part of that research, we found that a large number of the women had experienced a number of traumatic events, beginning in childhood, then later repeated in adolescence, and then later in adulthood (e.g., child sexual abuse, domestic violence)."

"Later, when federal funding became available through the Center for the Prevention and Control of Rape, I was funded for the Southern California Center for Rape Prevention: The CARE Project (Consultation and Rape Education). The project was a unique collaboration between DHCMH and the Los Angeles Commission on Assaults Against Women, a rape crisis center. These two programs set the stage for my continued work in trauma."

"In 1986, I founded PROTOTYPES, Centers for Innovation in Health, Mental Health, and Social Services, with my colleague, Maryann Fraser. PROTOTYPES' mission was to design new models for emerging community problems, test them through research, refine them, and then disseminate them to others in mental health, substance abuse, and health. One of our first programs was a residential substance abuse treatment program (the PROTOTYPES Women's Center in Pomona) for women, including women with children. Many of these women were multiply diagnosed with substance abuse and mental illness, as well as with HIV/AIDS. And, it soon became clear, many, indeed most of these women—and their children—had experienced numerous traumatic events. In our research studies, we found that up to 90 percent of the women had experienced sexual abuse, physical abuse, and/or neglect in childhood and domestic violence in adulthood."

"My work on "level of burden"[1] (as described in Chapter 1) showed that most of our clients did not just have one problem. In fact, they had an average of four (usually including mental illness, substance abuse, HIV/AIDS, other serious health conditions, trauma experiences, and/or cognitive impairments). This level of burden affected retention in treatment and treatment outcomes. The women often felt overwhelmed by the social and familial demands and expectations they were facing when entering treatment. It became clear to me that these clients needed more effective and integrated interventions that could address all of the issues with which they were dealing. These women were also subjected to another burden—the stigma and blame directed toward them by the systems and communities upon which they had to rely. This was especially true if they were mothers."

"I also want to mention that we found that physical abuse/domestic violence also led to cognitive impairment in some of the women. We started screening the women using the Luria Nebraska Screener and found a number of the women who reported physical abuse showed signs of cognitive impairment on the screener. Here was another burden on the women—and one which would have impact on their ability to understand and participate in treatment. In addition, many of our women clients were arrested because of their sex work and/or their drug use, then they were re-traumatized again in the criminal justice system. "

"When funding became available from SAMHSA (the Substance Abuse and Mental Health Services Administration) in 1998 for a five-year study of Women with Co-Occurring

Disorders and Violence/Trauma Histories (WCDVS), I eagerly submitted a grant application and was one of the nine sites funded.[2] PROTOTYPES was also one of four sites that received additional funding for a subset study on the children of the women. These two studies were extremely significant for trauma studies. Some of the lessons learned were: treatment that integrated substance use, mental health, and trauma showed better outcomes than treatment-as-usual; having peer staff (consumer/survivor/recovering staff) had a significant impact on engagement and retention of the women; implementing trauma-specific interventions were effective; trauma-informed practices were important in changing our systems of care; and it was critical to ensure that the clients and the consumer/survivor/recovering (c/s/r) staff had a voice in everything, including decisions on research questionnaires."

A Safe and Welcoming Environment

Patients who have been traumatized have an exquisite sensitivity to cues of threat. They are hypervigilant and always searching for indications that someone is going to hurt them. Since we do not know all the things that can trigger particular patients/clients, we can all trigger survivors unintentionally. When we provide a safe and welcoming environment, we are engaging in both harm reduction and improving the patient's experience. The client pathway through care is important. Is the system made easy and safe for clients to get the care they need?

As can be seen in many of the comments, safety is an important concept—and one that has roots in medicine. Safety has three levels: physical; psychological; and cultural. Physical safety includes: medical attention to any injuries; avoidance of any errors in medical treatments; attention to basic health needs; and establishment of a safe living environment. Psychological safety includes: screening for traumatic experiences, including screening for domestic violence and development of a safety plan; attention to patients' anxieties and fears about treatments; attention to cognitive impairment and whether the patient understands treatment options and procedures; financial security; and mobilization of caring and trustworthy people.

It is also important to provide safety for *staff* and to ensure that all our systems do not repeat adverse/abusive environments for patients or staff. Staff need to feel safe in order to respond to clients' anxieties and hostile responses, to bring gaps in treatment systems to the attention of leaders, to express their own anxieties and fears, and to learn new practices.

Paull: "Once we started taking in women, we noticed a couple of things. Most of them had been survivors of sexual assault or domestic violence. Most of them had mental health issues as well. And most of them were using drugs in addition to alcohol, especially benzodiazepines. But we couldn't treat those; we couldn't treat any of those because all we had was a substance abuse license."

"So, in no particular order, we got a licensed mental health clinic. We went to the state and said, 'We need to be able to detoxify people from drugs as well as alcohol.' And we had a local representative that got an earmark to give us eight drug detox beds. Also my nurses were enraged, because they didn't want to have to deal with those drug addicts. And so we had a lot of staff turnover."

"It's my goal to have any place that I run to feel like a place that I would want to go to or that I would want my family member to go to. And if it's not that, then we need to work on it. And trauma is just a part of it. I think when people think about drug treatment and battered women, they think they are going to go into these hellholes. Instead our centers are safe and warm and welcoming."

To have a place where you would want to go or where you would send your family members appears to be an important principle of trauma-informed care. Would you feel safe and comfortable coming into your emergency room or your residential treatment program or your outpatient facility?

Fallot: "I remember one man we talked to in Texas who had done a walkthrough of his own agency. He didn't realize, until after doing the walkthrough, that there were two parts of the intake interview. One part of the interview took place in one part of the building, and the second part took place in another part of the building; new clients had to walk a long way between the two of them. He said when he was made to do that walk himself, he realized that it felt like walking to the gallows. So, to make it different for other people, he decided that staff were going to accompany new clients and walk with them on that journey, every step of the way. By changing that aspect of the intake interview, he made a big difference in the way that the people perceived and felt about it."

Machtinger: "I realized that, when you walk into my program, the lobby is completely chaotic—totally chaotic and really loud, with some of the people there in conflict with the people at the front desk, who are in conflict with each other. There are a lot of people on drugs. It's a crowd, the providers are running late, they're really stressed, and they trigger their patients. Some providers—I, for example—are drawn to these environments. I wanted to work in a chaotic setting with lots of action and lots of conflict and lots of drama. Somehow that seemed exciting, but ultimately it is not healthy. The other epiphany that came later is that the whole system is a mirror of the trauma experience of our patients. This chaos and this reactivity on the part of both staff and patients is a reflection of the trauma of our patients and the trauma of our providers. And it is the norm for HIV care. This is what most HIV clinics look like."

"One of the things we are starting, which should be really exciting, is this thing called the 'clinic host.' When people came into the clinic previously, they just massed at the front desk, and the medical systems triggered all the patients. So, we are now going to have a person with a clipboard—like someone from a cruise ship—and that person is going to greet people at the front door and say something like, 'Welcome to clinic. I see you have an appointment, let me let the people at the front desk know you are here. Want to have a seat, breakfast burrito, coffee?' Or, 'Hey, I see you don't have an appointment here today. Are you here to see Beth the social worker, are you just here for food, can I do anything, do you need anything, do you need to see a nurse or something?'"

Harris: "As an example of how programs can promote safety, Community Connections formed a Safety Committee, which made a few changes in the daily routines of staff. These changes included: introducing themselves to each visitor and consumer and then escorting them throughout their visit at Community Connections from the waiting room to the suite they are visiting, and from there to the door out of the building; and wearing a Community Connections ID so that others know who they are."

Brown: "We really looked critically at all of our practices. What could re-traumatize someone? And that was extremely important because in a trauma-informed practice you do not want to re-victimize or re-traumatize. In states across the country, at this same time, people were trying to reduce the use of seclusion and restraint because it caused re-traumatization. So, in every practice we were doing, we looked at re-traumatization and spent time training the staff, which became a very important piece too. We undertook a major effort on that. Training every staff member, including clerical and house maintenance staff, on the basics of trauma was critical so that they would understand that some of the things we were doing could be unintentionally re-traumatizing people."

"We walked through our system and looked at everything. For example, we asked: 'As you approach the facility, is there enough light, enough security?' 'As you enter the building, are there signs that help you understand where you are supposed to go?' 'Is the waiting room comfortable?' 'Is it scary to children?' 'Should there be something separate for children?' Those are the kinds of things we looked at. Step-by-step, we asked ourselves whether we should change something to make sure people feel more comfortable. We have beautiful colors in our facilities. Artwork that is culturally sensitive and not triggering. Of course, in our staff training, we explain all of that, why we are doing that, what it means."

"From this experience and my experience with NIATx (National Improvement of Addiction Treatment), I developed a Walk-through Trauma Assessment, based on Harris and Fallot's work for other agencies to use."[3] (See Chapter 11 for more information.)

Training/Engaging of Staff

All of the interviewed sites had implemented trauma training for their staff and some of their collaborating partners. Two sites had developed trauma-specific curricula and trained their own staff and others across the country on their well-recognized interventions.

Paull:	"We have trainings all the time. With the new drug courts we received, the first thing we did was have Lisa Najavits (the developer of *Seeking Safety*) come down and teach the judges and the probation officers about trauma."
	"The other thing I found exciting was we had the supervisors take the trauma training with the staff. The students journaled about their jobs and what they did and how it applied to what they learned, and the supervisors used that journaling in their supervision. And talk about trauma. Staff understood now why sometimes traumatized people lashed out at them. They just thought they were 'being bad.' So again, the keys are education and promoting our staff, who are dedicated and wonderful. We've raised them up; we've changed their lives."
Fallot:	"You can have training at orientation for trauma-informed care, which is what a lot of places have adopted now. You train as soon as someone comes on board and get them involved in trauma-informed care. It's one of the things trauma-informed organizations are doing right. They say, 'This is what we do, this is why we do it, this is how we do it.' They start it with their orientation sessions."
	"One of the reasons we emphasize the training of staff and clients in this approach is because staff members have to feel safe and have a trusting relationship with their supervisors in order to communicate safety to their clients. Many agencies have decided to start with staff, rather than clients, as they adopt a trauma-informed approach to services. They decided to focus on staff needs rather than client needs because the staff is so vulnerable. Due to the lack of safety, and trustworthiness, and lack of empowerment. And they can't pass that along to anybody else when they are working until they are more solid themselves."
Harris:	"I think that the only other thing I would add is that, as with any other organization, repetition is critical. And the idea of making it part of an orientation, but even within ... I am teaching some of this again to people who have been here a number of years. And I think you've got to be prepared to talk about this over and over and over again and you can't assume that an initial introduction to some of these concepts and you're good to go."
Kassam-Adams:	"We have a couple of different ways that we do training. We have some online courses for nurses that build on the *DEF* idea. We started with "An Introduction to Pediatric Medical Stress," which gives one hour of nursing continuing education. Now we also have one hour of nursing courses on D and then on E and then on F. The D course is dealing with pain and helping your patients deal with pain, fear and worries, and stress. The E is what does your patient need now and how do you deal with that. And the F is about really focusing on family. Each of these training modules uses some clinical scenarios and, though

online, is a little bit interactive. It takes about an hour to go through it properly, so you get a one-hour nursing continuing education. They count as trauma hours, and many nurses need trauma hours. That's one way that we've done it, and we've been able to reach a whole lot of people." (See Appendix A for website, etc.) "We also frequently do grand rounds or a one-of-a-kind training session. So that is a second type of training. Finally, we have developed here, within Children's Hospital of Philadelphia (CHOP), and are getting ready to take outside a series of trauma-informed trainings for different units around the hospital. It's for different professions, it's not just for the health care providers. We are trying to take into account for each different unit what their particular concerns might be."

"Then we have the training around the specific interventions or assessments we have developed, like the *Surviving Cancer Competently* intervention program *(SCCIP)* that Anne Kazak and her team have developed. (See Chapter 10.) There are *SCCIP* trainings on how to implement that specific trauma-focused intervention. We can go and do those on-site if there are enough people to do it, or we have also offered them here for groups of people who want to come in from various places to do that. That's the other trauma-focused intervention I should have mentioned earlier."

"I think it is important that you are respectful and collaborative and willing to hear back from staff about their experiences. I can't speak to other institutions, but at CHOP our security officers are part of the trauma-informed workforce. And they were before we ever called it that. They are incredibly sensitive, and many of them have worked here for decades."

"There was a family-centered care training series on video (it was on an interactive CD-ROM, that's how old it is), created by the National Association of Emergency Medical Technicians (EMTs). The series was framed as focusing on family-centered care, but, when you look at it, you see trauma-informed care all through it. One of the points made is that, when you involve parents or family members at the scene as an EMT, you may do it in order to be family-centered, but you are also going to get a better history of what happened with the patient, and that is going to make your care better. You will get a better history if you are sensitive and don't push the family away, but, instead, involve them in the care."

Machtinger: "So we contracted with a psychologist out here in the Bay area who is very experienced in trauma, particularly in structural violence and implicit bias. She is leading three half-day workshops for our entire staff. We are going from Trauma 101 to talking about structural violence and bias, to skills building focused on identifying things staff can do to improve their understanding of why patients are acting the way they are or being the way they are. Instead of thinking in terms of 'what's wrong with them,' we want our staff to focus on 'what's happening to them.' We also want our staff to use language that is less triggering with each other and with patients."

Brown: "We have a large training division, and trauma is a major component of training for us. When we began screening for trauma, some staff members were uncomfortable asking about it. So, we added trauma screening to the training. As I do trauma trainings, part of my introduction about screening is that staff should say to clients: 'I may be asking you some questions that you may be uncomfortable with. If you are and you don't want to answer, please say "I don't want to answer. You don't have to lie to us."' It's amazing how many people do tell us about trauma(s) they have experienced. And, if they don't tell us at intake and screening, they will tell us later in groups. You have to be prepared that it may emerge later."

"The *Seeking Safety* training for our staff was extensive. We had Dr. Lisa Najavits, its developer, train us for two days,[4] and then we spent the next ten weeks training all the co-facilitators and clinical staff. When we did the Women with Co-Occurring Disorders study, we trained a large number of group facilitators on trauma-specific interventions. However, when we started the training, some staff would come up and say, 'I never dealt with my own trauma. I've dealt with my mental health, I've dealt with my substance abuse, but I've never dealt with my own trauma, and I don't think I can lead these groups.' We allowed them *not* to lead the groups and asked if they wanted help in dealing with their own traumas. We still had a large number of trained facilitators."

"We really developed multi-level training. Every staff member received basic training on trauma. Every single one. It's really important, because we talked to some of the clerical staff, and they said, 'A potential client will call, crying and screaming, and I don't know what to do. So I hang up.' That is when we realized it is really important for everyone to understand about trauma. So everybody got the basic training on trauma. Then, for the staff who would be implementing trauma-specific interventions, we had specific trainings on the interventions. Then we had trauma-informed practice trainings. We had trauma-informed supervision training for supervisors. Supervisors really have to be very sensitive and attuned, because staff who have been traumatized can also get triggered. We wanted supervisors to be sensitive to that."

"It is also important to repeat the trainings yearly, if possible, because of inevitable staff turnover and to ensure fidelity to the interventions."

Engaging with Clients/Patients to Continually Improve Services

In addition to the training of staff, several of those interviewed mentioned engagement with clients/patients as important for continually improving the quality of services.

Paull: "And so once a month I have a meeting in Open Access. I have a 'Talk to the CEO,' during which staff can tell me what's going on. And I meet with the patients and say, 'What do you like, what don't you like, what's happening, what should we be aware of, what's working well, what's not working well?' So I get to hear."

Kassam-Adams: "We also involve our families in designing new programs. We have a Family Advisory Group that is very important to us at our center. We run everything we develop past them. For example, we have just expanded our website section for parents, and that was very much influenced by the Family Advisory Group. It is made up only of parents at this time, but we would like to include children and youth. Family involvement is very important across the National Child Traumatic Stress Network (NCTSN)."

Brown: "Modeled after the practices of the therapeutic community, we always had a Resident Council or a Client Advisory Committee to give us feedback, not only on our current procedures and programming, but also on any new ideas or new grant proposals that we were working on."

Utilization of Peers/Expansion of Teams

Peer staff have been involved in treatment systems for health, substance use disorders, mental illness, trauma (rape, domestic violence, and combat), and HIV/AIDS. They have been called community health workers (CHOWs), outreach workers, consumer staff, mentors, peers—but, whatever they have been called, they are an important component of helping systems become more accessible, more engaging, and more sensitive to the needs of their clients. They help clients negotiate what are, all too often, non-responsive and fragmented systems, give them a sense of continuity as they move from one stage of treatment to another, and provide ongoing support when formal treatment ends. They serve as role models, counselors, outreach workers, recovery coaches, advocates, case managers, trainers, co-facilitators, research assistants, and directors of consumer-run agencies. In addition, I propose that they have reduced the burden on professional treatment staff and can do so even more.

Paull: "We're trying to keep up with all the changes in the ways peers can be part of a program. We've always had peers. We have always had wonderful frontline staff who are under-educated and have been in the very low paying jobs. So, in the last ten years or so, we have really tried to raise them up and provide education for them. We have the Trundy Institute, which does the addiction counseling training for the National Certifying exam. We give our staff some hours during their work day to attend, and they have to give us some of their own hours to attend. We will pay for the course, and they need to pay $75 for the books. If they pass the exam, then we give them the $75 back. Once they pass the exam, we give them a raise. Most of them get promoted to other positions. We also worked with Fred Rocco, who was Dean of Bristol Community College, so they get 15 college credits for passing the certifying exam."

Harris: "I think one of the things we have tried to do is use peers in some of these subsidiary roles, quite honestly. That's been a challenge because people bring some of their own baggage. Even though we talk about trauma sensitivity, we've had peers who see someone they knew out on the street, with whom they might have used drugs, and the peers may try to be conciliatory or thoughtful. Then woman comes in for services, says all kinds of nasty things, and our peers react! We do a lot of training, a lot of supervision."

"I think that people need to be carefully trained and supervised. What we are doing now could best be described as peer/professional staff collaborations. I run groups here, with peers, but there are times when I can see they are dissociating in the middle of the group. Then it becomes my responsibility to say to them, 'This happens to all of us sometime' or 'Jump in when you feel you can, don't when you feel you can't.'"

Fallot: "It always makes sense to have peers involved as advocates."

Paull: "And it's a win-win. It was a win for the organization and a win for the staff person and a win for the client. So why wouldn't you do it? I mean, it's not rocket science. But the peer things are all changing, and now there are more regulations. Now I have community health specialists and I have recovery specialists and I have case managers and I have care managers. And I have navigators. So I have five different things paid for by five different entities. I just want to say, 'Come on guys, let's pull it together. I don't know what you are calling them this week, but....'"

Brown: "Peers have always been part of the design for any of our programs since the 1960s—in outreach, drug counseling, and drug prevention. Then we began including peers in our mental health, trauma, and HIV/AIDS programs. We hired them as outreach workers, intake workers, counselors, group facilitators, case managers, data collectors, and recovery coaches. When clients are leaving, graduating, they may be going into another level of treatment, and the peers help with the transition."

"When our peer staff understood that they themselves had been traumatized and that some of their reactions were like those of the clients, that became very important to talk about. We had to teach them about transference and counter-transference and that, if someone has been traumatized from her childhood into her adulthood, triggers will arise. Those were important discussions. We taught our staff self-care. When the AIDS crisis hit, we had a large number of staff living with HIV/AIDS. Self-care was an important priority. We needed to include rest periods, etc."

"In the WCDVS Study, SAMSHA was very interested in what the children looked like and what we could do for them. Four of the sites, including PROTOTYPES, designed a children's intervention, and we thought the women were going to have problems letting us have their children in the group. So, the consumer/survivor/recovering staff of the four sites designed a letter for the mothers, telling them what the intervention was, what we were doing, why we were doing it, and assuring them that they would be available to them for information and support at any time. We never had a problem with the mothers consenting to having their children in the group after they received the letter."

Machtinger: "I believe that isolation is the biggest obstacle to healing from trauma. When you have HIV and you are not out about your HIV status or when you have had trauma and you are not out about your history of trauma and you are keeping your secrets, you can't really make friends who can support you. So when we did our partnership with the Madea Project, we had this group of women who were coming together and slowly opening up to one another. One of the women, a real peer leader, came in one day and had been beaten by her husband—in front of her granddaughter. The granddaughter had been taken away from her parents by CPS because her mother was in prison for seven years, and this meant that we would have to report this incident to CPS. And that was a very tense period in our relationship with the grandmother; she felt very angry at us for doing that. But, within six weeks, she had gotten this guy out of her apartment, filed for divorce, and had gotten back into care with us ... and forgiven us. And the only reason was that the group of friends/peers at Madea said, 'This isn't Eddie and Beth's fault that they called CPS. It's your fault if you don't kick this #### out of your house. Because this guy beat you up in front of your kid. This is not acceptable. We can't have that happen.'"

Collaborations with Others

Collaboration is another core component of a trauma-informed approach. There is collaboration of provider with client, collaboration of provider with other providers, and collaboration of provider with other systems. In all these collaborations, trust is one of the most important elements. Just as patients/clients must be able to learn to trust their providers—to keep them safe and "do no harm," to hear them and understand them, to share in the decisions about their care, to respect their preferences and choices, and to offer a number of interventions for their healing—team members in the collaborations also need to feel safe, heard, understood, and respected.

Destructive dynamics can also undermine collaborations. Team members can withhold information, pressure individuals to conform, cast blame, and/or split off into competitive subgroups. Shared information is essential because it gives the collaborative a common frame of reference, helps establish goals/objectives and outcomes, helps the group make the best decisions, and increases efficiency. One method of understanding one another is to visit each member's organization/workplace and experience some of the procedures and constraints that member may be experiencing.

Teams need the right mix and number of members with a balance of knowledge and skills. In a collaborative, individuals are inclined to see themselves belonging to a subgroup, not as one cohesive group (e.g., "our unit," "our function," "our region," "our culture"). This can create tension and hinder collaboration. It can also foster sharing incomplete information. Shared information is the cornerstone of effective collaboration.

It has been reported repeatedly that follow-through on referrals from health/ primary care to mental health, substance abuse treatment, or other needed services is low, with estimates ranging from 10 percent to 50 percent (Katon 1995). Having everyone sitting at the table is an important step in changing this and bringing about effective collaboration and collaborative care.

Machtinger: "We started a partnership with the Positive Women's Network, USA that has been, to this day, one of the couple most important professional partnerships that I've ever made. Naina Khanna, their Executive Director, mentored me on the power of policy and advocacy and public opinion and publicity. So, together we convened a group of leading policy makers, government officials, community organizations, and people living with HIV and trauma at the Aspen Institute in Washington, D.C. for two days to talk about how to take this growing body of literature associating trauma with poor health outcomes, specifically in women living with HIV, towards a practical model of trauma-informed primary care."

"What they've just developed is a curriculum, a 12-step curriculum that can help women develop the skills they need to come out to each other about their HIV status and then develop the confidence that their stories matter. Developing a voice with which women can advocate for something that is very important to them. We want to support them whether it's HIV, whether it's crime, whether it's improved schools for their kids, whatever it is they decide to advocate for."

"The first study we did was in partnership with a group called Cultural Odyssey: Theatre for Incarcerated Women. Specifically, we collaborated with their Medea Project. Rhodessa Jones for 25 years had worked in jails with incarcerated women, bringing them together in groups, have them write their stories then read their stories out loud to one another and then choreograph certain ones of their stories and then put on a production of their life stories. Ostensibly it was to prevent recidivism to jail. But it was more of an empowerment group, where women would learn to value their stories and develop the skills and confidence to tell their stories and realize that by telling their stories they could have a meaningful impact on those who heard their stories. Rhodessa is a dynamo and one of the best advocates I have ever met. She's irreverent, a "wild woman," but with a laser focus on what matters and what helps and what's wrong and what needs to be done. Together, we got a grant for a collaboration between a health organization and an arts organization from the William Ford Hewlett Foundation; it was specifically for that type of collaboration. Rhodessa came out of the jails to work with a group of our patients living with HIV to do that same process. None of the women who had participated had ever exposed their HIV status publicly before."

"So, you had this group of women who were coming together and slowly opening up about their histories of trauma and their being HIV positive to a small group of other women—and then beginning to write and reflect on their experiences and to read publicly of their experiences. Many of these women had never written before. And then they choreographed and turned this into a play called *Dancing with the Clown of Love*, and the first theatre run was seen by over 1,000 people. There was a documentary made of it, and people described the impact on women as transformative. And we, as researchers, really needed to understand that better. So we did a very in-depth, qualitative study on the impact of the women's lives through highly in-depth interviews with each of the women about where they were at the beginning and where they were now and the various impacts that going through this process had on them. And what were the facets of the program and the experience that led them to those impacts."

"So from that experience analyzing that data, we realized that by going through this form of therapy—it's called Expressive Therapy—the women had five impacts: sisterhood; catharsis; self-acceptance; developing safer and healthier relationships; and gaining a voice to change the social norms that led them to being HIV positive and having trauma in the first place."

Collaborations and partnerships take many forms, and some of the interviewees ensured that their collaborations included funding through grants.

Machtinger: "The Robert Wood Johnson grant that we got went almost entirely to the Trauma Recovery Center based in San Francisco General Hospital. Previously the Trauma Recovery Center only saw recent victims of crime in San Francisco, violent crime, and victims of torture. They could not see patients of ours who had complex cases of PTSD from having been serially raped as children and were addicted to crack cocaine because of that and were cycling in and out of substance abuse centers because they hadn't dealt with their traumas. The premier trauma agency in the city didn't have a track to deal with our patients. The Robert Wood Johnson grant allowed us to fund an 80 percent time position, within the Trauma Recovery system, who is now stationed with us and working with our psychosocial team to figure out which of our clients are appropriate candidates for referral to the Trauma Recovery Center."

"The Ryan White AIDS care program was so innovative because it recognized that AIDS was not purely a medical disease, that an AIDS clinic needed to have psychosocial and mental health services alongside medical services. And those administering the program embraced the idea that community organizations—advocacy organizations, social support organizations, financial services organization, religious organizations, housing groups, and job training groups—could come into clinics and work alongside clinic staff to provide comprehensive care for AIDS patients. That conception of comprehensive care was really pioneered by the Ryan White AIDS care system."

Kassam-Adams: "We have different collaborations with different medical settings that are doing different things around the country. Sometimes the collaboration takes the form of a phone call from another program, which ask us, 'We are trying to think through this. Can you help us think about what type of trauma-informed care we need here?' Other collaborations are longer-term projects. For example, we worked with a group in Maine that wanted to do a quality improvement project in a large hospital with a pediatric floor, but a small PICU. They wanted to know if they could take our *DEF* concept and use it to change the bedside nursing assessment. So, we helped them implement that for six months and measure whether or not it made a difference. We do that kind of technical assistance."

Brown: "PROTOTYPES Women's Center provided not only substance abuse treatment services, mental health services, trauma services, and medical services, but also job training on-site and job placements in the community, housing on-site and in the community, parenting programs, children's programs, including both a Head Start and an Early Head Start program right on campus, and coordination with ongoing care through partnerships in the community, such as ongoing health care (general and HIV/AIDS related) when the women graduated from the program."

"Our onsite medical team helped the women become more trusting of medical providers, feel more comfortable with physical exams (since many of them had experienced trauma, they were often triggered by physical tests), reduce their utilization of the emergency room as the primary provider of health care, and understand the need for ongoing monitoring of their pregnancies and their children's development by the health teams. Our HIV/AIDS programs for women ranged from outreach to women throughout Los Angeles, two on-site programs at hospital/medical settings, collaboration with USC AIDS (WIHS) program, an outpatient program, our integrated residential treatment program, and AIDS training program for health, mental health, and substance abuse treatment providers throughout all of Los Angeles County. We also had one of the first domestic violence shelters (STAR House) for women with substance abuse, mental health disorders, and HIV/AIDS."

"I also developed a Local Experts Group, which included all of the Directors of the County departments of mental health, substance abuse, child welfare, as well as other agency providers, researchers, and consumers. That group went through the five years of the WCDVS grant with us. That was very important because during that time in California the Mental Health Services ACT (MHSA) was passed. That was a 1 percent tax on the second million dollars of individual's income, which led to some major expansion of mental health services. One of the things that we felt we were able to do was help get implemented the requirement that for every grant and contract paid for with MHSA funding, you had to demonstrate that you were thinking about trauma-specific interventions and trauma-informed practices."

"And I had such support from all the County Directors. As an example, at one of the Local Expert Group meetings, one of the domestic violence program directors said that they hadn't taken women with mental illness because they didn't know what to do for them, they hadn't been trained. The Director of Mental Health, Dr. Marvin Southard, said, 'I will get you a consulting psychiatrist'. Right in the meeting. Instantaneous change. And he is very good about fulfilling his promises. It's that kind of thing that makes a real difference in collaborations."

"There was an overall evaluation of the WCDVS study, and the evaluators went to the sites and interviewed those involved. One of the things they noted at our site were all these heads of departments sitting there with the researchers and providers. All these individuals said they came to this meeting 'because Vivian asked them to.' The evaluators said to me, 'It's like this personal thing.' And, I said, 'Yes, we have known each other, grown with each other, worked together, and pushed one another's systems. This is how things change.' It was funny to me that the evaluators presented this almost as a criticism, that everybody knew me personally and wanted to come to the meeting."

"Los Angeles County is a very odd system. It is larger in population than many states, you can't move it quickly and that we were able to move it as much as we were able to move it is, I think, incredible. The directors of county and state agencies, who have known me for many years, understood that what we were trying to do at PROTOTYPES was try new models. *Seeking Safety* became one of the evidence-based practices that LA County Mental Health trains all the county-based agencies to do. And they learned about it from sitting on that Local Expert Group."

"I think providers who are interested in expanding trauma-informed care have to reach out in their county, city, state to find people who know and care about trauma. This includes providers in mental health, substance abuse, child welfare, health departments, and academic institutions. PROTOTYPES has collaborative relationships with all of them. There are so many people who are willing to help support programs as they attempt to integrate trauma."

Voice and Choice for Clients

Another important component of a trauma-informed approach is client choice and empowerment. The leaders I interviewed all expressed this concept in varied and innovative ways.

Paull: "We instituted Open Access, where an individual with any problem—drug, alcohol, mental health, domestic violence, health—goes through the same intake point. We've had five overdoses in our Open Access waiting room since we started.

And, knock on wood, we have saved every one of these clients. Thank God we have the Primary Care Center right there. In addition, in the outpatient program, no appointments are scheduled. Clients choose which provider/therapist they want to see. Clients have the program's group schedule, can see when staff members might be available, and can just show up."

"We had a male physician who was examining patients newly admitted into detox. In our program, you are admitted by a nurse who is generally a woman, and the nurse does the admission physical. But within 24 hours, the medical doctor has to follow-up. Well the saintly Dr. Lepreau was on vacation, and we had someone else doing the post-admission physical. The woman would not disrobe for him to listen to her heart. And he said, 'Well if I can't check you out, then you are going to have to leave.'"

"Again, he's concerned about his liability, what's she hiding, what does she have that is going to prevent her—that she wants to be here is clear but what is she hiding that is going to make me responsible in something that is going wrong? Does she have a bad heart? Is she going to stroke out here and then I have to say I admitted her? So at that time, we sat down—we have group meetings—sat him down and said, 'Look this is what we think, this is our history, everybody has the right, there are questions you could have asked like, 'Are you comfortable with a male? Would you like me to get a female physician?' Not that we had a female physician right then, but these are the questions. And he got it! It didn't happen again. It's not like it's tremendously difficult to understand."

Some of the leaders discussed how to handle situations and procedures that could be triggers for patients/clients who have been traumatized, but that are mandatory. These include urine testing in substance abuse treatment or monitoring client residences for illegal activities.

Fallot:	"You can be more trauma-informed and less trauma-informed in the ways you implement procedures. If staff are coming into an apartment or a residential treatment room where they are not announced in advance, they can come in, be polite, and say 'I'm here, not because I want to be, but because I have to be. This is why I have to do this. I will be as unintrusive as I can be. That is the way it is, and I wanted to let you know that in advance.'"
Harris:	"That's right, you need to give clients any choice you can. I think Roger's example about the apartment is something that I think would make sense to put into a monograph. You can always make a modification in your system to lessen the clients' sense of violation and lack of privacy."
Brown:	"That is what we have to do with urine testing, to make it a little more trauma-informed. You still have to do it, but you can do it better. You can ask, 'Is there some way I can do it that will make you a little more comfortable?'"

"We also needed to change our policies on medication. We trained staff that we must really listen to the patient and, if the client is scared of a medication for any reason, we should take the time to discuss it with her and give her a choice. We explained how each medication might help and asked hesitant clients if they would be willing to do an experimental trial."

"Our psychiatrists spent more time explaining why it might be a good idea to try it. Again that trial, that choice. Choice is one of those important parts of trauma-informed, to give people choices. When they have been traumatized, choice has been taken away from them. So we want to give the choice back. And when people have choices, despite what we think, they often choose the right things."

"We gave people choices, including choices of groups. In our residential program, we had 25 core groups. That's a lot. We wrote up the descriptions in short, little blurbs, we read the blurbs to the client in case the person didn't read well, and we asked, 'Which ones would you like to start with?' It is very important to give back control and choice to people."

Screening

Each of the sites implemented some form of trauma screening.

Paull: "The *PTSD Checklist*[5] is the main screener we use. But, with our new combined computerized medical records system, we are looking to pick a new screener. I don't know if we'll add 17 questions, because at a primary care visit it won't happen."

Machtinger: "There are two types of trauma in general: intimate partner violence and lifelong abuse and the consequences of lifelong abuse. Almost everyone in our program has had lifelong abuse. So we don't necessarily screen for lifelong abuse in people. We don't take comprehensive trauma histories of everyone in our program. We assume that everybody has had lifelong abuse, and we screen for the consequences of lifelong abuse—like depression and PTSD, substance use, isolation, and non-disclosure."

"One element of our program that we are going to be implementing is a comprehensive screening of and response to intimate partner violence. The U.S. Preventative Services Task Force now calls for screening for intimate partner violence. The Affordable Care Act now calls for screening for intimate partner violence. The Joint Commission (JACHO) on hospital accreditation calls for screening for intimate partner violence. So now we are instituting a process called the *Danger Assessment*, which was created by Jacquelyn Campbell, who was on this group with us in D.C. This assessment includes: all members of the staff; literature in the waiting room; prompts in our electronic medical records; and an algorithmic response."

"We did a study looking at a subset of our patients. We did a detailed interview with them about many aspects of their lives, including substance use, trauma, and mental health. And then we asked which factors were associated with failing anti-retroviral medications. In other words, of the subset of people in our clinic who didn't have an undetectable viral load, we wanted to find out which were the factors that were associated with their being unsuccessful with those medications. Of all the factors we looked at, recent trauma leapt off the page. Those were the individuals who reported trauma within the past 30 days, who answered yes to the question, 'In the past 30 days have you been abused, threatened or been the victim of violence?' When we looked at the data, it was a small subset of patients. It was only 113 patients. We didn't really have the power to look at the contribution of crack smoking or race or depression or medication non-adherence, but none of those were independent factors for why people were failing their medications."

Brown: "We used a number of different screening tools: the *Adverse Child Experiences (ACE) Questions*, the *Life Stressor Checklist-Revised (LSC-R)*,[6] and the *Enhanced COJAC Screener*. (See Appendix B.) I almost forgot to mention that I was Chair of the Screening and Treatment Subcommittee for COJAC, the State of California Co-occurring Joint Action Committee. We developed a screener that had three questions assessing mental health, three questions assessing substance abuse, and three questions assessing trauma. Then we took that basic screening and enhanced it so that it would qualify for *SBIRT (Screening, Brief Intervention, and Referral to Treatment)*.[7] We added two questions from *PHQ-9 (Patient Health Questionnaire)* and three questions from the *NIDA Quick Screen*. We piloted that and had a number of different staff members, including consumer staff and medical assistants, implementing it. People responded quite well to the *COJAC Screener*." PROTOTYPES and Tarzana Treatment Center did the piloting for the *COJAC Screener*. We had medical assistants and peers doing it, and no client complained about the questions. We also tested it on adolescents, and there was no problem. We picked up a high frequency of suicidal intent, which was very important to know about."

"I should also mention the *Stages of Change Tool* we developed in collaboration with the Measurement Group. It was designed based on our work on level of burden, which showed that most of our clients had at least four problems facing them, and on our concept that if you had more than one problem to work on, you were likely at different stages of change for each problem. The *Stages of Change Tool* allowed each participant to show us what level of change they were at for each of four problem areas: mental health, substance use, domestic violence, and HIVAIDS." (See Chapter 1.)

Trauma-Specific Interventions

Machtinger: "The other biggest epiphany I've had in this field of trauma has to do with realizing that people can heal from trauma. It turns out there is actually a solution to this. There are many evidence-based interventions to help people heal from trauma that are incredibly effective and not terribly expensive."

"There are proprietary therapies. One is called *STAIR Narrative Therapy*,[8] something invented by a woman called Marylene Cloitre at the VA. The first eight sessions are about skills building. And the second eight sessions are done individually and focus on developing a new narrative, as a survivor and an empowered person. Another is *LIFT*."[9]

"*Seeking Safety*, as you know, is a group intervention for people who have substance abuse and PTSD. We did it with transgender women living with HIV, which is actually a hard population to reach because they are so traumatized. The *Seeking Safety* group had very significant benefits in both PTSD and substance use. These types of therapies are about rebuilding connections with others. The other element of rebuilding connections with others is peer-based empowerment, group therapies. And we have two partnerships, one with the existing mental health agency in our clinic, called South End Health and Behavioral Health Services, and another, as noted earlier, with the Trauma Recovery Center."

Brown: "For the WCDVS Study we implemented *Seeking Safety* as our trauma-specific intervention. The women loved it, and, after completing it, they wanted to go through all the sessions (32) again. In my entire career, I have never heard people so enthusiastic about a group therapy. People would run up to me on the campus and say, 'Dr. Brown, I just love *Seeking Safety*.' So, *Seeking Safety* has now been implemented in a number of our programs—residential, outpatient, mental health, juvenile justice, HIV/AIDS. For children, we have staff who are trained in another evidence-based practice, *Trauma-Focused Cognitive Behavioral Therapy (TF-CBT)*. We also had a few staff members, including myself, who were trained in *EMDR (Eye Movement Desensitization and Reprocessing)*. So that was available. And we also had our staff trained in *Trauma Empowerment and Recovery (TREM)*, and that is being used in our domestic violence program."

Paull: "We are doing *Seeking Safety* and we're also doing *Surviving and Thriving*. (See Appendix C.) Those are the two trauma-specific interventions we are using."

Prevention

One of the unique features of the work of the Center for Pediatric Traumatic Stress (CPTS) is its focus on prevention as it cares for children and their families. As discussed earlier, one of the reasons this book focuses on trauma, rather than solely on PTSD, is because we want to identify trauma experiences and treat trauma symptoms early enough so that we can prevent the emergence of PTSD. CPTS is doing an excellent job developing new prevention programs in the area of trauma.

Kassam-Adams: "I think we have a bit of a benefit in the pediatric health care world. It is clear to people who've worked directly with or think about sick, ill, or injured kids and their families that this is a really tough thing they are dealing with. So, of course, we are going to bring in a framework that helps them make sense of it and see how we can help. I think we have an easier sell than other fields where we might see our clients or patients or consumers—whatever you call them—as somehow "blame-worthy" even though they really aren't. We don't have a lot of blaming of sick and injured kids, though there may be some blaming of parents from time to time. In that way being a pediatric program is helpful."

"Even in the health care field, it gets a little harder to think beyond kids. That's a really important thing for us. It's not good enough to get all the pediatric-focused clinics or all the children's hospitals in the country doing a trauma-informed approach. It has to be all the other settings as well. Even if you just think within health care, think of a young man alone on a trauma unit who has just been shot. It doesn't matter if you're 23 instead of 6, you feel the same inside. Yet, you may get treated as if you ought to be able to handle it somehow."

"I think the other really wonderful thing about a traumatic stress framework for understanding medical events and families is that it is not blaming. There is a way to do it without it even feeling to the client that it's being identified as a mental health issue. There is this very difficult thing happening and, of course, you are struggling. Some of those struggles interfere with functioning and might even be eligible for a diagnosis of something—PTSD or depression or something—but there is a plain language version of that that makes a lot of sense to families and can be accepted without the family feeling that its competence is being questioned.

I think it's a framework that health care providers can understand. Especially in the pediatric world, but probably even in the adult world."

Brown:	"I think it's interesting Sandra Bloom talks about using 'injury' as the real concept to take away the stigma. And that sounds like you as well."
Kassam-Adams:	"Well, even after an injury, in a non-trauma-informed health care setting one might look at an injured kid who is really struggling to get over it or a parent of an injured kid who is distraught and see them having something wrong with them. We might focus on that instead of asking them the classic trauma-informed question, 'What happened to you?' We need to understand the trauma history that these folks had before this incident and how that might impact their response to it. That makes sense to families, and it makes sense to health care providers, too."

"I think our research, and many people's research now, helps show that trauma is in the data and that a trauma-informed approach is a useful framework. And I think it has the potential to shift how we act in health care settings, not just about the trauma(s) that people bring in, but about the things we ourselves do that are potentially traumatic. Often, the treatment itself is potentially traumatic. Sometimes, particularly with serious illness or injury, we could maybe modify how we do the scary things in order to mitigate the trauma a little bit. Also, the health care setting is a place where we often see people who just had a traumatic experience that isn't just medical. They were just in a car crash or a natural or manmade disaster. Medical providers are often first responders in the really early aftermath of traumatic exposure. This gives us the opportunity for changing how we respond in a way that might shift the post-trauma trajectory in one way or another."

"Think of all the traumas in the world—sexual abuse, sexual assault, war—where people don't appear in front of a helping professional in the early aftermath of that happening to them. Yet the health care setting is one of those places where we will see people who just had something potentially traumatic happen. And maybe we can at least be sensitive in our response. Whether it makes a long-term difference or not, we should do that as human beings. But maybe we can make a difference in whether or not that trajectory goes toward resilience and healing or toward more trouble. That is why I really like thinking about this stuff in a health care setting."

Kassam-Adams: "My work has focused primarily on that secondary prevention time. Not treating either PTSD or just significant symptoms once they develop, but what can we do in the early period after trauma to prevent the development of those things. What can we do to prevent the trauma from turning into—for the child or their family—long-term posttraumatic stress and/or long-term depression? So, one of the things that we developed and tested was an intervention designed to be delivered, not by psychologists or psychiatrists, but by nurses and social workers in our pediatric trauma care unit. By trauma, I mean injury. The intervention was called *Stepped Preventive Care*. Based on our prior screening work, each child in the study got assessed as early as possible for his/her risk factors for persistent traumatic stress. Those we thought were at risk got randomized to this extra intervention, and the others got usual care. It was a small trial, about 40 in each group."

"In the end, we did not find a difference in outcomes between the two groups. But what the nurse and social worker did was to perform another assessment of the children during their time in the hospital and one more about two weeks post-discharge. What they did was target the assessment to what that child and the family's needs were. We framed the assessment around our *DEF* framework (see Chapter 5) of distress and emotional support in family. Was this child having extra pain? If so, the nurse and social worker would make sure that pain management was happening optimally. If the child and/or family were particularly distressed emotionally, then the nurse and social would suggest something else that the child or parents could do to help themselves cope better and work better with the treatment team. In terms of the parents, we looked at whether there were any barriers to emotional support for this child (that's the E) and how the family was doing (that's the F)."

"It was pretty low-level intervention, not that potent, which was probably why it didn't make a difference. We did feel that we figured out that it didn't take that much time, that you really could embed these extra services in care. But I think for it to have actually have made a difference, we would have had to do more. It might be that the interventions had to happen later. So there are questions about timing and how potent the intervention has to be."

"The other intervention we've done and had better findings from was an online intervention for kids, framed as a kind of game, kind of like playing a video game. We called it *Coping Coach* and tested it in small, randomized trial with about 35 kids in each group. They were kids with any kind of medical event: injury, illness, anything that had acutely just happened for them and had brought them to the hospital. They needed to have a little bit of distress from it. They needed to say that this was something they thought they were going to need to cope with. We did this trial as a universal intervention. You didn't have to have major initial acute distress."

"We did a waitlist control this time. The kids either got to play this game right away or they had to wait until the 12-week assessment to play it. Because we also looked at the question about timing, this was really a pilot study. The game was designed to target being able to identify emotions that might happen after a traumatic event in order to shift appraisals, a lot like cognitive behavioral therapy. If you are appraising things as threatening, you can make just a small shift early on and nip in the bud any burgeoning avoidance. Of course, we should avoid things that are really dangerous. However, if you are avoiding things that are not actually dangerous, but are just making you feel nervous, that may be leading you into a trajectory toward posttraumatic stress. So, there was a little bit of work in the game about approaching things that make you nervous, instead of avoiding them."

"There were characters in the game dealing with things that make you nervous, and then the player has to deal with that as well. There is a storyline, there is a plot, and it looks kind of cool. We found out a couple of things: The kids played it for an average of almost an hour, which was great. And we found that we had a slight impact on posttraumatic stress symptoms. Certainly in the kids who played it right away. And a borderline effect in the kids who played it 12 weeks later. So, much more has to happen, that's not enough to say, 'Let's make it available to the world.' But we also found that it did no harm."

"We also found out that playing the game did not harm those that were not at high risk initially. And it seemed to provide the most help to those who were most at risk. So we think the next steps are maybe to do a trial and ongoing work with those who are at most risk and try to refine the game with them. What I like is that it needs no provider time, other than introducing it."

"We need potent interventions that can be very helpful to kids who have the most trouble. We also need interventions that are perhaps only somewhat helpful, but can reach millions of kids. We have millions of kids with medical events, and we won't reach them all with psychologists and psychiatrists and clinical social workers. We think this could be an adjunct to other kinds of treatment."

As you can see, the Directors of the programs interviewed shared what they considered to be core components of trauma-informed practice: a safe and welcoming environment; training and engaging staff in the process; the utilization of peers in many important roles; collaborations with other programs to enhance services; providing choices for clients and engaging them in the transformation of practices; screening; trauma-specific interventions; and prevention. In the next chapter, the interviewees voice their opinions about and experiences with issues important in transforming organizations to become trauma-informed. These include: using crises in their communities as motivations for change and finding areas of shared concern with other providers, organizations, and systems. They also describe those program components and practices that were easiest to change, as well as those that were most difficult.

Notes

1 (Brown, Huba, and Melchior 1995)
2 Actually, the funding was divided into two phases. Phase I (two years) included 14 sites and was designed to plan the longer study. For Phase II (three years), a second grant proposal was submitted, and nine sites were funded for project implementation.
3 (Brown, Harris, and Fallot 2013)
4 For *Seeking Safety*, not only is there a manual, but Lisa Najavits has developed four excellent DVDs. PROTOTYPES has used those for trainings. (See Appendix C.)
5 (Weathers et al. 1993)
6 (Wolfe and Kimerling 1997)
7 See Chapter 4 for a description of *SBIRT*.
8 *STAIR* is an acronym for *Skills Training in Affective and Interpersonal Regulation*. See Appendix C.
9 *LIFT* is an acronym for *Living in the Face of Trauma*. See Appendix C.

References

Brown, VB, Harris, M, and Fallot, R 2013, Moving Toward Trauma-Informed Practice in Addiction Treatment: A Collaborative Model of Agency Assessment, *Journal of Psychoactive Drugs*, vol. 45, no. 5, pp. 386–393.

Brown, VB, Huba, GJ, and Melchior, LA 1995, Level of Burden: Women with More Than One Co-Occurring Disorder, *Journal of Psychoactive Drugs*, vol. 27, no. 4, pp. 339–346.

Katon, W 1995, Collaborative Care: Patient Satisfaction, Outcomes, and Medical Cost-Offset, *Family Systems Medicine*, vol. 13, pp. 351–365.

Swenson, S, Pugh, M, McMullan, C, and Kabcenell, A 2013, *High-Impact Leadership: Improve Care, Improve the Health of Populations, and Reduce Costs, White Paper*, Cambridge, MA, Institute for Healthcare Improvement.

Weathers, FW, Litz, BT, Herman, DS et al. 1993, The PTSD Checklist: Reliability, Validity, and Diagnostic Utility, Presentation at Annual Meeting of the International Society for Traumatic Stress Studies, San Antonio, TX.

Wolfe, J and Kimerling, R 1997, Gender Issues in the Assessment of Posttraumatic Stress Disorder, in JP Wilson and TM Keane (eds.), *Assessing Psychological Trauma and PTSD*, New York, NY, Guilford Press, pp. 192–238.

Chapter 8

Stages of Adoption and Inroads to Change

As providers of health, mental health, and substance abuse treatment, we know that significantly changing the behavior of a single person can be exceptionally difficult work. We have to show over and over that what the person is doing is not getting her/him what s/he wants; we show, we explain, we interpret behaviors that are self-defeating. We help our patients/clients learn new skills, e.g., how to communicate their needs clearly, how to develop or find positive relationships; it is the emotional reactions of the client and the therapeutic relationship that helps move the change process along.

Now picture trying to move an entire agency of 50 people, and then an entire system of hundreds of people, toward change. In order to change the agency/system, the people involved need to feel a sense of urgency. This is why crisis intervention works so well—there is urgency, and the individual is ready to make a move. In general, people will resolve crises by themselves in one of three ways; (1) their functioning deteriorates; (2) they go back to their usual ways of coping, which may often be maladaptive; or (3) they show growth. We want to ensure that the outcome of our urgency to change our system is growth.

There are a number of cultural shifts that will need to be made as you attempt to adopt a trauma-informed approach in your agency/practice/system (Kotter and Cohen 2002).

1. Begin with the patients that are at high risk and those that are the most bothersome to your providers—those who over-utilize services or are noncompliant, depressed, using drugs and/or alcohol, etc. The clinical team and office staff should be given an opportunity to talk about how the psychosocial aspects of care are currently handled and to identify some of the more difficult patient populations with which they need help. New ways of working, even if they are clearly improvements, can be very upsetting to staff. They may feel as if they have been doing something wrong. I like to frame the discussion of implementing a trauma-informed approach by saying that we now know more about trauma than we did before. By doing this, I communicate that these changes don't imply any criticism of previous practice, but rather are focused on the implementation of new knowledge.

2. Decide on a pilot project. Ask for volunteers from staff so that you start with an enthusiastic group. Devising trial procedures with one or more of the populations identified (Plan-Do-Study-Act)[1] can help staff feel that everyone has a part in the process. The more successful the pilot project is, the higher the

morale and excitement of the project staff and the more the rest of the organization around the project may feel left out. Therefore, you want all the staff to have a say in the designing of the pilot. Ensure that you have given the pilot project a realistic time frame. Decide on what you will measure to evaluate the success of the pilot.

3.   Hold regular meetings to update the group on the progress of the pilot project. The updates should include the telling of stories (e.g., describing a problem a patient presented; what was done differently; what the provider learned; describing "blind alleys" that led to no better service). Harvest the wisdom from the pilot.

4.   When the pilot project is to be moved to broader implementation, again ask for volunteers from staff to take the next steps. Identify a "trauma champion" from the group. This staff member will: keep updated on the latest trauma research and keep others informed about it; coordinate trauma trainings; and keep everyone informed about the latest developments in implementation.

The individuals interviewed for this book discussed the stages that they went through in adopting a trauma-informed approach and the important "inroads" to change that helped in the transformation of their organizations. The leaders discussed using crises as inroads to change and finding key issues, like safety, that providers across different fields understand. Then they discussed what was the easiest to change and what was most difficult.

Crises as Opportunities for Transformation

Crises signal both danger and opportunity. The AIDS crisis, as discussed in the interviews (see Chapter 7), opened up a number of opportunities related to trauma and trauma-informed practices. Young people who had been healthy were suddenly dying, gay men were being told that their illness was a "sign from God," injection drug users were being told that they were at high risk of dying, and many did—and we all struggled about how to stop the onslaught of terrible things happening to our clients/patients, friends, and family. This was one of the times when the communities that were affected had to help one another; the government response was too slow. One of the most important results of the crisis was that many community-based and university-based HIV programs integrated substance abuse treatment, mental health treatment, and trauma-informed care. This integration was assisted by Ryan White funding from the federal government, but many of the programs had already begun the integration before the funding became available.

Now, we are facing another crisis; the misuse of and addiction to opioids, such as heroin and prescription pain medications, are now serious national problems. An estimated 1.9 million people in the U.S. suffered from substance use disorders related to prescription opioid pain medicines in 2014, and 586,000 suffered from a heroin use disorder (SAMHSA 2015). Research has shown that prescription opioid misuse is a risk factor for heroin use; 80 percent of new heroin users started by abusing prescription pain medications. This has become a public health crisis with devastating consequences, including fatalities from overdoses.

Annual overdose deaths involving heroin, for example, increased to more than 10,500 in 2014.

Numerous controlled studies have reported significantly better outcomes when individuals who are addicted receive medication-assisted treatment (MAT), utilizing medications such as methadone, buprenorphine, or naltrexone. These medications are effective for helping clients achieve abstinence from other opioids, reducing symptoms related to opioid use, and decreasing disease transmission and crime. Despite the research, MAT is underutilized by many addiction treatment programs. However, most programs that admit patients with co-occurring disorders do utilize MAT. As substance use disorder treatment is integrated into health care, this will mean expanded treatment options for individuals with opioid use disorder. In order to respond to the opioid crisis, in March 2015 the Secretary of Health and Human Services launched an initiative that included: improvements in prescription practices; increased deployment of naloxone to reverse the effects of overdoses; and enhanced access to MAT.

With regard to crises, we have become increasingly concerned about mass shootings, terrorism, and other disasters. After the Oklahoma City bombing in 1995, the Compassion Center was designed to provide a safe, protective environment to meet the physical and emotional needs of family members of those killed and injured in the bombing. Their children remained in physical proximity to them while being offered a separate place of their own to play and be with their peers. This was a trauma-informed approach.

A crisis in the community offers an important inroad to change. When there is a crisis, such as the HIV/AIDS epidemic or the spread of crack or opiates throughout communities, providers and community-based organizations move quickly to develop programs and interventions. Driven by the urgent need to do something about the crisis, providers and consumers move together to save lives and reduce community disintegration. Three of those individuals interviewed talked about the role of crises in their organization's adoption of trauma-informed care.

Paull:	"When HIV first came into the picture, we had many more HIV-positive women than we had men. And they were seroconverting faster than the men, which I don't know if anyone has studied. It was overwhelming. So, we said, 'We need to add this to our array of services.' However, there were no infectious disease doctors in the city of Fall River, there was nobody to treat them. That is when we decided we were going to provide health care ourselves. Dr. Lepreau said, 'These are our patients and we need to treat them well.' And so we opened a health center. The Community Health Center community was really unhappy. They didn't want us stealing their dollars; they had just gotten a big pot of money through legislation, and they saw us as competitors. We went in with another health center and became a Federally Qualified Health Center (FQHC) Look-Alike."
Machtinger:	"When the AIDS crisis hit, I became active in the AIDS movement, in the gay men's health crisis, and in ACT-UP. I was really moved by AIDS because AIDS brought together so many issues that were so relevant: sexuality, discrimination,

drug use, politics, fear. I keyed in at that age that this was a really historical epidemic. People were really dealing with it quite poorly, and the federal government was absent in a way that was profoundly negligent."

"At the Gay Men's Health Crisis, I was a buddy to many people living with HIV. I was just a kid, so they would just put me with somebody who was dying and I would be his support person. And that was very heavy for me. The people I was paired with were not these perfectly psychologically intact people all the time. These were people in crisis and coming from backgrounds that were not necessarily familiar to me. So, it was really hard. But it was motivating, and so I had an idea that I would be an AIDS doctor."

"We looked at what existed in the literature around the evidence on effective interventions and came up with a framework of what are the core components of trauma-informed primary care. We did that so that someone like me, a clinic director who is really interested in embracing trauma-informed care and dealing with trauma in my patients, would know where to begin. Because I think when I first started I really, really had no idea, or even what the definition of trauma was. What was the scope of trauma? What can you do for trauma? How do you help people heal from trauma?"

Brown: "As someone who has always focused on the co-occurring disorders of substance abuse and mental health, it was a natural next step for me, when the HIV/AIDS crisis hit, to design programs for persons living with HIV. We began providing HIV outreach services for women at risk through the WARN (Women at Risk Network) program.[2] The high-risk women included women who were injecting drug users and/or women who were sexual partners of male injecting drug users. Not only did we outreach to hundreds of women, but we also added an HIV/AIDS component to our women and children's residential treatment program, and we formed collaborations with the Women's Interagency HIV Study (WIHS) at the University of Southern California (USC), AIDS Healthcare Foundation, and AltaMed Healthcare."

"Some of the important lessons learned were that: (1) our outreach workers did an incredible job engaging women in the community and getting them to HIV testing and to treatment; (2) women were afraid to ask partners to use condoms because their partners might physically harm them; and (3) that most of the women we worked with had experienced childhood sexual and physical abuse and, later, domestic violence."

There are certain components of a trauma-informed approach that fit with what providers/organizations are already doing something about (e.g., safety) and/or see as part of their job/mission already (e.g., screening, even if it doesn't include screening about trauma). This can help make the first steps toward transformation much easier. In addition, once providers understand how perfectly trauma-informed practice fits with patient-centered care, family-centered care, recovery, and collaborative care, it is easier for them to learn about the pervasiveness of trauma in the lives of their patients/clients and to address that.

Building on What Is Already Being Done

Harris: "In certain systems, for example, Medstar, which is the biggest health care provider here, there is a Chief Safety Officer. Safety outcomes are important to them; in fact, it's one of their primary goals for the improvement of their health care system. I think if you went in to places where there was a Chief Safety Officer, it would give you the sense that already the system values safety. And safety is a key part of trauma-informed practice."

Kassam-Adams: "I think all of these ideas about trauma-informed care are congruent with what we already do. They are not exactly the same as, and they add something, but they are congruent with all the things that pediatricians already know how to do. Or already think is their job. Similarly, I think it's congruent with a lot of things that nurses—pediatric or not—already know how to do, already see as part of their job. And, as in other service systems, it fits with things that people already see as part of what they do or they already have skills to do, maybe we just tweak that or add an element to it."

"Trauma-informed care fits well with both family-centered, patient-centered care and the Joint Commission (JCAHO) requirements. If we are asking people to do something different, the more we can ally it as something they already have to do for someone else, the better. I think that's not medical, that's across the board. There is a JCAHO requirement for every hospital, for every health care setting, is that you have to assess pain well. Assessing pain and optimizing pain management isn't the sum total of trauma-informed care, but it's an important element. If we can say, 'Yes, please do that and do that better and do that really well,' then we are doing trauma-informed care. You have to do it to stay accredited as a hospital."

"It is a similar story with patient and family-centered care. Not every place is doing this well, but there has been a culture shift, and I think most places aspire to do better at patient-centered and family-centered care. And there is some patient-centered care expectation written into the Affordable Care Act."

"That's also true of other systems. If you want trauma-informed judges, what are the ways in which judges or courts perform better when courts are trauma-informed? What are the things on which judges are being evaluated that happen to overlap with trauma-informed care? Let's go with that."

"We can't sit as the mental health trauma experts from outside these systems and come in and tell people what to do. First of all, it's just disrespectful. Second of all, we don't know what that job is like. I know what it's like to have some people tell me I need to add something on top of my job. But we need to figure out how to work with folks within those systems and take advantage of opportunities that already exist."

Easiest to Change

Implementing Trauma-Specific Interventions

If groups are part of what you do (e.g., in substance abuse and mental health treatment), then there is no problem with adding trauma-specific group interventions. If not, then it is important for providers to know the resources available in their communities.

Paull: "It's been a battle for women and for our population all of my life, especially women because women are more stigmatized in this disease [addiction] than men. There was never a battle about trauma. I think there needed to be education, but, generally, once the staff got educated, they just embraced it. I think that's because we're women, we're run by mostly women. If you really look at your patient, you get it. It's not difficult! We've had a couple of situations here where our staff has been scared by partners of women who have come searching for them, but we feel pretty empowered. It's being sensitive to the people that you are treating and understanding what they are facing. I don't know anybody who hasn't had a traumatic situation, myself included, and there are issues around those traumas. You have to have people that are kind and gentle and take their time with you."

Brown: "The easiest thing to change was to put the *Seeking Safety* group into the treatment program. No problem. One, it was based in our residential and outpatient programs, where it was seen as just another group. Most of the staff knew that many of our women had been traumatized, so adding a group like this made sense. And many of the group facilitators wanted to learn it and were very excited about it. The structured curriculum was a bit different for many of the staff, but, as I said before, we spent a great deal of time on the training. The staff and clients, who, of course, were partners in this too, felt that they were comfortable with the curriculum in about two months of doing it. The women loved it. It was quite a surprise how much the women loved it. That was definitely a very important piece of information for me."

"I also want to mention that one of the other easy things to change was the addition of male clients to many of our treatment and prevention services. Many of the men in our substance abuse outpatient treatment who had custody of their children wanted parenting groups and *Seeking Safety* groups. Many of the men in our programs for individuals with serious mental illness also wanted the *Seeking Safety* groups, and in our juvenile justice programs, the young men and women engaged in *Seeking Safety* groups (separate groups for each)."

On-Site Health Care/Behavioral Health Teams

A few of the programs that began as substance abuse or mental health treatment programs were quite willing and able to add onsite medical teams, so that their clients would have readily available health care services.

Brown: "Our onsite medical team helped the women become more trusting of medical providers, feel more comfortable with physical exams (since many of them had experienced trauma, they were often triggered by physical tests), reduce their utilization of the emergency room as the primary provider of health care, and understand the need for ongoing monitoring of their pregnancies and their children's development. Our HIV/AIDS programs for women ranged from outreach to women throughout Los Angeles, two on-site programs at hospital/medical settings, collaboration with USC's WIHS program, an outpatient program, our integrated residential treatment program, and an AIDS training program for health, mental health, and substance abuse treatment providers throughout all of Los Angeles County. We also had one of the first domestic violence shelters (STAR House) for women with substance abuse, mental health disorders, and HIV/AIDS."

Paull: "I said to the doctors in our health center, 'If you want to be the god-like doctor, this is not the place for you. Your purpose is to check out the clients' medical issues and tell us what they need in order to be successful in improving their health. Whether it's case management, whether it's nutrition, whether it's housing, whether it's you name it! We want to know what you know so we can help the person and make sure it doesn't fall all on you.'"

"I wish I had Dr. Lepreau's biography to give you. He was a famous surgeon here in Massachusetts, but he got bored with it. Then, he decided to go to Haiti, where he ran the Schweitzer Clinic. He was here at our program seven days a week to see patients. I paid him $7,000 a year. He set the tone for the entire staff. If you were a new nurse, you were scared to death of him because he would quiz you. If you weren't being respectful to the clients, he would call you on it. But he was also the kindest and sweetest man alive."

"He got interested in alcoholism because he had alcoholic patients when he worked in Appalachia. So, he started to go to AA meetings to learn about it. That is what got him going. And he worked here until he was 89 years old. We had somebody who went into cardiac arrest in our detox unit, and Dr. Lepreau was down on the floor doing the CPR. At that point, I think he realized, 'I am just not well enough to do this.' And he said, 'I'm retiring, at 89.' I said, 'You can't retire until I retire!' He just died last year. We miss him. He was an angel. He set the tone for our entire medical staff."

Most Difficult Issues

When asked about the most difficult issues they faced in integrating trauma-informed practice into their programs, the individuals I interviewed discussed funding issues, regulations, staff resistance, electronic health records (EHRs), staff turnover, and barriers related to time.

Funding

Harris: "Funding streams are incredibly important. They are flipping here in the District right now from fee-for-service reimbursement to a health home model. How to integrate a trauma-informed perspective in those two models is a real challenge. We are not going to change health homes here in the District. And I may or may not think it is a good model, but it is the model into which I have to move my program and find a way to deal with the doctors, the nurses, all of those folks we are going to have to encounter, in a way that is trauma-informed from our end and provides some trauma education at their end."

"I can ask you again—and this is my CEO hat—how do you pay for it? Because one of the things we tried, we were fee-for-service billable. So then we have to train peers to do the things that get reimbursed. So we have thought, we want peers down in our waiting room, talking to people, making things more comfortable for them. Now I have to pay the peers and nobody pays me for the service they deliver."

"I think the money drives some of what we can do. Now the city here has gotten into a sort of peer specialist training. If someone has been sort of designated as a peer specialist, there is a reimbursement for them. However, I was just talking to the head of human resources (HR). We have a gentleman who has been great. He was a peer specialist intern with us. We hired him into a full-time position, but, now that he is hired, we have to do a background check. And, while he was out there using [drugs], he picked up three assault charges. So, our head of HR had to talk to him and say, 'Look, we can't do this.' It was very stressful for her. I think those are the kinds of barriers we encounter when one system clashes up against another."

"Pay attention to the system you are going into. We have lived, at least in mental health, in a fee-for-service system for the last 15 years. And a lot of the interventions, trauma-informed and otherwise, were built into a fee-for-service system. I think that there will have to be modifications as health care moves to this sort of health/home model. The challenges will not be the same as those we've already had to deal with."

Fallot: "Inpatient services cost a lot of money because they have seclusion and restraints and more injuries to staff. Staff injuries are a major concern in some of these settings. One program told me their costs went down by a factor of five after trauma-informed care treatment was implemented. Those are the kind of outcomes that are meaningful in that setting."

Harris: "What I hear you saying, Roger, is that preventing injuries and reducing costs are outcomes that a particular system values, and that we've got to talk the language of that system. We've got to say, 'If you do this, what you really are looking for will change.'"

"What we are going to be measured on with these new health homes is whether we can flip the chronic illness trajectory. If women don't go in to get their blood pressure checked because they are afraid to go to the doctor, if nobody goes to the dentist because they are afraid to open their mouth, if people don't go to regular gynecological care, things get missed. We are using the trauma behavioral health intervention to bring about better health care outcomes. Because health care outcomes, right now, are what the system cares about. I think the way we're pitching this is that the way to get people to comply with the health care system is to deal with their trauma issues that make them scared and resistant to going for health care. But we're going to have to prove that, honestly. Because what they're measuring is BMI, hypertension, and other things like that."

Kassam-Adams: "This question is not unique to health care settings, but it is extremely important. Who pays for what? Many of the things we would like health care settings to do to be trauma-informed are not extra services and would not take any more time. It's just how you do what you are doing. However, to the extent we are asking for extra things, who pays for that? If it makes the session take longer, that just can't happen. If the business model works a certain way, it can't work if something takes longer. Or if you are asking for services to be delivered, then it's not clear who can pay for it. Again, not unique to medical, but certainly an issue."

Policies/Regulations/Electronic Health Records

Harris: "We are dealing with this issue of trust right now in terms of the integration around medical records. We have one system, Georgetown University has another system, the District of Columbia is mandating another system, and the issue now is how will this data talk to one another? Part of it is a trust issue, part of it honestly is a HIPPA[3] issue. I think the conversation about trust has to include the information technology people. We live in a world where the regulations are up to your eyeballs."

"We're taking over a new building in another part of the city. But it will have children, families, and adults. From a trauma-perspective, we wanted two separate waiting rooms, two separate entrances. But there are regulations. We have to go to the regulatory board, we will have to go to lawyers, and that is just to have two different doors. One of the things that the architect told us, because we are getting a certain amount of money per square foot to rehab, is what it would cost us to have two waiting rooms. And if we do, it will take away from other things that we need to do. I think when you talk to administrators and people who have to juggle those multiple balls, it's a different set of issues. I think people are going to have to prioritize and maybe stage changes."

"And what is our liability? We have 46 buildings that we run to house people. And a number of those buildings have apartments for people who have had addiction disorders. Now we have to make sure that drugs are not being used or trafficked in those apartments. So, we have to do spot-visits. Now, it totally invades somebody's space, it is not in any way a trauma-informed practice. However, if somebody dies on our property of a drug overdose, we're liable for that."

"The rules and regulations often get written by people who have no practical, on-the-ground experience. So they come up with this plan, but you know and I know there is no way in hell that you are going to get a doctor to do some of these things. More burden, less money, more time."

Turnover/Retirement of Staff

Paull: "When I went to 'open access,' a lot of our staff left because they didn't want to give up their offices. They didn't like the fact that they weren't going to be the primary clinician and that our program was going to be more team-based. So we had turnover right away. But I think if you walk through the halls and ask, "How long have you been here?' I think you will see there are people who have been here 20, 30 years that just love it. When we did the open access, I changed the primary clinician, who said, 'How could they survive without me?' Well, look, the clients are surviving very well, thank you. So, we had turnover then. But, what we are starting to go through is the graying of the agency. And that means a different kind of turnover. I can't tell you any department that doesn't have someone who has been there a long time and is thinking about retiring. Now that they are leaving and new people are coming in, we have to be sure those values are there in the new people."

"The health care staff is a whole other ball of wax. Yes, they were trained in trauma at the time they came to us, but none of those people are still here. We just had a tremendous turnover in health care, and, quite frankly, it's because of dollars. ACOs[4] (Accountable Care Organizations) are developing, and their goal is to get as many patients under their ACO as possible. They raided all the Health Center medical staff. Now I have a new group of great people who have come in, who want to be here. Dr. Carter was one of the top docs in Rhode Island. His practice got bought by a hospital, and he was unhappy so he came here. And I have another older doctor, who didn't want to see 27 patients as day, as his organization wanted him to. That is what I am attracting. Because we take our time with our patients."

"Dr. Carter wasn't a top doc in Rhode Island because he didn't have a good bedside manner. He's the kindest. I've had patients come up to me and say, 'This is the best doctor I've ever had.' But the problem is that he's my age. He'll be here five years and retire. So we have hired a lot of young nurse-practitioners. We're also looking to hire young graduates from Brown University who have their M.D. degree, but who also have a degree in population health management. Because I hope that will be a sign that these people really want to work with this population."

Harris: "We have high staff turnover, so this can never be a one-time intervention. I was with a large case management team just the other day, and the person who ran that department asked people to go around and introduce themselves and say how long they had been here. The average length of stay of staff, of young staff, was seven months. So if we did an initiative, a treatment training in August, we could expect by December that we would have to do it again."

As noted earlier, one issue related to turnover is retirement of leadership and/or key staff members.

Paull: "So I think for us, staff turnover is an ongoing thing, but what I'm really looking at is a new challenge—retirement of staff."

Brown: "I retired recently and went through the difficult process of finding a replacement who would, I hoped, understand the culture of our agency, support trauma-informed practice, and retain it. You also need to find a person who has the passion for what you have created. The best thing we did was have my co-founder, Maryann Fraser, stay on to help the new CEO for a few years."

Staff Acceptance/Resistance

Fallot: "I'm seeing things that are sometimes more flexible than people sometimes portray them to be. Sometimes Child Protective Services are very responsive, sometimes they are not. Sometimes the courts are very responsive, and sometimes they are not. It depends a lot on the locale or the local issues that are going on in that particular location."

"Acceptance is quite variable from place to place. I was asked to go up to New York state to talk to the child welfare programs and the court systems dealing with child welfare cases. They are very interesting because they are trauma-informed. The judge working with me on this occasion warned me that some of the people were going to be very resistant to trauma-informed practice. She said that right up front. She said, 'There are a lot of judges that aren't going to like it. They will think it's nonsense.' But there are other people who are going to be into it. So, you have to go into the training and consultation on trauma-informed practice with that mindset. Some people are going to listen and some people might not listen from the beginning."

"I was in Michigan recently. We went to talk to the staff of a program about trauma-informed care and we asked people why they were there today. One guy said, 'I'm here today to find out the next thing the state is pushing down our throats.

I don't think it's going to last. I don't think any of the state's things have lasted. Over the last five years, nothing has lasted.' That was his position. And, then, there are some people just not interested in hearing about this trauma-informed stuff because it sounds to them like an excuse to let clients off the hook, so they just don't want to hear about it."

Harris: "I think one of the things that needs to be highlighted, in terms of barriers, is that people need to know that this won't be more work and it won't cost more. As crass as that may sound, if people think it is going to be harder or more expensive, they will close the door before you even get to start talking. And some of the really resistant people have to quit. There are a couple of people who just really dig their heels in and obstruct at every point, and you just have to hope they find another job someplace."

Kassam-Adams: "I think there are stereotypes about medical providers and their openness to thinking about psychosocial things. Some of those stereotypes come from reality, but many of them are overblown or don't always apply when it comes down to their patients, particularly their pediatric patients. So I'd say that, on the whole, individual barriers in terms of people's willingness to think about this are relatively low."

"Certainly, it's important to speak in a language and manner that fit the setting you are in. For example, if you are a mental health practitioner, particularly a psychologist, you are used to writing multi-page reports and going into great background when discussing your clients. The medical setting is one in which things happen quickly. So, whether it's doing a training or whether it's talking about a patient, we need to give a quick, 'How does it affect this situation here and now?' I think there can be barriers when mental health trauma experts come in and expect the medical setting to adapt to their style, rather than the other way around."

"That's not unique to the medical setting. That's true of every setting. You need to be conscious about the setting you enter. You don't want to walk into a court and not do it the way the court does it. That's true for our mental health agencies as well. We have our own cultures in a place centered on mental health."

Time Barriers

Kassam-Adams: "I think there are systemic barriers that, again, are not unique to medical settings. Providers do not have enough time to do what they are already doing. So if you ask them to do something else, it had better fit. And then there's 'bandwidth'—how many more things can someone pay attention to? Do we want people to pay attention to a really careful differential diagnosis and do you have to throw this in as well, so you are just challenging people's bandwidth?"

Adopting a trauma-informed approach gives us a different lens with which to view all our interactions with our patients and clients, as well as with our colleagues. Providing trauma-informed care means more than being compassionate; it means recognizing that our patients come to us with their own histories of traumatic events and their own, unique meanings of these events. It also means that we recognize that our "care" itself (whether it be medical, mental health, or substance abuse treatment) can be traumatizing to our clients. As providers, we all strive to minimize the suffering of our patients; however, it is crucial that we keep in mind that their suffering is both physical and emotional/psychological. Trauma-informed care does not have to be time-consuming; as discussed in this chapter, there are many ways to incorporate it into the myriad interactions that take place in our daily practice. In the next chapter, I expand upon the core concepts in trauma-informed care and suggest practice changes for health care, mental health, and substance abuse treatment systems.

Notes

1 The PDSA or Plan-Do-Study-Act cycle is part of the Institute for Healthcare Improvement's model for quality improvement. PDSA is shorthand for evaluating a change in practice by planning it, trying/testing it, observing the results, and acting on what is learned.
2 Principal Investigator, Josette Mondanaro, M.D. The program was funded by the National Institute on Drug Abuse.
3 HIPPA is the acronym for the Health Insurance Portability and Accountability Act (1996), which provided the first nationally recognizable regulations for the use/disclosure of an individual's health information.
4 An accountable care organization is a health care organization with a payment and care delivery model that seeks to tie provider reimbursements to quality metrics and reductions in the total cost of care for an assigned population of patients.

References

Kotter, JP and Cohen, DS 2002, *The Heart of Change*, Boston, MA, Harvard Business School Press.
Substance Abuse and Mental Health Services Administration (SAMHSA) 2015, *National Survey on Substance Abuse—2014*, Rockville, MD, Center for Behavioral Health Statistics and Quality, U.S. Department of Health and Human Services.

Part III

Chapter 9

Recommended Practice Design Changes

The interviews and site visits (Chapters 7 and 8) illuminated core concepts and components of effective trauma-informed programs. This chapter expands on a number of these concepts/components and suggests practice changes that can help transform programs and organizations. Safety, including cultural safety, collaboration, peers, and task-shifting are discussed.

Safety

Safety is one of the most important concepts in a trauma-informed practice. Experiences of physical and sexual abuse and other traumatic experiences not only violate an individual's sense of physical safety, but also damage his/her emotional well-being and safety. Physical, psychological/emotional, and cultural safety all need to be considered when designing and implementing trauma-informed programs.

Psychological safety involves the patient trusting the provider with "doing no harm." To patients, "feeling safe" means having confidence that they will be listened to seriously, treated with respect and dignity, and not unduly hurried, disbelieved, or judged negatively. Some, especially those with a history of drug/alcohol abuse and/or mental health problems, worry that their accounts of physical symptoms will be attributed to these conditions and therefore, often, don't admit these other problems when reporting to the doctor. Berwick (2003) stated that, "Health care tends to regard human interactions more as a toll or price than as a goal or product. The system tends to act as if interactions were the burden it must bear so that it can deliver the care ... here, we know that interaction is not the price of care; it is care itself ... to perfect care, we must perfect interactions" (Berwick 2003, pp. 207–208).

Daker-White and colleagues (2015) implemented a meta-analysis of studies of patient safety in primary care. Forty-eight studies were included: These studies looked at patients' perspectives on safety, staff's perspectives on safety, medication safety, systems issues, and the primary/secondary care interface. With regard to patients' perspectives, findings were organized around errors related to access issues, communication problems, relationship breakdowns, technical errors, and inefficiency. Examples included under relationship breakdowns/communication problems were: rude staff; disregard for patient concerns; racial bias; insensitivity and miscommunication; and provision of insufficient information about medication(s).

From a staff perspective, safety issues included: physical limitations common to the elderly; patients' difficulty keeping track of medications; memory limitations;

adherence errors; low literacy; and anger and mistrust on the part of the patients. It should be noted that providers emphasized patient errors only and that most of the errors mentioned would be very common among patients with trauma, chronic conditions, and comorbid conditions. System issues included: lack of follow-through and confusion within the office; long waits for appointments; the gatekeeping role of service staff; offices being too busy; incomplete or scattered patient information; electronic health records; lab tests being done in other settings that do not send results back; insufficient communication between primary care and other providers; staffing changes; and doctors and other staff working around system problems rather than trying to solve them. The authors noted that, "Findings from all ... groups referred to the complex symptomatology and physical or cognitive disadvantages found especially in elderly or multimorbid patients" (Daker-White et al. 2015, p. 29). They conclude that relying on patients for information, adherence to medications, and self-monitoring may be compromising their safety, especially for patients who have been traumatized.

The Emergency Room (ER), where acute injuries present the most obvious links between trauma/abuse and health, is the setting that is least likely to have the elements in place to support patients experiencing abuse. These missing elements include sufficient time to calm the patient, a relationship with the health care providers, and privacy. Since the onset of PTSD/overwhelming anxiety, depression, and other signs of psychological distress may occur months after the injury, it is important to provide proactive support throughout an extended care period. However, this is not the typical case in the ER (Frank and Rodowski 1999).

Safety is also an important issue for emergency (ER) staff, who are confronted with high levels of acute and traumatic stressors and unpredictable work conditions (Adriaenssens et al. 2011; Potter 2006). Johnston and colleagues (2016) reviewed 31 key studies of the ER working environment. The literature presents a mixed picture of emergency departments (EDs) as a clinical area filled with stressors, but also as an exciting and challenging environment. Synonymous with both these views, high levels of staff turnover, clinician burnout, and posttraumatic stress have been noted. One of the stressors most consistently mentioned was staff workload and perceived time pressures. In addition, most of the studies mentioned emotional drain as critical; three-quarters of the studies examining nurses' perceptions mentioned the emotional burden of working in the ER/ED, while only one-quarter of medical staff did so. Given that these issues often lead to staff burnout, it is important that strategies for reducing the stressors be in place for ER staff.

The American Psychiatric Nursing Association's (APNA) Institute for Safe Environments (ISE) has focused on key elements that affect safety in psychiatric treatment environments (Polacek et al. 2015). APNA has identified patient engagement as one of the key factors that can improve safety. Engagement means developing a trusting relationship with the patient. Trust is a two-way street. When patients build trust in the provider, they may also feel trusted by the provider (e.g., "I am not just a mentally ill person; I am not someone to fear"). When nurses demonstrate caring toward, support for, and shared decision-making with patients, and the atmosphere of the unit fosters a calm, peaceful, and safe environment, then a positive experience and recovery is more likely to result. Nursing care that patients considered as negative included nurses: not initiating communication; showing favoritism; staying in the nurses' station; not listening; not asking for patients' input on their treatment plans; and making patients feeling judged. From the perspective of the nurses, those things that hinder their engagement with patients included patients' denial of illness; refusal of medications; cognitive deficits; and being triggered by procedures that are experienced as re-traumatizing. Other things that hinder engagement for nurses include: stigma around mental illness; vicarious traumatization; viewing patients as dangerous; threats of violence; and lack of adequate training and supervision.

Delany and Johnson (2008) discuss how patient safety on acute psychiatric wards is narrowly defined in physical terms (e.g., number of incidents on wards), while the psychological safety of patients is disregarded. Initially, many patients report feeling safe on admission to acute care because they have been separated from the daily stresses of life outside the ward. However, this initial feeling of safety may diminish as patients recognize the threats present in the ward environment. Aggressive behavior by other patients is common. Patients expect the nurses to keep them safe.

When addressing physical safety in our programs, we need to walk through our facilities looking through a "trauma lens" and ask:

- Is the treatment site in a safe neighborhood? Are there security measures—guards, alarm systems, barriers—in place to keep out dangerous individuals (e.g., a batterer seeking to harm a woman client)?
- Are there clear signs indicating where a patient/client needs to go? Is there a waiting room that is calming (e.g., not too crowded, not too noisy)? Is there a warm and supportive receptionist? Is there a play area for patients' children?
- If the treatment site is residential, is there separation of male and female patients/clients? Are there separate corridors, bathrooms, sleeping quarters?
- Is there availability of safe time-out space when clients are experiencing emotional distress and when it makes sense to decrease the impact of interpersonal stimulation?
- Is there availability of same-gender staff? Is the patient's preference for working with a same-sex staff member honored?
- Is the treatment site warm, nurturing, inviting? Are spaces (e.g., waiting rooms, offices, exam rooms) large enough so that patients do not feel enclosed and/or restricted?
- Is there available a safe time-out space where staff can de-stress?

When addressing emotional safety, it is important for staff to understand that patients who have experienced trauma may feel vulnerable and unsafe in places and situations that may seem unthreatening to the staff under normal circumstances. Traumatized individuals may experience a flood of feelings and worries that make it difficult to make decisions, follow plans, and take care of responsibilities.

Intake/Reception Procedures

Reception staff should be included in the trauma training, so that they understand how to assist anxious, fearful, or hostile patients/clients. Having pamphlets in the waiting room on sexual and physical abuse can convey to patients/clients that the practice/agency is aware of and ready to help with these issues. Programs need to reflect on whether staff approach clients with nonjudgmental questioning. Staff should be trained to speak with respectful language. It is also critical to ensure that our intake processes are not burdensome, repetitive, or intrusive. Clients should know that they are allowed to state that they do not want to answer any question that is asked. Intake staff can say, for example, "I am going to ask you a number of questions. Some may be about sensitive issues. If you do not want to answer a question, please just tell me that you do not want to answer." If a patient states that she does not want to answer a question about domestic violence, this should be noted in the intake, since this is important information.

During intake, clients should be informed about policies, rules, and procedures. Knowing what to expect decreases anxiety and may prevent the patient from being triggered by unanticipated events. Rules and procedures need to be repeated. Each individual has her/his own pattern of situations that can trigger her/him and her/his own pattern of things that can comfort her/him. You can use the *Massachusetts DeEscalation Scale*[1] (see Appendix B) as part of the intake; this asks patients what upsets them and what comforts them. This important data can be utilized by staff when the client becomes distressed. For the patient, learning to recognize emotional triggers and soothing behaviors restores a sense of safety. For staff, this information can help prevent some of the disturbing events and/or help them comfort and stabilize the client when s/he is upset.

A trauma history may also impact medication adherence, because the patient may fear that taking medications will result in a loss of control. Given that trauma has removed choice and control from them, whenever possible patients should have choice and control in their treatment. For example, the provider can say: "For many people, this can all be overwhelming. We don't have to solve every problem right away. Is there one thing you would like to work on first?" Or, "We have a number of groups you could attend. Which one would you like to attend first?" And always ask, "What can I do to make this easier for you?"

Health Care/Physician Visits

Many health care visits involve the provider being close in proximity to the patient and touching the patient's body. This can be very triggering for patients who have been traumatized. There are several steps that can be taken to minimize any "triggering" effects. Prior to any physical examination, the provider can present a brief summary of what parts of the body will be involved and offering patients choices that will not hinder the exam but will increase the patient's sense of control. In addition, it is important to ask patients what can be done to make them more comfortable during the appointment.

Physical examinations, including pelvic exams, breast exams, rectal exams, and oral exams, can be triggering for patients who have been sexually or physically abused. In addition, any medical procedure that takes place in confined spaces and/or restricts mobility (e.g., MRIs, CT scans) can also be quite disturbing. Therefore, the provider needs to explain what the test is for, why it is important to do, and what will be involved. Following this explanation, the provider should ask the patient what can be done to make her/him more comfortable. Again, it is a good idea to ask, "What can I do to make this easier for you?" Other strategies to decrease the potential of patients being triggered are:

- Ask if the patient would like someone else (a friend, family member, or nurse) to be in the room with her/him. Also ask if the patient prefers a male or female physician.
- If a client needs to disrobe for an exam or procedure, explain what will happen next, what level of undress is required, and why.
- Reduce interruptions and other staff walking into the exam room.
- Allow the patient to monitor the procedure (if possible) by using a mirror.
- Ask permission before performing each part of the exam.
- Be mindful of your body position. Do not approach the patient quickly and do not lean over him/her in a way that might feel threatening. Tell the patient where you will be touching them. Even a simple exam of the patient's thyroid (where your hands will be around her neck) can be triggering for a woman who has been a victim of interpersonal violence.
- Take your time and slow down your pace.
- Be aware of nonverbal signs of the patient's fear and anxiety, including extreme tenseness or cringing when you touch her/him. Allow the patient to stop a procedure.
- Allow breaks during the examination, during which you check on the patient's comfort level.
- During the exam, talk about what you are doing, why you are doing it, and what you see.

With regard to unhelpful behaviors, there are a few cautions:

- Do not say, "Just relax" if a patient is showing signs of anxiety and fear. Instead, help the patient by suggesting some specific steps, such as, "Focus on breathing—take deep breaths while I do this exam."
- Do not say, "Don't cry" or, "Don't be scared" when a patient expresses a negative emotion by crying. Say, "I can see you are frightened" and, "No matter what we find, I will be with you throughout this whole process."
- Don't interrupt patients when they are trying to tell you their concerns or why they came to the visit. You may miss the most important information they have to give you.

See Appendix E for further training resources.

An excellent resource, *Handbook on Sensitive Practice for Health Care Practitioners* (Schachter et al. 2009), was written by and for primary care practitioners in Saskatoon, Canada who work with adult survivors of child sexual abuse. The authors identified nine things that can facilitate a sense of safety among these patients during interactions with health care practitioners, including:

- Showing respect—seeing the patient/client as a particular and situated individual, with unique beliefs, values, needs, and history.
- Taking time—being rushed or treated like an object diminishes a survivor's sense of safety.
- Sharing control—the process of informed consent is a vital part of sharing control, as well as a legal responsibility. Informing, consulting, and offering choices are all part of sharing control.

- Understanding non-linear healing—the degree to which a survivor is able to tolerate or participate in treatment may vary from one health care encounter to the next.
- Demonstrating awareness and knowledge of interpersonal violence—many abuse survivors look for indicators of a clinician's awareness of issues of interpersonal violence. In addition, male survivors may also be looking for an indication that the provider is aware that men also experience interpersonal violence.

Dentistry

Another important area for establishing safety in health care is dentistry. Dental fears are associated with less frequent or irregular dental visits, as well as cancellations and/or deferrals of appointments, which in turn can lead to poor dental health and more costly, painful, and invasive procedures. Adults with histories of sexual abuse victimization may experience increased difficulties in tolerating dental exams and treatments. Since the sexual abuse may have involved the victim's mouth, dental treatments may be threatening and trigger unwanted memories (Larijani and Guggisberg 2015).

From the literature on this, we know that one of the issues for dental patients is lack of control. Individuals studied expressed various degrees of helplessness and powerlessness. Some of the proposed strategies to increase patients' sense of control are: (1) collaboration with patient about treatment decisions; (2) asking permission before performing dental treatments; (3) following the rule "inform before you perform" by explaining to patient what you will be doing and why, and asking, "Is this OK?"; (4) allowing breaks during treatments, checking on patient's comfort levels, and using an agreed-upon stop signal (e.g., raise your hand); and providing written material about the procedures being done (this is particularly important for patients who disassociate when dealing with providers).

Patients can experience flashbacks or involuntary recurrences of the memories of traumatic experiences as if they were occurring in present time. Conditions that may be triggers in dental care include: being placed in a horizontal position; the physical proximity of the dentist; the gender of the dentist; oral manipulation; instruments being placed in the mouth; and the smell of latex. Proposed strategies to decrease the potential of patients being triggered are:

- Place patients in semi-supine positions whenever possible, covering them and allowing monitoring of the procedures (via mirror). If this is not possible for certain procedures, give detailed explanation for why the supine position is needed.
- Have the patient bring a chaperone (trusted friend or family member) with them to decrease his/her stress.
- Leave the door to the exam/treatment room open.
- Ask patient who he/she may feel more comfortable with (e.g., male or female dentist, dental hygienist).
- Be mindful of your body position during treatment and do not lean in towards or touch the patient's body.
- Use relaxation, distraction, and desensitizing techniques (e.g., music).

- Ensure that all members of the dental team have been taught how to identify the nonverbal signs of patients' fear and anxiety, including extreme tenseness, gagging when their mouths are intruded, and cringing when the dentist touches them.
- Ask, "Are there any parts of the dental treatments that are difficult for you?" and, "Is there anything we can do to help you feel more comfortable?"

Substance Abuse Treatment

Substance abuse treatment providers have underestimated the effects of trauma on their clients. There are certain procedures that can be re-traumatizing, such as: urine testing; aggressive confrontation; sudden discharge from treatment; and supervised visits with children who may be in foster care. Some recommendations to drug abuse treatment staff to reduce re-traumatization and to become trauma-informed are:

- Do a walk-through of your program from first contact by a potential client through the entire treatment process. Look at issues such as how many contacts clients have to make before they get an intake appointment and how many steps it takes to complete the intake.
- Participate in trauma training at your site or at conferences.
- Routinely screen clients for traumatic experiences. Those programs that routinely use the *Addiction Severity Index (ASI)* can begin by using the trauma items embedded within that instrument. Then, the program can decide on additional screening items.
- During urine testing, try not to stand too close to the client, assure the client you know this procedure can be uncomfortable, and ask, "What would make this more comfortable for you?"
- If a client is triggered in a group session, stop the action and introduce grounding strategies (Covington 2003; Najavits 2002).
- Reduce aggressive confrontation, which can be seen as provoking retaliation of the part of clients who have been physically assaulted or proving increased anxiety and fear in clients who have been sexually or physically abused. Instead, provide firm feedback in a supportive environment.
- Do not discount a client's report of a traumatic event.
- Help decide on which trauma-specific intervention (e.g., *Seeking Safety, Beyond Trauma, TREM*) fits best in your program. Participate in the training for the intervention selected.
- Speak to clients with respectful language.
- Link "triggers" for using drugs and alcohol to "triggers" for re-experiencing traumatic events.
- In residential treatment, when entering the rooms at night (for monitoring): Knock on the door; identify yourself; say, "I'm coming in"; and ask if clients are okay.
- In relapse prevention, when discussing triggers for using drugs/alcohol, focus upon situations that increase the client's physical discomfort, bring up unpleasant emotions, provoke conflict with others, and remind the client of losses. These situations appear to have a strong impact (i.e., increasing the likelihood of relapse) for clients who have substance use disorder-PTSD.

- Find ways to give clients choices. This is not "enabling" the client, as many staff in substance abuse treatment fear. Examples of choices are: which groups s/he would like to start with (after all the groups available have been described); how the client would prefer to be contacted (phone, email, or through a regular phone-in time set up for the client). Allowing the client to decide how contact with him/her will be made can be quite important for ensuring the safety of a client experiencing domestic violence.

Mental Health Treatment

While trauma and PTSD treatments reside in the mental health arena, the mental health treatment system has been slow to adopt trauma-informed practice. Mental health providers can do these things to decrease re-traumatization of their patients:

- Do a walk-through of your program/practice from first contact by a potential client through the entire treatment process. Look through a client's eyes and a trauma lens.
- Find ways to give clients choices. Examples of choices are: what problem s/he would like to start with; how the client would prefer to be contacted (phone, email, or through a regular phone-in time set up for the client). Allowing the client to decide how contact with him/her will be made can be quite important for ensuring the safety of a client experiencing domestic violence.
- Provide parenting skills training for clients who are parents or who are pregnant. This will enhance the client's ability to: recognize and regulate emotional responses; accurately read the child's cues and respond effectively; and develop predictable routines to increase the child's sense of safety and improve his/her self-regulation.
- Provide walk-in appointments for patients in crisis.
- Participate in trauma trainings at your site or at conferences.
- During the intake process (screening, assessment, and treatment planning), listen to and use the patient's own terms for what s/he is experiencing. Routinely screen clients for traumatic experiences.
- Implement *Motivational Interviewing*.
- Provide anticipatory guidance to parents/adults about stress reactions in themselves and their children and about effective ways of coping with these.
- Ask, "Since the last time I saw you, has anything happened that was upsetting or scary?"
- Understand that an individual's perception of the severity of a traumatic event and the meaning of the event to her/him is what makes it traumatic. When talking to a patient about a potentially traumatic event, it is important to explore these two features.
- Use the *Massachusetts DeEscalation Form* to identify what upsets this particular client and what helps him/her de-escalate. Make sure to review this form throughout the period of treatment; don't just file it and forget it.
- In inpatient facilities, reduce the use of seclusion and restraint to 1 percent of all de-escalating procedures.

Cultural Issues

As we have become more aware of the importance of taking culture into account as we provide care to the diverse populations in our systems, our ideas about how best to do so have moved through a continuum from cultural awareness to cultural sensitivity to cultural competence to cultural humility to cultural safety. Cultural competency involves more than gaining factual knowledge about the different populations we serve; it also includes examining and changing our attitudes toward our clients. Cultural humility requires the provider to engage in continual self-reflection and self-critique and to acknowledge "privilege" if that is relevant (Tervalen and Murray-Garcia 1998). As providers, we must be both humble and bold enough to look at ourselves critically and to be willing to change our attitudes and behavior. It is also essential that our staff examine their own patterns of unintentional and intentional racism, classism, and homophobia. Cultural humility may be especially important in order to develop a strong working relationship with a client who is culturally different. The provider must be able to overcome the natural tendency to view one's own beliefs and values as superior and, instead, be open to the beliefs and values of the client. Cultural humility involves the ability to work with the client to understand how the client's various identities (e.g., man, worker, Hispanic, father) intersect and how they affect the therapeutic alliance. Providers also must understand that the client is the expert on his/her own life, symptoms, and strengths.

I believe that cultural safety offers us one more step to enhance our understanding of the way culture affects our practices. The concept of cultural safety was first articulated in 1988 and emerged from the experiences of the indigenous people of New Zealand.[2] It is a model for negotiated and equal partnership that moves beyond awareness or sensitivity to more attuned action or behavior in a range of cultural contexts. The Nursing Council of New Zealand (2011) further developed the concept: "[Cultural safety is] effective nursing practice of a person or family from another culture, and is determined by that person or family…. The nurse delivering the nursing service will have undertaken a process of reflection on his or her own cultural identity and will recognise the impact that his or her personal culture has on his or her professional practice. Unsafe cultural practice comprises any action which diminishes, demeans or disempowers the cultural identity and well being of an individual" (Nursing Council of New Zealand 2011, p. 7). One of the key principles set forth by the Nursing Council is the need for nurses to recognize that both contemporary and historical inequities, including those resulting from colonization, affect health care interactions and that the attitudes, beliefs, policies, and practices of providers can act as barriers to effective care. This principle, while developed for nursing, is applicable to a wide range of other health and behavioral health professionals.

This concept really helps us to understand safety through both a trauma lens and a cultural lens. There is no "post" or "past" traumatic stress when you feel your body is in danger because of your race, ethnicity, religion, gender, sexual orientation, etc. American Indian/First Nation peoples and African Americans may not feel safe when their lives can be taken by those who have been held up as their protectors. I believe that cultural safety is a key concept in understanding that, although we are trying to help our patients—through our medical practice, mental health treatment, and addiction services—the patients may not experience our help or their safety. An essential feature of cultural safety is that the patient/client define whether or not the practice, the practitioner, and the environment are culturally safe. What cultural safety asks us to do is to "ask" the client.

Ramsden (1992) conceptualized a continuum from cultural awareness to cultural competence to cultural safety. Cultural safety turns the focus away from the cultural understanding and knowledge of the health care practitioner and onto the power inherent in their professional position. Ball (2007a) regards the concept as a paradigm shift rather than the last step of a continuum. She sees the central question about cultural safety as, "How safe did the service recipient experience a service encounter in terms of being respected and assisted in having their cultural location, values, and preferences taken into account in the service encounter?" (Ball 2007a, p. 1). Ball also set forth five principles necessary for cultural safety: (1) protocols—a respect for cultural forms of engagement; (2) personal knowledge—understanding one's own cultural identity and sharing information about oneself to create a sense of equity and trust; (3) process—engaging in mutual learning, checking on cultural safety of the service recipient; (4) positive purpose—ensuring the treatment process yields the right outcome for the service recipient according to the service recipient's values, preferences, and lifestyle; and (5) partnerships—promoting collaborative practice (Ball 2007b). What is most important is that the person who receives the service defines whether it is culturally safe.

There are two other concepts that are relevant for enhancing our understanding of the ways in which trauma affects our patients/clients and ourselves: intersectionality and historical trauma. Each is discussed below.

Intersectionality

I remember the first time I experienced—in a meeting about women's services— what intersectionality really meant. We were discussing the barriers women experienced in drug treatment programs and in health care, when one of the African American women in the group stated that we were missing an important piece of the puzzle. She asked us to understand that Black women's experience was not just like white women's experience. Some of the women present wanted to ignore the comment, but some of us asked her to explain. She brought to our attention the concept of intersectionality.

Intersectionality draws attention to the meaning and consequences of multiple categories of identify, difference, and disadvantage. As an example, an African American woman who has been battered has experienced trauma and discrimination on three (if not more) levels—as a woman, as an African American individual, and as a person who has experienced physical abuse. Interventions based solely on women who do not share the same race or class or sexual orientation may not be relevant for her. African American feminists found themselves having to explain to their white colleagues that Black women had unique experiences with discrimination, which cut across all kinds of lines (color, class, gender). In her 1991 publication, "Mapping the Margins: Intersectionality, Identity Politics, and Violence Against Women of Color," Crenshaw (1991) explained that feminist efforts to politicize the experiences of women and anti-racist efforts to politicize experiences of people of color have "frequently proceeded as though the issues and experiences occur on mutually exclusive terrains" (Crenshaw 1991, p. 1242).

In exploring the race and gender dimensions of violence against women of color (e.g., domestic violence/interpersonal violence), she (Crenshaw 1991) stated that the interests and experiences of women of color were frequently marginalized within both race and gender. Each patient is uniquely qualified to help providers understand the intersection of race, ethnicity, religion, class, gender, age, sexual orientation, etc., in his/her life and to clarify the relevance and impact of this intersectionality on the present illness.[3]

Following a brief field study of battered women's shelters located in minority communities in Los Angeles, California, Crenshaw described the dynamics of structural intersectionality. In most cases, the physical assault that led the women to the shelters was only the most immediate manifestation of the subordination they experience on a daily basis. Many women of color are also burdened by poverty, childcare responsibilities, and the lack of job skills. "These burdens, largely the consequence of gender and class oppression, are then compounded by the racially discriminatory employment and housing practices women of color face" (Crenshaw 1991).

These intersecting systems structure the experience of the battered women of color and point to the need for treatment/advocacy services to be responsive to all the needs, not just one, e.g., domestic violence. This is also true for women survivors of rape.

People of color often must weigh their interest in avoiding the highlighting of issues that might reinforce distorted public perceptions of their communities (e.g., "violence") against the need to acknowledge and address intra-community problems. Race and culture contribute to the suppression of domestic violence in other ways; viz., women of color are often reluctant to call the police, fearing that their abuser will be harmed by the police. In addition, battered women shelters that do not admit women who use drugs/alcohol or are diagnosed with mental illness or do not speak English are also compounding the harms and increasing the burden these women face.

Historical Trauma

A type of trauma that can also be seen as a component of identity and is often overlooked is historical trauma. It has been described as multigenerational trauma experienced by a specific cultural group. Eyerman (2001) stated, in reference to African American identity in the U.S., that cultural trauma was not just constituted in those who were enslaved, but also in their descendants. Fassin and Rechtman write: "The memory of the Holocaust is clearly the starting point for the contemporary manifestation of collective trauma in the public arena" (Fassin and Rechtman 2009, p. 17). Among the many groups that have been identified as experiencing historical trauma there are American Indians/First Nations people, African Americans, Jewish people, and Japanese Americans. These populations have been traumatized by: expulsion from their homelands; loss of economic status and self-sufficiency; removal of children and separations of families; loss of social ties; and torture and murder.

For American Indians, the forced relocation onto reservations and the sending of children to Indian Residential Schools led to significant losses of cultural identify and cultural methods of healing, as well as sexual and physical abuse in the schools.

Taken together, these losses and traumas have led to high rates of suicide, domestic violence, and alcoholism.

African Americans sustained psychological and physical injury as a direct result of slavery. The violence and abuse continued after slavery officially ended with Black Codes, convict leasing, lynching, threats against African Americans' lives and property, and Jim Crow segregation. Inequality and racism persist today, with the most extreme and visible manifestation being the killing of unarmed Black men and women by the police.

For Jewish people, the memory of the Holocaust represents the most extreme reach of violence. The delay between the event itself and its painful exposure to public gaze led to the urgent need to "bear witness" and not forget. Survivor guilt, which often persists in the next generation, became the defining symptom of this trauma. Survivors and their families also experience psychic numbing, unresolved grief, and a "death imprint."

Collaboration with the Community and Community Agencies

In trauma-informed care/approach, collaboration is twofold; collaboration with the patient/client and collaboration with the community and community agencies. As I have noted many times, health problems and behavioral health problems have multiple determinants, including those over which individuals have little or no control. Collaboration with community agencies can have a number of benefits, including greater buy-in from community leaders and residents, more acceptable and culturally relevant messages, better follow-up with referrals, and greater use of services. There is an important distinction between providing services "in" the community and conducting services "with" the community. When services are intended to be empowering, when they attend to social inequities, and when they are designed and delivered in collaboration with respected community service providers, then the collaboration is *with* the community.

When determining membership in a collaborative (i.e., who should be at the table) it is recommended that those who deliver the interventions (agency staff), those who receive the interventions (community residents and others), and those who evaluate the programs should all be part of the collaboration. This "three communities" model for identifying critical stakeholders, particularly for HIV/AIDS work and work with populations diagnosed with severe mental illness, has been described by Reed and Collins (1994).

All of my work, beginning with the writing of the grants that funded projects, was based upon equal partnerships with community groups and community members. That meant that goals and objectives were decided upon together, staff from the community were hired and trained (and the training was often done in partnership with other community agencies), and the results of evaluation/research were shared with the community (in language that was meaningful to them). In the Women with Co-Occurring Disorders and Violence Study (WCDVS), consumer/survivor/recovering (c/s/r) staff participated in all aspects of the program and the research, and all publications had at least one c/s/r as an author.

In the domain of health promotion, many collaborative efforts have focused on developing empowerment models and conducting research linking health outcomes to the degree of control we experience over our lives. Empowerment has been defined as an intentional process centered in the local community, through which residents lacking an equal share of valued resources gain greater access to and control over those resources (Rappaport 1994). Empowerment emerged as an important goal in feminist research, in PAR, in HIV/AIDS, and in work with populations diagnosed with severe mental illness. The motto "Nothing about us, without us" is part of this empowerment movement.[4]

Lack of trust, inequitable distribution of power and control, a lack of clarity about who represents the community (communities), and a variety of potential areas of conflict involving different priorities, values, and roles all play a part of success or failure of the collaborative effort. In addition, tensions between the service agenda and the research agenda, as well as potential differences between the funders' priorities and the community's priorities, can cause major conflict. There may be three kinds of interests among collaborators, viz., shared, differing, and opposing. Sorting these out is a critical aspect of the collaborative dynamics. Collaborations, by their very nature, reflect differing goals, vested interests, and world-views on the part of the different parties involved. Though often viewed as negative, conflict between members may serve critical positive functions if negotiated properly (Trickett and Espino 2004).

Two preconditions for a successful collaboration are shared commitment to collaboration and an organizational willingness to change. A certain degree of trust must be developed among/ between collaborators. Trust is multi-leveled, existing at the individual, organizational, and inter-organizational levels of the collaboration. The dynamics of collaboration, particularly in the early phases, may revolve around "tests of trustworthiness." Because collaboration involves trust, credibility, dependability, and mutual respect, individuals lacking these qualities tend to give the collaborative a "bad name" in the community and divert needed project resources to damage control.

Issues of trust are heightened when White staff members work in ethnic minority communities. White researchers are likely to be seen as informers attempting to get inside information that can subsequently be used against those who are providing the information. Black communities have become accustomed to informers and have devised methods to keep them happy by feeding them what is frequently bogus information. Fullilove and Fullilove (1995) focused on the potential suspicion with which outsider research is greeted in communities of color. They point out that, when research/evaluation is any way race-based, the researchers need to clarify specific hypotheses, whether or not interracial comparisons will be made, and how race is thought to be related to the other variables of interest. First Nations people have also learned to hold on tight to cultural information for fear of it being used against them.

It was easier for us at PROTOTYPES, because our agency and its multi-racial, multi-ethnic staff (many from each of the communities we serve) worked on drug use, mental health, domestic violence and other trauma, and HIV/AIDS in communities where we worked and lived for many years. The racism and historical trauma were an explicit part of our conversations with staff. In one meeting, where we were speaking of racial tensions in the community, some of the staff looked at me anxiously as staff members spoke of some of the racist behaviors of white people. I stated that "my people [the Jews] were also killed by white people." It has been our experience that community perception of agency knowledge, of openness and honesty, and of concern and care for the community aid in attaining trust and credibility.

Trust must be earned. The Tuskegee experiments showed why community vigilance around outside researchers and doctors, particularly when race and power issues are involved, represents an adaptive, rather than a "paranoid" response. I explained to my staff (with our research partners) that we were collecting data not because it was mandated by the funding agencies, but because we believe that data and evaluation are key to our making our services better for our communities. We trained staff, from outreach workers to clinicians, to understand how evaluation/research works. When we had collected the data, we shared it with them, and asked what they thought about what we had found. There were some very exciting discussions around the data, including what changes to our practices it suggested should be made.

A learning-oriented, trauma-informed system embraces teamwork and collaboration in an environment that values continuous improvement and encourages staff to propose ideas for improvement without fear. Such a setting needs a strong leader/leadership to support the aim of continuous learning, translating that aim into practice at all levels, removing barriers that threaten staff improvements, and supplying resources to accomplish the improvements. Often when successful collaboration has occurred, it has depended largely upon the drive and personal investment of key individuals in leadership positions. As a result, the sustainability of the collaborative efforts is threatened when changes in leadership take place.

Peers/Reducing the Burden on Staff

One of the important components of collaboration and the sharing of tasks is the addition of peers to our teams. Task-shifting is a method of strengthening and expanding the health care and behavioral health care workforce by distributing service delivery tasks among a broader range of providers. This practice is not new and is currently in place in many developed countries (Australia, England, the U.S.), where nurses, nursing assistants, medical assistants, and pharmacologists provide services once only provided by doctors. In addition, as discussed above, community health workers and other peer specialists now provide health, mental health, and substance abuse services in many settings. For example, despite strong evidence of the efficacy of specific treatments, approximately 90 percent of primary care patients with depressive and anxiety disorders do not receive treatment (Wang et al. 2007).

The history of the peer movements is discussed in Chapter 5. More recently attention has focused upon the effectiveness of peer-delivered services. For example, Chinman and colleagues (2006) reviewed the literature and conducted interviews, focus groups, and a brief survey of administrators, providers, and patients at three large Department of Veterans Affairs (VA) clinics in order to determine the feasibility and acceptability of consumer provider (CP) services for patients with serious mental illness. The authors suggest that consumer providers can address the patient and system level factors that contribute to poor outcomes among this group of patients. At the patient level, poor outcomes are, in part, a result of social isolation, demoralization, and disconnection from services and supports. The consumer provider can enhance social networks by role modeling and by facilitating peer support groups and activities, can engage patients and make treatment more relevant, and can teach coping skills and provide hope. At the systems level, providers are overburdened and services are often fragmented. The consumer provider can: reduce the burden on providers; provide case management and system navigation to increase access and deal with fragmentation; and advocate for community integration over symptom stabilization.

The study showed that most of the members of the three groups (administrators, providers, and patients) agreed that CPs could play a supportive role for patients and that CPs could be strong role models and provide hope of recovery to other veterans. All three groups were enthusiastic about using CPs as "a bridge between the mental health system and the patient to improve service delivery," who can help patients navigate the system, help providers and patients understand each other's needs, and help providers to better engage patients to remain in treatment.

Other studies have identified three unique contributions of peer support: (1) the instillation of hope through positive disclosure; (2) the exploration of new ways of using "street smarts," to deal not only with the illness, but also with low income, stigma, discrimination, and a maze of service systems; and (3) a relationship characterized by trust, acceptance, and cultural understanding. Davidson and colleagues (2012) investigated whether peer support might decrease rates of hospitalization and days spent in the hospital for patients with histories of multiple hospitalizations. The peer staff members, who named themselves "recovery mentors," were trained to provide functions of advocacy and community integration. Participants were randomly assigned to usual care or usual care plus a peer recovery mentor. There were statistically significant findings for the number of hospitalizations and the number of days spent in hospital, with participants assigned recovery mentors doing significantly better than those without a recovery mentor on both measures. In addition, consistent with other studies, there was a significant decrease in substance use and depression and an increase in hope and self-care for patients with recovery mentors.

Despite these positive results, there were several reservations expressed by providers, including the belief that CPs might overly rely on their own experience and might force patients to conform to their own path of recovery. Several providers were also concerned that CPs could potentially harm patients by projecting their own illnesses onto the clients or talking negatively about medications. Many providers were also concerned that CPs "may fall apart" or experience a significant reoccurrence of their symptoms as a result of their exposure to the stress of the CP job. All three groups did discuss ways to overcome some of these concerns, including screening applicants carefully and providing adequate training and supervision.

Community Health Workers

The concept of community members to render basic health services to the communities from which they come has a 50-year history, beginning with the Chinese Barefoot Doctor program (Shi 1993; Zhu et al. 1989). A number of countries then began to experiment with the Village Health Worker (VHW) concept (Sanders 1985). Both Tanzania's and Zimbabwe's VHW programs were set in the political context of systematic transformation (decolonization and the Ujamaa movement in Tanzania and the liberation struggle in Zimbabwe), and both focused on self-reliance, rural development, and the eradication of poverty and social inequities. In general, community health workers (CHWs) carry out the following roles:

- Bridging the gap between communities and the health care system, by:
  - Enhancing care quality by aiding communication and clarifying cultural practices between provider and patient;
  - Educating community members how to use health services; and
  - Educating the health care system about community needs.

- Helping patients navigate the health and human services systems, by:
  - Increasing access to primary care through outreach and enrollment strategies;
  - Providing follow-up care;
  - Linking clients to available community resources; and
  - Providing support to clients throughout their different treatments.

- Providing direct services, by:
  - Providing culturally appropriate health information to clients and providers;
  - Assisting clients in self-management of chronic illnesses and medication adherence;
  - Organizing and facilitating support groups;
  - Conducting health-related screenings; and
  - Becoming members of patient-centered health teams.

Peers are serving increasingly important roles in health homes and in disease management programs. The Health and Recovery Peer Program (HARP) is a model of a peer-led disease management program, and the Chronic Disease Self-Management Program (CDSMP) is the most widely developed peer-led self-management intervention in general health care settings (Lorig et al. 2001). Peer support programs are also used in military medicine, particularly for amputees (Gajewski and Granville 2006; Marzen-Groller and Bateman 2005). Berwick and colleagues noted that, "Such programs have been shown to encourage an optimistic future outlook, decrease the sense of isolation, and promote coping abilities and self-management" (Berwick, Downey, and Cornett 2016, p. 279). Peer support services have been recognized by the Center for Medicare and Medicaid Services (CMS 2007) as an evidence-based practice. They are Medicaid-reimbursable in more than 30 states. Currently, 37 states have adopted standards for training and certification, and others are in the process of doing so.

Peers can also play an important role in the delivery of trauma-specific interventions. Upshur and colleagues (2016) conducted a quasi-experimental study that compared women in two prenatal care settings who screened positive for PTSD. The study was conducted in two federally qualified community health centers; both centers had a prenatal care team consisting of paraprofessional prenatal advocates, nurse midwives, and physicians. As part of routine prenatal care, all women were screened for domestic violence, smoking, substance use, depression, and PTSD. The prenatal advocates were trained to conduct *Seeking Safety*, which, as noted in Chapter 2, is a trauma-specific intervention addressing PTSD and substance use. The advocates were all bilingual/bicultural and had extensive prenatal care training and between five and 20 years of experience as community health workers. Women in the intervention group (usual prenatal care plus *Seeking Safety*) attended significantly more prenatal care visits and more mental health visits, as compared with the usual care group (only usual prenatal care). Women in the intervention group had higher negative coping skills, and they decreased these skills significantly more than did the usual care group. In addition, there was a greater decrease in PTSD symptom severity at follow-up in the intervention group.

Shared Medical Appointments

Dealing with chronic diseases is an important issue as they continue to increase. The traditional one-on-one model of medical visits may not be the optimal intervention for the approximately 60 percent of primary care visits that are due to chronic conditions. This may be true both for the patients and for the primary care physicians.

Shared Medical Appointments (SMAs) were first implemented in the US in 1996. They have been used for adults with type 2 diabetes, heart disease, hypertension, arthritis, metabolic syndrome, cancer, COPD, and obesity. There are two models of SMA developed by health psychologist Edward Noffsinger: *Drop In Group Medical Appointment (DIGMA)* for follow-up visits and the *Physical SMA (PSMA)* with the opportunity for private physical exams (Noffsinger 2009; Noffsinger 2012). Shared medical appointments do not replace individual appointments. SMAs have been implemented in the U.S., Canada, and the Netherlands. Patients who may not be a good fit for SMAs are: patients that speak a different language than the rest of the group, patients with severe hearing impairments, and patients with dementia.

The care team for SMAs is typically led by a general practitioner or advanced practice nurse. The team can also include a pharmacist, dietician, psychologist (who may be the facilitator), health educator, exercise specialist, and a documentation specialist. The sessions are typically 90 minutes and involve ten to 16 patients, and involve history taking, examination, medical decision-making, and education. Added value comes from the facilitated peer interaction, particularly around aspects of self-management and empowerment. The SMA provides group support, reduces patient waiting lists, allows the doctor more time with the patients at a more relaxed pace, reduces problems with "No Shows," provides supporting contributions from other professionals (e.g., pharmacist) immediately within the group setting, and reduces costs.

A review of randomized control trials of SMAs for patients with type 2 diabetes showed positive outcomes, including fewer urgent care and ER visits, improved glycemic control, fewer specialty care visits, improved diabetes knowledge, increased patient satisfaction, and improved provider productivity (Edelman et al. 2012). SMAs have been found to reduce costs by 20 to 30 percent (Clancy et al. 2008). In a systematic review of all relevant studies published from 1947–2012, Housden and colleagues (2013) found that SMAs led to significant reductions in HbA1c. Patients also reported improvements in quality of life.

Open Access Scheduling

Medical practices, and other practices in mental health and substance abuse treatment, need ways to operate more efficiently and increase their capacity to care for patients when the patients need care. One way to do this is through open access scheduling (see interview with Nancy Paull, Director of SSTAR). It is a model that allows patients to schedule non-emergency visits on the same day. In traditional scheduling, some appointment slots may be left for emergencies. However, this system usually means double-booking, which overburdens providers, fosters no-shows, and diverts patients to urgent care facilities or ERs. With open access, patients can be seen on a first call, first serve basis. Practices offering same day appointments frequently see a drop in their no-show rate. Not all appointments are the same-day in open access. Patients can continue to make traditional appointments and schedule follow-up appointments for low-demand times. For finding the right balance, on Mondays or Tuesdays (when appointments are typically in high demand), you might want to devote most of your appointments to same-day. On days that are not so busy, you can devote a larger number of appointments to traditional visits. Allowing patients to schedule same-day appointments also reduces wait times and often allows the patient to be seen by their own personal physician; this is likely to increase patient satisfaction.

The model has been used in a number of places, including Kaiser Permanente in Roseville, California; HealthPartners Medical Group in Bloomington, Minnesota; Mayo Clinic's primary care pediatric/adolescent medicine team; the Alaska Native Medical Center; and the Fairview Red Wing Clinic, in Red Wing, Minnesota. In order to implement open access, the staff needs to reduce the backlog of appointments. This will be the step requiring the most work, but it should be able to be accomplished in six to eight weeks. Contingency plans should address who else on the team can help the physician during times of excessive demand (e.g., a nurse, a colleague).

Motivational Interviewing (MI)

In 1991, Miller and Rollnick (1991) published an important book focusing on patients' problems with alcohol and other drugs, entitled *Motivational Interviewing: Preparing People to Change Addictive Behaviors.* The focus of the book was on helping these clients talk about and resolve their ambivalence around behavior change. *Motivational Interviewing (MI)* is a practice that fits well within a trauma-informed approach. Both trauma-informed practice and MI seek to empower clients by supporting their self-efficacy and emphasize respect, empathy, and acceptance. The focus is on behaviors that survivors can control, including safety planning, self-care, addictions, and health. *MI* is both person-centered and guidance-oriented, and it allows providers to carry out the goals of a trauma-informed approach without the imposition of control or provider bias. Many substance abuse treatment providers are already implementing *MI* in their programs. It became apparent that this method could be used in other systems outside the addiction system, and, in 2008, Rollnick and colleagues (Rollnick, Miller, and Butler 2008) published *Motivational Interviewing in Health Care.*

Training staff in *MI* can be an important step in respectfully assisting patients/clients in behavior change. The "guiding" approach in *MI* involves you/the provider listening carefully and empathically to the client/patient in order to understand her/his issues. Then you ask her/him about the various options s/he is considering. Then you both explore, together, the pros and cons of each option.

The well-intentioned efforts of providers can express themselves in a "directing" style that compromises quality care and renders patients/clients the passive recipients. Much as we would like to make the "right" choices for a patient, our ability as providers to do so is constrained by the patient's beliefs, motivations, and own behavioral choices. Doctors often use the "ask-inform" pattern of communication with patients. When you take a directing style with an ambivalent patient/client, you are taking up the side of their ambivalence. A common patient response to this is to fill in the other side of the ambivalence, by saying, "Yes, but..." (away from change). Adding listening each time will help move the patient toward change (ask-inform-listen). There are several pre-commitment types of "change talk." These are known as DARN:

- D=Desire (I want to...)
- A=Ability (I could...)
- R=Reason (I would feel better if I...)
- N=Need (I need more sleep)

As DARN motivations are voiced, commitment to change gradually strengthens, and the patient may take initial steps; these two things (commitment and taking first steps) predict behavior change. Helping a client with "change talk" tells you what matters to them. Asking open questions allows patients to tell you things that you might not have asked about, but that are potentially important. For example, you might ask: "Tell me about a typical day when you drink"; or "What are you worried about?"; or "How are you getting along on the medications?"

Practical strategies in *MI* include the following:

1. Use open questions and reflection.
2. Slow down.
3. Use truthful positive messages, which can increase the patient's responsiveness to hard facts.
4. Consider the amount of information the patient wants. For example, ask, "What would you like to know and in what detail?" Give the message in an accessible way (avoiding technical terms) and check to see whether your patient understands what you have said.
5. Offer a variety of options and ask the patient to choose among them.
6. Beware of the "righting reflex." A common response to fear is to become defensive and shut down; scaring a patient will not lead to behavior change. It can also put a patient off if you rush in with your solution (e.g., "You've got to take a proton pump inhibitor..."). Instead the provider should ask questions like these: "Many people in your situation (HIV positive) find it hard to take their medications all at the same time. How do you do it?" Or, "I can tell you how other patients stopped smoking and what might help you. Would that be of interest to you?"
7. Engage in agenda setting. This is a strategy for developing a compromise between your aspirations (for the client's behavior change) and that of the client her/himself. Summarize how the patient is feeling and your understanding of her/his aspirations. Then, proceed with agenda setting. For example, you might say, "Let's just take a step back for a minute and look at our progress. We

both want you free of pain, and we can talk about different ways of getting there. There's taking more painkillers, something you want that I have some concerns about, and then there's getting more exercise, which I favor and you have concerns about. So, where do we go from here?"

The suggested practice changes discussed in this chapter are the beginning of a cultural change in our systems of health care, mental health, and substance abuse treatment. If implemented, they will lead to reduced client burden, as well as reduced treatment staff burden. This is the promise of a trauma-informed approach. In the next chapter, I discuss the research that has been done to measure the success of the trauma-informed practices in the programs highlighted in the book.

Notes

1 *Commonwealth of Massachusetts Department of Mental Health De-Escalation Form for DMH Facilities/Vendors.* See Appendix B.
2 Research on cultural safety is an emerging field. While cultural safety was first conceptualized in New Zealand, with respect to health care for Maori people, Canadian practitioners have furthered the idea of culturally safe practices for First Nations communities at risk (Smith 2003).
3 Hook and colleagues (2013) conducted four studies testing a client-rated measure of therapists' cultural humility. They demonstrated that clients' perceptions of their therapists' cultural humility was positively associated both with developing a strong working alliance and with improvements in therapy.
4 An example of "non-empowerment" and "non-participatory" was described by Earls and Carlson when they were implementing research in collaboration with children and youth in their Project on Human Development in Chicago Neighborhoods. In the description of the development of the project, they stated, "Throughout this entire period, there was no record that any serious consideration was ever given to consulting youth about the observations and assumptions we adults were making about their lives" (Earls and Carlson 1999, p. 4). They found that the inclusion of youth promoted positive developmental outcomes among those adolescents involved as collaborators.

References

Adriaenssens, J, De Gucht, V, Van Der Doef, M, and Maes, S 2011, Exploring the Burden of Emergency Care: Predictors of Stress-Health Outcomes in Emergency Nurses, *Journal of Advanced Nursing*, vol. 67, pp. 1317–1328.
Ball, J 2007a, *Creating Cultural Safety in Speech-Language and Audiology Services*, PowerPoint Presentation at Annual Conference of the British Columbia Association of Speech-Language Pathologists and Audiologists, Whistler, Canada, p. 1.
Ball, J 2007b, *Supporting Aboriginal Children's Development*, Victoria, Canada, University of Victoria Early Childhood Development Intercultural Partnership.
Berwick, DM 2003, *Escape Fire: Designs for the Future of Health Care*, San Francisco, CA, Jossey-Bass.
Berwick, D, Downey, A, and Cornett, E (eds.) 2016, *A National Trauma Care System: Integrating Military and Civilian Trauma Systems*, Washington, DC: The National Academies Press.
Centers for Medicare and Medicaid Services (CMS) 2007, *State Medicaid Director Letter—Peer Support Services SMDL #07–011*.
Chinman, M, Young, AS, Hassell, J et al. 2006, Toward the Implementation of Mental Health Consumer Provider Services, *Journal of Behavioral Health Services and Research*, vol. 33, no. 2, pp. 176–195.
Clancy, DE, Dismuke, CE, Magruder, KM et al. 2008, Do Diabetes Group Visits Lead to Lower Medical Care Charges, *American Journal of Managed Care*, vol. 14, pp. 39–44.
Covington, S 2003, *Beyond Trauma: A Healing Journey for Women*, Center City, MN, Hazelden.

Crenshaw, K 1991, Mapping the Margins: Intersectionality, Identity Politics, and Violence Against Women of Color, *Stanford Law Review*, vol. 43, no. 6, pp. 1241–1299.

Daker-White, G, Hays, R, McSharry, J et al. 2015, Blame the Patient, Blame the Doctor or Blame the System? A Meta-Synthesis of Qualitative Studies of Patient Safety in Primary Care, *PLOS One*, vol. 10, no. 8, pp. 1–42.

Davidson, L, Bellamy, C, Guy, K, and Miller, R 2012, Peer Support Among Persons with Severe Mental Illnesses: A Review of Evidence and Experience, *World Psychiatry*, vol. 11, pp. 123–128.

Delany, KR and Johnson, ME 2008, Inpatient Psychiatric Nursing: Why Safety Must Be the Key Deliverable, *Archives of Psychiatric Nursing*, vol. 22, pp. 386–388.

Earls, F and Carlson, M 1999, Adolescents as Collaborators: In Search of Well-Being, unpublished paper, Harvard University.

Edelman, D, McDuffie, JR, Oddone, E et al. 2012, *Shared Medical Appointments for Chronic Medical Conditions: A Systematic Review*, Washington, DC, U.S. Department of Veterans Affairs.

Eyerman, R 2001, *Cultural Trauma: Slavery and the Formation of African American Identity*, New York, NY, Cambridge University Press.

Fassin, D and Rechtman, R 2009, *The Empire of Trauma*, Princeton, NJ, Princeton University Press.

Frank, JB and Rodowski, MF 1999, Review of Psychological Issues in Victims of Domestic Violence Seen in Emergency Settings, *Emergency Medicine Clinics of North America*, vol. 17, no. 3, pp. 657–677.

Fullilove, M and Fullilove, R 1995, Conducting Research in Ethnic Minority Communities, in G Botvin, S Schinke, and M Orlando (eds.), *Drug Abuse Prevention in Ethnic Minority Youth*, Thousand Oaks, CA, Sage, pp. 46–56.

Gajewski, D and Granville, R 2006, The United States Armed Forces Amputee Patient Care Program, *Journal of the American Academy of Orthopaedic Surgeons*, vol. 14, special no. 10, pp. S183–S187.

Hook, JN, Davis, DE, Owen, J et al. 2013, Cultural Humility: Measuring Openness to Culturally Diverse Clients, *Journal of Consulting Psychology*, vol. 60, no. 3, pp. 353–366.

Housden, L, Wong, ST, and Dawes, M 2013, Effectiveness of Group Medical Visits for Improving Diabetes Care: A Systematic Review and Meta-Analysis, *Canadian Medical Association Journal*, vol. 185, no. 13, pp. E635–E644.

Johnston, A, Abraham, L, Greenslade, J et al. 2016, Staff Perception of the Emergency Department Working Environment: Integrative Review of the Literature, *Emergency Medicine Australasia*, vol. 28, pp. 7–26.

Larijani, HH and Guggisberg, M 2015, Improving Clinical Practice: What Dentists Need to Know About the Association Between Dental Fear and a History of Sexual Violence Victimization, *International Journal of Dentistry*, Article ID 452814, pp. 1–12.

Lorig, KR, Ritter, P, Steward, AI et al. 2001, Chronic Disease Self-Management Program, 2-Year Health Status and Health Care Utilization Outcomes, *Medical Care*, vol. 39, no. 11, pp. 1217–1223.

Marzen-Groller, K and Bateman, K 2005, Building a Successful Support Group for Post-Amputation Patients, *Journal of Vascular Nursing*, vol. 23, no. 2, pp. 42–45.

Miller, WR and Rollnick, S 1991, *Motivational Interviewing: Preparing People to Change Addictive Behaviors*, New York, Guilford Press.

Najavits, LM 2002, *Seeking Safety: A Treatment Manual for PTSD and Substance Abuse*, New York, NY, Guilford Press.

Noffsinger, E 2009, *Running Group Visits in Your Practice*, New York, NY, Springer.

Noffsinger, E 2012, *The ABC of Group Visits*, London, England, Springer.

Nursing Council of New Zealand 2011, *Guidelines for Cultural Safety, the Treaty of Waitangi and Maori Health in Nursing Education and Practice*, Wellington, New Zealand, Nursing Council of New Zealand.

Polacek, MJ, Allen, DE, Damin-Moss, RS et al. 2015, Engagement as an Element of Safe Inpatient Environments, *Journal of the American Psychiatric Nursing Association*, vol. 2, no. 3, pp. 181–190.

Potter, C 2006, To What Extent Do Nurses and Physicians Working Within the Emergency Department Experience Burnout: A Systematic Review, *Australasian Emergency Nursing Journal*, vol. 9, pp. 57–64.

Ramsden, I 1992, *Kawa Whakaruruhau: Guidelines for Nursing and Midwifery Education*, Wellington, New Zealand, Nursing Council of New Zealand.

Rappaport, J 1994, Empowerment as a Guide to Doing Research: Diversity as a Positive Value, in EJ Trickett, RJ Watts, and D Birman (eds.), *Human Diversity: Perspectives on People in Context*, San Francisco, CA, Jossey-Bass, pp. 359–382.

Reed, G and Collins, B 1994, Mental Health Research and Service Delivery: A Three Communities Model, *Psychosocial Rehabilitation Journal*, vol. 17, no. 4, pp. 69–81.

Rollnick, S, Miller, WR, and Butler, CC 2008, *Motivational Interviewing in Health Care*, New York, Guilford Press.

Sanders, D 1985, *The Struggle for Health: Medicine and the Politics of Underdevelopment*, London, England, MacMillan.

Schachter, CL, Stalker, CA, Teram, E et al. 2009, *Handbook on Sensitive Practice for Health Care Practitioners: Lessons from Adult Survivors of Childhood Sexual Abuse*, Ottowa, Canada, Public Health Agency of Canada.

Shi, L 1993, Health Care in China: A Rural-Urban Comparison After the Socioeconomic Reforms, *Bulletin of the World Health Organization*, vol. 71, no. 6, pp. 723–736.

Smith, MS 2003, "Race Matters" and "Race Manners," in J Brodie and L Trimble (eds.), *Reinventing Canada: Politics in the 21st Century*, Toronto, Canada, Prentice Hall, pp. 108–130.

Tervalen, M and Murray-Garcia, J 1998, Cultural Humility Versus Cultural Competence: A Critical Distinction in Defining Physician Training Outcomes in Multicultural Education, *Journal of Health Care for the Poor and Underserved*, vol. 9, pp. 117–125.

Trickett, EJ and Espino, SLR 2004, Collaboration and Social Inquiry: Multiple Meanings of a Construct and Its Role in Creating Useful and Valid Knowledge, *American Journal of Community Psychology*, vol. 34, no. 1/2, pp. 1–69.

Upshur, CC, Wenz-Gross, M, Weinreb, L, and Moffitt, JA 2016, Using Prenatal Advocates to Implement a Psychosocial Education Intervention for Posttraumatic Stress Disorder During Pregnancy: Feasibility, Care Engagement, and Predelivery Behavioral Outcomes, *Women's Health Issues*, vol. 26, no. 5, pp. 537–545.

Wang, PS, Aguilar-Gaxiola, S, Alonso, J et al. 2007, Use of Mental Health Services for Anxiety, Mood, and Substance Disorders in 17 Countries in the WHO World Mental Health Surveys, *The Lancet*, vol. 370, pp. 841–850.

Zhu, NS, Ling, ZH, Shen, J et al. 1989, Factors Associated with the Decline of the Cooperative Medical System and Barefoot Doctors in Rural China, *Bulletin of the World Health Organization*, vol. 67, no. 4, pp. 431–441.

Chapter 10

How to Recognize Success

Most of the organizations/programs I visited have implemented or participated in a number of research projects. This chapter combines the interviewees' responses to my questions about their research with brief summaries of the research findings.

Research from the Center for Pediatric Traumatic Stress (CPTS) at CHOP

CPTS's research includes work on screening, interventions, and its trauma-informed approach to care. With regard to screening, Kassam-Adams spoke about many of CPTS's research projects in her interview.

> *Kassam-Adams:* "I have also been involved in some work that is developing measures of acute stress in children, which are important both clinically and for researchers. We have done a lot of creating of checklists and things that are quick and easy to use. For example, we developed the Acute Stress Checklist. First, we created a version in English, but then we created a version in Spanish, through a careful process. We did a multi-site study enrolling both Spanish- and English-speaking children to make sure it is valid across both groups. I think that in the U.S., at least, it is important to think beyond English, at least into Spanish and maybe into other languages as well. As a Center, when we create materials, we create them in both English and Spanish. We'd love to go beyond that, and maybe that is something we will do in the future, into other languages."

Winston and colleagues (2003) sought to develop a stand-alone screening tool for use during acute trauma care to identify children and their parents who are at risk for significant, persistent posttraumatic stress symptoms. A sample of children admitted for treatment of traffic-related injuries—and one parent per child—completed a risk factor survey assessing potential predictors of PTSD. Families completed a follow-up assessment. The *Screening Tool for Early Predictors of PTSD (STEPP)* contains four questions asked of the client, four questions asked of the parent, and four items easily obtained from the emergency medical record. The authors state that the *STEPP* should be "viewed as a triage tool to identify from among all injured children and their parents those for whom a subsequent mental health evaluation is required" (Winston et al. 2003, p. 647).

In 2015, Kassam-Adams and colleagues (2015b) further studied a predictive screening protocol for risk of later posttraumatic stress (PTS) and depression outcomes. They also replicated studies of two previously published screening tools, the *STEPP* and the *Child Trauma Screening Questionnaire (CTSQ)*. The screening protocol demonstrated: excellent sensitivity and good specificity for the prediction of posttraumatic stress at six months after the injury; moderate sensitivity and good specificity for depression in the same time period; and excellent negative predictive value for both outcomes. However, mixed replication results for the *STEPP* suggested that it would be premature to rule out other risk markers as predictive.

> *Kassam-Adams:* "We have tried to create an even shorter version of our 29-item checklist, to be practical for certain settings where we would like to see people assess traumatic stress responses soon after an event. In those settings, say a busy medical center or a court, it may not be the main thing or the only thing being assessed. We have under review right now a paper where we look at making a three- or six-item version of that. We wanted to have a quick screener that approximates the longer version. So, we think we have three or six questions that can help with that."

Enlow and colleagues (2010) developed a short-form (four items), user-friendly scale to measure traumatic stress responses in injured children (hospitalized with burns or other acute injuries). The new scale was created from the *Child Stress Disorders Checklist (CSDC)*, a 36-item measure, using standard psychometric scale development techniques. The four-item scale *(CSDC-SF)* demonstrated comparable reliability and validity to that of the *CSDC*. The study authors stated that, due to its ease of use, the *CSDC-SF* has the potential for widespread utility. They recommended that the new scale be tested in other traumatized populations (e.g., maltreated children) and in different settings (e.g., pediatric primary care practices).

> *Kassam-Adams:* "When people want to use our Psychosocial Assessment Tool (PAT), they need to agree to give data back. PAT is a tool that started within the oncology population, but now has been adapted for other populations. Its intention is to help teams in the hospital get a sense of which children and families are likely to need more psychosocial support. It includes, but is not limited to, traumatic stress. PAT is empirically validated, and it can be scored on the web, which makes it much easier to use. Many sites around the country are using the PAT. Our Center backs that up; it provides the PAT, provides the technical assistance to get them going with it, and then collects data. We ask those using PAT to report quarterly on how many patients and families they have assessed and what the levels of risk were."

Distress shortly after hearing a pediatric cancer diagnosis is normal; over time, however, most families return to baseline functioning. Children and parents with high and/or escalating distress need interventions to reduce the stress. Kazak and colleagues (2012) identified conceptual models to guide screening and specific psychosocial risk screening tools during pediatric cancer treatment. Two empirical approaches to screening were identified: the *Distress Thermometer (DT)* and the Psychosocial Assessment Tool *(PAT)*, which was discussed earlier. The *DT* provides a very brief, unidimensional rating of distress. The *PAT* (Kazak et al. 2001) is a brief parent report screening tool and maps onto classification of risk levels in the Pediatric Preventative Psychosocial Health Model (PPPHM) (Kazak et al. 2007). *PAT* has strong psychometric properties and high rates of participation. It can identify a need for intervention at an early point in cancer treatment and therefore serve as a preventive intervention for PTSD. The authors recommend targeting specific transitions in care (e.g., relapse, end of treatment) for re-screening.

Kassam-Adams and colleagues (2015a) assessed both post-injury posttraumatic stress symptoms (PTSS) and depression symptoms in children and parents, as well as the relationship of these symptoms to parent reports on their children's overall recovery. Study results showed that 19 percent of children and 18 percent of parents reported significant symptoms of either PTS or depression. At follow-up, most parents reported that their clients had completely recovered from the injury, but a significant minority (17%) reported no or partial recovery. Authors state that when a child or parent exhibits significant distress, emergency clinicians can minimize frightening or painful aspects of injury care.

> *Kassam-Adams:* "We are getting closer to really understanding what best practices should be with children and families who are facing illness and injury. There is a huge number of them. There are hundreds of millions of children around the world who are injured, tens of thousands of children a year who have cancer, and probably in the hundreds of thousands of kids who have other life-threatening chronic illnesses that they will always be dealing with. Think of conditions like asthma, diabetes, sickle cell disease. They are scary because of what can go wrong—and lead to an emergency room visit, a painful episode, or frightening symptoms."

In 2005, Kazak (2005) summarized the existing reports on psychological interventions for children with cancer and their families. The DSM-IV added the experiencing of a life-threatening medical condition or the observing of it in a close family member as a qualifying event for PTSD. While rates of PTSD in childhood cancer survivors are low (5 to 10%), higher rates are reported for survivors of childhood cancer when they are young adults (15 to 21%).

An intervention designed to reduce PTSS was evaluated in a clinical trial. The *Surviving Cancer Competently Intervention Program (SSCIP)* (Kazak et al. 1999) integrates cognitive-behavioral and family therapy in a four-session, one-day program involving adolescent cancer survivors and their family members. The results of the randomized trial indicated that families in the *SSCIP* condition showed significant reductions in PTSS, particularly for survivors and fathers (Kazak et al. 2004).

> *Kassam-Adams:* "There is another thing we've done that's not quite an intervention, but that we have tested to see if and how it helps parents. It is 'aftertheinjury.org,' an informational, psychoeducational website. It's not meant to decrease posttraumatic stress symptoms; we can't go that far. But we wanted to see if it

would help parents understand how to help their child after an injury and promote the adaptive coping. We were able to show changes in the parents' ability to better understand traumatic stress reactions; they know better what to look for. It includes: some brief videos for parents on how to talk with their children about injury; audio clips of parents talking about how they have helped their children; information about traumatic stress symptoms; and information about how to take care of a cast, how to use crutches, how to work with a health care team, how to help your child with pain, and what to do if your child isn't sleeping well. It is focused on traumatic stress, but has a lot of other information on the other things that we have found concern parents. We have about 25,000 hits a month on the website, and most of those come through Google searches and Google ads."

"We are thinking about different ways of disseminating that are not our traditional ways. If you are recognized by Google as a non-profit, there are ways to get a Google grant. It's not money, but it's a budget to use for those sponsored search ads that appear on the side or the top. We received one of these grants, and it has allowed us, at no cost to us, to run a sponsored search ad that helps parents find that website. And that's how we get tens of thousands of hits a month. Even if those who find it are only 1 percent of those who need it, it's still hundreds of thousands of people a year. We are very grateful for the support from Google, and it's been a real learning experience for us."

Marsac and colleagues (2011) surveyed parent knowledge of child injury reactions, including posttraumatic stress symptoms, and evaluated parent satisfaction and learning outcomes following a web-based or video intervention. Results showed that, while parents' knowledge of expected injury reactions was high at baseline, the knowledge was focused on physical injury recovery; parents were less likely to identify emotional recovery as issues for them to follow. No significant differences emerged between parents' pre/post-intervention knowledge scores. However, most parents reported that they learned new information. Parents reported high levels of satisfaction with both the web-based and video intervention materials. The *AftertheInjury* web and video tools were designed to help parents promote emotional recovery in their children by increasing knowledge in three areas: (1) the normal course of emotional responses after injury, including traumatic stress; (2) what parents can do to help their children; and (3) when a child's responses warrant seeking additional help. Results were promising in each of these three areas. Future studies were planned by the authors.

Kassam-Adams and colleagues at CPTS have also implemented research on trauma-informed approaches to care. For example, in a recent article, Marsac and colleagues (2016) discuss the ways in which trauma-informed care minimizes the potential for medical care to trigger traumatic events, addresses patients' distress, provides emotional supports for the family, and provides anticipatory guidance regarding the process of recovery. "A trauma-informed approach incorporates an understanding of trauma into routine care and treatment of illness or injury with a goal of decreasing the effect of potentially traumatic events (PTEs)" (Marsac et al. 2016, p. 70). PTEs are events in which an individual experiences or witnesses death or threatened death or serious injury. These events usually require children and their families to enter pediatric health care settings. However, medical care also may include painful and frightening procedures, which add to the trauma and affect how patients experience medical care. For those children who have been exposed to abuse, neglect, domestic violence, and/or community violence, the risk of posttraumatic stress symptoms is even higher.

In a trauma-informed approach, we use "universal precautions"; that is, we assume all children and family members may have experienced trauma and we do everything we can *not* to re-traumatize them. We also recognize that medical/health care staff, who unintentionally may cause additional pain and fear, may experience compassion fatigue and burnout. Some health care staff may have experienced traumatic events in their own lifetimes, and this can increase the risk of adverse outcomes for staff. "One trauma-informed approach that all professionals providing direct care can adopt, regardless of specialty, is the *DEF (Reduce Distress, Emotional Support, and Remember the Family)* protocol for pediatric health care professionals. (*http://www.healthcaretoolbox.org*)" (Marsac et al. 2016, p. 73).

> *Kassam-Adams:*   "When we redid our DEF cards (see Chapter 5) and produced a second edition, we added a culture card. We thought that was very important because we need to think about the cultural impact, or variation, or even flavor of trauma. And we also added a self-care card to help our providers. The culture card asks the provider to attend to distress in the way the family defines it, to ask about the family's decision-making practices in advance, and to connect the family with community resources they trust. The self-care card is designed to make the provider understand: how s/he reacts to stress; that s/he needs to attend to her/himself in order to attend to patients; and that s/he needs to maintain a balance between personal and work life."

Research from the Women's HIV Program (WHP) at UCSF

> *Machtinger:*   "We did an analysis of the patient deaths in our program over the past decade, and what we found was that only 16 percent of the patients who died did so from HIV. Of the patients who died, 84 percent died from murder, suicide, addiction-related illnesses and overdose, and other medical conditions that were either directly linked to murders or indirectly like other conditions related to trauma. Even the people who were dying from HIV weren't really dying from HIV, they were dying from hopelessness. Because what happened to them is that they stopped taking their HIV medicines. So, the people who were dying from HIV also had preventable deaths. Almost everybody who died in the program, with the exception of one person who died of pancreatic cancer, died from a preventable cause of death. And most of those preventable causes of death were either directly or indirectly correlated to trauma."
>
> "And when I say trauma, I mean capital T Trauma—childhood abuse, sexual abuse, physical abuse, inter-partner violence,

adult sexual abuse, and then things like community violence, police violence, and structural violence, like race phobia and homophobia and transphobia. Or xenophobia. All the different causes of structural violence that caused this experience of toxic stress in someone's life."

"But those people who had reported recent trauma within 30 days had over four times the likelihood of failing their HIV retroviral therapy. And that study was very powerful because it linked trauma with what everybody was so focused on, that is, having people's viral load be controlled. Most of these people are not dying from HIV, they are dying from violence. The huge, very statistically significantly link between recent trauma and this conservative medical marker, which was then published in a top tier science journal, was an epiphany for me. It then got a lot of recognition by people who knew this truth very well, but were looking for the evidence to convince policy makers to actually deal with this issue."

Machtinger and colleagues (2012a) analyzed data from a prevention-with-positives program to understand if socio-economic, behavioral, and health-related factors are associated with antiretroviral failure and HIV transmission-risk behaviors among HIV-positive biological and transgender women. Among the participants, 71.7 percent were biologically female and 64.6 percent African-American. Recent trauma (within the past 30 days) was reported by 17.3 percent; lifetime trauma was reported by 71.8 percent. Recent coercion to have sex was reported by 8.2 percent; lifetime sexual coercion by 64.5 percent. Low social support was reported by nearly half (48.7%) of participants. The median CD4 cell count (nearest to the time of enrollment) was 387; the majority (56.3%) reported being on anti-retroviral therapy (ART). Among those, adherence was reported by 23.8 percent. Drug use within the past six months was reported by 40.5 percent; injection drug use was reported by 9.8 percent, almost half of whom (45.5%) reported sharing needles and over half (54.5%) had detectable virus. Recent trauma was the single statistically significant correlate of ART failure on univariate analysis. Patients reporting recent trauma had greater than four times the odds of ART failure than those who did not report recent trauma (OR = 4.3). Low social support was the only statistically significant correlate of ART adherence (OR = 5.6). The authors suggest that screening for "recent trauma" among HIV-positive women may effectively identify patients at high risk for poor health and transmission risk outcomes and allow for more resources, trauma-specific interventions, and ART adherence support.

Machtinger: "So, we did a medical analysis combining the results of many studies that included over 5,000 patients to calculate rates of trauma among women living with HIV. And the results showed that the rates of trauma among women living with HIV were startlingly high, even compared to the rates in the general population of women, which are already startlingly high. Fifty-five percent of women living with HIV have experienced intimate partner violence. That is approximately twice the rate in the general population. Sixty percent of the women living with HIV have experienced sexual abuse, which is almost five times the rate in the general population. And 30 percent of women living with HIV have acute recent/current PTSD, which is six times the rate of the general population."

Machtinger and colleagues (2012b) employed meta-analysis to clarify rates of trauma exposure and PTSD in HIV-positive women. The results of the meta-analysis showed that: The estimated rate of recent PTSD in HIV-positive women was 30.0 percent; the rate for IPV was 55.3 percent; and the rates for adult sexual abuse and adult physical abuse were 35.2 percent and 53.9 percent, respectively. The analysis also found that the estimated prevalence of child sexual abuse and child physical abuse among HIV-positive women were 39.3 percent and 42.7 percent, respectively; both of these estimated rates are approximately twice those documented in a national prevalence sample of women (Cougle et al. 2010). The rate of lifetime sexual abuse among HIV-positive women was estimated at 61.1 percent.

In 2015, Machtinger and colleagues (2015) reported on a study to determine the impact of a community-based expressive therapy disclosure intervention on the lives of women living with HIV. The intervention was based on the Medea Project, which was first developed to help incarcerated women. Five core themes emerged from the data that described the impact of the intervention on the lives of the participants: sisterhood, catharsis, self-acceptance, safer and healthier relationships, and gaining a voice. Participants expressed their feelings that the intervention helped them experience a freedom from the burden of secrecy about HIV, childhood and adult traumas, and other stigmatizing experiences. Women also expressed being more able to develop open and authentic relationships, and some reported leaving unhealthy relationships.

Machtinger: "We were awarded a grant from the Robert Wood Johnson Foundation to become one of the sites for a national demonstration project on trauma-informed primary care. We also received funding from the University of California, a large trust, and three other foundations. All this funding allowed us to implement a trauma-informed primary care program and formally evaluate it. To our knowledge, this will be among the first, if not the first, formally evaluated trauma-informed primary care program in any disease state. Again, we are by no means the only people doing this. But I think we may be the only people who are funded right now to evaluate trauma-informed primary care that focuses on both intimate partner violence and lifelong abuse."

"We are doing a very comprehensive quantitative study of all of our patients who have signed up for this project. We are getting baseline data about depression, PTSD, substance use, trauma history, as well as access to their medical records, so we can also look at obesity, diabetes, heart disease, viral load, and other markers of their health. The intervention has begun. The first part of our intervention is educating all of our staff and providers about the tenets of trauma-informed primary care. We are giving them both the knowledge to understand why people who have experienced trauma act why they do and are the way they are and the skills to help them communicate with patients and with each other in a way that is more compassionate and less triggering."

"I'd like to see the entire Ryan White Primary Care system for men and women living with HIV become a trauma-informed care system. It takes care of 600,000 low-income individuals and it already is multi-disciplinary, it already has the infrastructure. If you could demonstrate the effectiveness of trauma-informed care within the federal HIV care system, it would be a very influential national demonstration project for primary care clinics that care for people who have obesity and diabetes, people who have lung disease, people with Hepatitis C, and people with depression or substance use. If we can demonstrate it throughout the Ryan White Care system, I am hoping that accountable care systems across the country adopt trauma-informed care principles as their guiding philosophy for how they keep people healthy."

Research by PROTOTYPES

Brown: "In fact, the Women with Co-Occurring Disorders and Violence Study (WCDVS) had over 75 publications. PROTOTYPES has quite a few publications, and I continue to have some new publications." (See Chapters 1 and 2 for PROTOTYPES/Brown studies on level of burden and WCDVS.)

"The Principal Investigators in the WCDVS formed a National Trauma Consortium and published a monograph[1] on the different trauma-specific interventions we used, how you could pick them, what were the different characteristics, etc. It's one of the most downloaded publications from the study. It was an important piece."

"I think the product I am most proud of, besides the *COJAC Screener*,[2] which is a brief screener for trauma, substance abuse, and mental health disorders, is the *Trauma-Informed Agency Assessment* (Walk-Through).[3] I have used it throughout the country with family drug-court systems, and it is being broadly adopted. A little background might be helpful. Maxine Harris and Roger Fallot had developed a self-assessment model that was a pre-post.[4] Building on that, as well as what I had learned in the WCDVS and in my work with NIATx (National Improvement in Addiction Treatment Network), I designed a *Trauma-Informed Agency Assessment* that allowed agencies and systems to "walk-through" their systems and processes and develop an action plan for transforming into a trauma-informed program."

"We walked through our own agency (PROTOTYPES) and found a number of things that needed to be changed, including the admissions process (and the way our telephones were answered) and the process of urine screening. Based on the walk-through findings, we decided to assign a peer to each client early in the treatment process to help her feel more comfortable, enhanced security measures to help clients feel more safe, and established an Orientation Group so that new clients could learn more about what to expect in the program."

"What the walk-through gives you is something unique and strong. It feels quite different than an audit. If you are in an audit and the auditors ask, 'Do you do x and y?' you say, 'Of course.' When you do a walk-through, you (the team) are actually experiencing the processes. That is a very different thing. As you walk through an agency or a system, you really see things that staff may not see. In addition, the different members of the team see different things. Consumers often see things that the rest of us miss entirely. Walking through allows you to look at the program through the client's eyes."

Research by/on Community Connections

Community Connections and its director, Maxine Harris, have been in the forefront on work on trauma beginning in the 1990s. Goodman and colleagues (1995) examined the lifetime prevalence of physical and sexual assault among 99 homeless women, all of whom had been diagnosed with a serious mental illness. Results showed that 87 percent of the women had experienced physical abuse and 65 percent sexual abuse in childhood. As adults, 87 percent had suffered some form of physical assault and 76 percent had been sexually abused. When the two types of abuse (physical and sexual) were examined together, 87 percent of the women sampled had been abused as both children and adults; when physical and sexual assault were combined, 92 percent of the total sample had been abused in childhood and adulthood. Only three of the 99 women reported no experience of physical or sexual abuse. The authors state that "three imperatives emerge from the findings of the present study" (Goodman, Dutton, and Harris 1995, p. 476). These are: (1) there needs to be regular and ongoing inquiry into women's present and past experience of abuse; (2) shelter and mental health center staff who work with this population need training regarding trauma and abuse; and (3) broad-based interventions need to be developed to address victimization histories among homeless, seriously mentally ill women and "a physically safe environment must be ensured for them" (Goodman, Dutton, and Harris 1995, p. 477).

This study led to a number of additional ones showing the need for more integrated and trauma-integrated services. In 1998, Harris published *Trauma Recovery and Empowerment: A Clinician's Guide for Working with Women in Groups* (1998). Known as *TREM*, this intervention is a 33-session group designed to meet weekly. It is divided into three separate components: (1) an empowerment section that helps women to acquire or reinforce skills such as limit-setting and self-soothing; (2) a trauma recovery module designed to address the specific sequelae of physical and sexual abuse; and (3) a skills enhancement section focused on helping women develop skills in communication, problem-solving, and emotional modulation. *TREM* was one of four trauma-specific interventions used in the Women with Co-Occurring Disorders and Violence Study (WCDVS). In 2001, Fallot and colleagues (2001) published the *Men's Trauma Recovery and Empowerment Model (M-TREM)*.

In 2001, Harris and Fallot published, *Using Trauma Theory to Design Service Systems* (2001b). This book has been one of the most cited references regarding trauma-informed services. The authors defined the difference between trauma-specific interventions and trauma-informed practice, as well as describing the five values of safety, trustworthiness, choice, collaboration, and empowerment.

Fallot and colleagues (2011) studied the effectiveness of the *TREM* group for 251 women within the Washington, DC site of the WCDVS. Significant differences were found for two of the four primary outcomes of the study; viz., women in the intervention/*TREM* group showed greater reduction in alcohol and drug use severity than women in the usual care group. Changes over time were significant for clinician rating on the *TREP*, which measures 11 trauma recovery skills (e.g., self-protection, self-soothing, etc.).[5] However, *TREP* ratings were not collected from the comparison group.

A randomized controlled trial of *Seeking Safety (SS)* and *M-TREM* (Wolf et al. 2015) examined the effectiveness of the group interventions for PTSD and addiction disorders[6] among incarcerated men compared to a waitlist control group. Results showed that, within the treatment group, there was significant improvement on all outcome variables as compared to baseline measures. The mean score on the *Clinician-Administered PTSD Scale (CAPS)*, which looks at PTSD severity, declined by 13 percent; the percent of men with full PTSD declined by 19 percent. For the waitlist group, significant improvement was found in PTSD and mental health symptoms over the three-month waiting period, but there was only a 3 percent decline in *CAPS* score and a 10 percent decline in full PTSD. Overall, study results modestly supported the effectiveness of both *SS* and *M-TREM* for incarcerated men.

In a study (Toussaint et al. 2007) examining the effects of the *TREM* intervention on women with substance use disorders and trauma, women in the intervention group showed greater improvements in mental health symptoms, dissociative symptoms, sense of personal safety, and ability to cope with trauma, as compared with those in the treatment-as-usual comparison group. Among *TREM* participants, an increased dose of intervention (extra sessions) was related to greater improvements in those outcomes. However, there were no differences between the control and comparison groups on alcohol or drug use. The authors state that the incorporation of *TREM* into residential substance abuse treatment appears to be effective in reducing trauma-related symptoms without affecting substance abuse outcomes.

It should also be noted that Harris and colleagues have published a number of significant clinical papers and books on trauma-specific interventions and trauma-informed practices. (See Appendix C and Appendix D.)

Research by/on SSTAR

Paull: "We have a great researcher, whose name is Dr. Genie Bailey. She worked at Women and Infants Hospital, went on a trip with us to Armenia, and ended up here. So she is a psychiatrist who is also in charge of our dual diagnosis unit next door. But she has really been interested in research. So, we were asked to join the NIDA (National Institute on Drug Abuse) Clinical Trial Network, with Harvard as our academic center. We have done several trials with them. And we also work with Brown

[University]. And Dr. Michael Stein is someone we have done a number of clinical trials with. We did a trial with Harvard, with Dr. Shelly Greenfield, on single-sex groups vs. co-mingled groups. It was surprising that we didn't find many differences in outcomes."

"The other one that was kind of shocking was a study we did for NIDA on outpatient treatment. One arm was treatment as usual. The other arm was an individual session and then a session with a special computer program. The patients did better in the computerized arm! So now we're looking at mobile apps and are working with the University of Wisconsin. We are about to start another trial with a mobile app as a support."

In a study exploring life concerns of prescription opioid and heroin users, Stein and colleagues (2015) explored 43 health and welfare concerns of 529 participants in SSTAR's inpatient opioid detoxification center. Compared to prescription opioid users, heroin users had significantly higher levels of concern about drug problems, lower levels of concern about alcohol-related problems, and significantly higher concerns about sexually transmitted diseases. Participants rated health issues and mental health issues as less concerning than economic issues. The authors stated that it may be necessary to engage in a discussion of what are seen by detox patients as their most pressing concerns, including recent trauma, in order to engage them in aftercare. One of the important components of SSTAR is that the program has integrated services for health, mental health, trauma, and substance abuse on the same campus. Therefore, introducing detox clients to other services and other service staff can be done easily.

In a recent study, Najavits and colleagues (2014) evaluated a new brief screener for behavioral addictions in a sample of clients with substance use disorder at SSTAR. This study was part of a larger project funded by NIDA to develop an automated telephone screening for SUD and comorbidities. On the mental health screens used in the study, 27 percent of the patients sampled were positive for PTSD and 18 percent for depression. The most commonly reported behavioral addictions were shopping/spending, eating, work, computer/Internet, and sex or pornography. The least commonly reported were gambling, self-harm, and exercise. A positive PTSD screen was associated with exercise addiction, and a positive depression screen was associated with eating and computer addiction. The authors suggested that, although most behavioral addictions do not yet have specific treatments, applying substance abuse treatment strategies, such as motivational interviewing, relapse prevention, and cognitive-behavioral therapy, would make sense at this time.

SSTAR was one of the programs in the WELL Boston site of the WCDVS; however, the SSTAR data could not be presented separately. SSTAR is also one of the programs in the Northern New England Node of the NIDA Clinical Trial Network and has participated in three clinical trials. Two of these were not trauma-related; the third was. In that study, one of the first to explore the role of gender in a large-scale effectiveness trial of a computer-assisted treatment for substance use disorder, Campbell and colleagues (2015) reported that gender did not moderate treatment outcomes of abstinence, retention, social adjustment, or craving. They also reported that men and women derived similar benefits from the computer-assisted intervention. Adherence was also high (76 to 80% of 62 modules completed). Acceptability of the intervention differed based on abstinence status at study entry among women; women who were negative for drugs/alcohol at entry reported higher acceptability of the computer-assisted intervention. This was not the case for men. The study authors speculated that, since women with substance use disorder at entry had experienced more childhood trauma and intimate partner violence than the other women, they may have felt the need for more personal contact in their intervention.

As can be seen in the variety of research projects implemented by and about the programs I visited, there has been an emphasis on showing the importance of screening, of trauma-specific interventions, of a trauma-informed approach, and of collaborations with community agencies. The research done by these programs have led to a movement toward trauma-informed practice in other programs and systems in the U.S. and other countries. In the next chapter, these other systems will be discussed.

Notes

1 (Finkelstein et al. 2014)
2 See Chapter 6 for a discussion of the *COJAC Screener.*
3 (Brown, Harris, and Fallot 2013)
4 First, the assessment is completed by staff before they receive training and technical assistance (pre) and then it is completed again after the training and technical assistance (post).
5 (Harris and Fallot 2001a)
6 Substance use disorder was not included as an outcome measure because use of drugs and alcohol while incarcerated is a chargeable offense.

References

Brown, VB, Harris, M, and Fallot, R 2013, Moving Toward Trauma-Informed Practice in Addiction Treatment: A Collaborative Model of Agency Assessment, *Journal of Psychoactive Drugs*, vol. 45, no. 5, pp. 386–393.

Campbell, AN, Nunes, EV, Pavlicova, M et al. 2015, Gender-Based Outcomes and Acceptability of a Computer-Assisted Psychosocial Intervention for Substance Use Disorders, *Journal of Substance Abuse Treatment*, vol. 53, pp. 9–15.

Cougle, JR, Timpano, KR, Sachs-Ericsson, N et al. 2010, Examining the Unique Relationships Between Anxiety Disorders and Childhood Physical and Sexual Abuse in the National Comorbidity Survey-Replication, *Psychiatry Research*, vol. 177, no. 1–2, pp. 150–155.

Enlow, MB, Kassam-Adams, N, and Saxe, G 2010, The Child Stress Disorders Checklist-Short Form: A 4-Item Scale of Traumatic Stress Symptoms in Children, *General Hospital Psychiatry*, vol. 32, no. 3, pp. 321–327.

Fallot, R, Harris, M, Affolter, HU et al. 2001, *Men's Trauma Recovery and Empowerment Model (M-TREM)*, Washington, DC, Community Connections.

Fallot, RD, McHugo, GJ, Harris, M, and Xie, H 2011, The Trauma Recovery and Empowerment Model: A Quasi-Experimental Effectiveness Study, *Journal of Dual Diagnosis*, vol. 7, no. 1–2, pp. 74–89.

Finkelstein, N, VanDeMark, N, Fallot, R et al. 2004, *Enhancing Substance Abuse Recovery Through Integrated Trauma Treatment*, Sarasota, FL, National Trauma Consortium.

Goodman, LA, Dutton, MA, and Harris, M 1995, Episodically Homeless Women with Serious Mental Illness: Prevalence of Physical and Sexual Assault, *American Journal of Orthopsychiatry*, vol. 65, no. 4, pp. 468–478.

Harris, M and the Community Connections Trauma Work Group 1998, *Trauma Recovery and Empowerment: A Clinician's Guide for Working with Women in Groups*, New York, NY, The Free Press.

Harris, M and Fallot, R 2001a, The Trauma Recovery and Empowerment Profile (TREP), unpublished manuscript.

Harris, M and Fallot, R (eds.) 2001b, *Using Trauma Theory to Design Service Systems*, New Directions for Mental Health Services, San Francisco, CA, Jossey-Bass.

Kassam-Adams, N, Bakker, A, Marsac, ML et al. 2015a, Traumatic Stress, Depression, and Recovery: Child and Parent Responses After Emergency Medical Care for Unintentional Injury, *Pediatric Emergency Care*, vol. 31, no. 11, pp. 737–742.

Kassam-Adams, N, Marsac, ML, Garcia-Espana, JF, and Winston, F 2015b, Evaluating Predictive Screening for Child's Post-Injury Mental Health: New Data and a Replication, *European Journal of Psychotraumatology*, vol. 6, no. 1.

Kazak, AE 2005, Evidence-Based Interventions for Survivors of Childhood Cancers and Their Families, *Journal of Pediatric Psychology*, vol. 30, no. 1, pp. 29–39.

Kazak, A, Alderfer, M, Streisand, R et al. 2004, Treatment of Posttraumatic Stress Symptoms in Adolescent Survivors of Childhood Cancer and Their Families: A Randomized Clinical Trial, *Journal of Family Psychology*, vol. 18, pp. 493–491.

Kazak, AE, Brier, M, Alderfer, MA et al. 2012, Screening for Psychosocial Risk in Pediatric Cancer, *Pediatric Blood Cancer*, vol. 59, no. 5, pp. 822–827.

Kazak, A, Prusak, A, McSheary, M et al. 2001, The Psychosocial Assessment Tool (PAT): Development of a Brief Screening Instrument for Identifying High Risk Families in Pediatric Oncology, *Families, Systems and Health*, vol. 19, pp. 303–317.

Kazak, A, Rourke, MT, Alderfer, MA et al. 2007, Evidence-Based Assessment, Intervention and Psychosocial Care in Pediatric Oncology: A Blueprint for Comprehensive Services Across Treatment, *Journal of Pediatric Psychology*, vol. 32, no. 9, pp. 1099–1110.

Kazak, A, Simms, S, Barakat, L et al. 1999, Surviving Cancer Competently Intervention Program (SCCIP): A Cognitive-Behavioral and Family Therapy Intervention for Adolescent Survivors of Childhood Cancer and Their Families, *Family Process*, vol. 38, pp. 175–191.

Machtinger, EL, Haberer, JE, Wilson, TC, and Weiss, DS 2012a, Recent Trauma Is Associated with Antiretroviral Failure and HIV Transmission Behavior Among HIV-Positive Women and Female Identified Transgenders, *AIDS Behavior*, vol. 16, pp. 2160–2170.

Machtinger, EL, Haberer, JE, Wilson, TC, and Weiss, DS 2012b, Psychological Trauma and PTSD in HIV-Positive Women: A Meta-Analysis, *AIDS and Behavior*, vol. 16, no. 8, pp. 2091–2100.

Machtinger, EL, Lavin, SM, Hilliard, S et al. 2015, An Expressive Therapy Group Disclosure Intervention for Women Living with HIV Improves Social Support, Self-Efficacy, and the Safety and Quality of Relationships: A Qualitative Analysis, *Journal of the Association of Nurses in AIDS Care*, vol. 26, no. 2, pp. 187–198.

Marsac, ML, Kassam-Adams, N, Hildebrand, AK et al. 2011, After the Injury: Initial Evaluation of a Web-Based Intervention for Parents of Injured Children, *Health Education Research*, vol. 26, no. 1, pp. 1–12.

Marsac, ML, Kassam-Adams, N, Hildenbrand, AK et al. 2016, Implementing a Trauma-Informed Approach in Pediatric Health Care Networks, *JAMA Pediatrics*, vol. 170, no. 1, pp. 70–77.

Najavits, L, Lung, J, Froias, A et al. 2014, A Study of Multiple Behavioral Addictions in a Substance Abuse Sample, *Substance Use and Misuse*, vol. 49, no. 4, pp. 479–484.

Stein, MD, Anderson, BJ, Thurmond, P, and Bailey, GL 2015, Comparing the Life Concerns of Prescription Opioid and Heroin Users, *Journal of Substance Abuse Treatment*, vol. 48, pp. 43–48.

Toussaint, DW, VanDeMark, NR, Bornemann, A, and Graeber, CJ 2007, Modifications to the Trauma Recovery and Empowerment Model (TREM) for Substance Abusing Women with Histories of Violence: Outcomes and Lessons Learned at a Colorado Substance Abuse Treatment Center, *Journal of Community Psychology*, vol. 35, no. 7, pp. 879–894.

Winston, FK, Kassam-Adams, N, Garcia-Espana, F et al. 2003, Screening for Risk of Persistent Posttraumatic Stress in Injured Children and Their Parents, *Journal of the American Medical Association*, vol. 290, no. 5, pp. 643–649.

Wolf, N, Huening, J, Shi, J et al. 2015, Implementation and Effectiveness of Integrated Trauma and Addiction Treatment for Incarcerated Men, *Journal of Anxiety Disorders*, vol. 30, pp. 66–80.

Part IV

Chapter 11

Trauma-Informed Practice in Other Systems

We are not alone in this journey. Other systems have been working on becoming trauma-informed: child welfare, education, criminal justice, and military/veterans services. Some of their efforts to do so are described below.

Child Welfare

In 2013, more than 3 million children in the U.S. required services from child welfare agencies (ACF 2015). As discussed in Chapter 9, many children served by the child welfare system have experienced at least one major traumatic event, and many have complex trauma histories. These children, especially those in the foster care system, have a higher prevalence of mental health problems than the general population (Leslie et al. 2004; Taylor, Wilson, and Igelman 2006). Practices in the child welfare system, such as removal from home, multiple placements in out-of-home settings, and separation from family and existing social supports add to the trauma burden these children already bear.

Several initiatives are underway to promote trauma-informed practices in child welfare. Child welfare workers, foster and adoptive parents, and courts play important roles in facilitating trauma recovery for both the children and the parents. To assist them, since 2000 the Center for Mental Health Services of the Substance Abuse and Mental Health Services Administration has funded the National Child Traumatic Stress Network (NCTSN). NCTSN is a group of treatment and research centers across the U.S., whose mission is to raise the standard of care and improve access to services for trauma-exposed children and their families. The network integrates research on best practices for trauma with their clinical application in community-based organizations. The NCTSN partners with established systems of care, including health, education, child welfare, and juvenile justice.

In addition to the work of the NCTSN, the Arkansas Division of Child and Family Services (DCFS) trained 102 (75%) of DCFS area directors and supervisors in trauma-informed approaches and evaluated this initiative (Kramer et al. 2013). Results from comparison of pretest and three-month follow-up suggest that the use of trauma-informed practices increased significantly, and that there was a significant increase in reported use of trauma assessment. The most commonly chosen action steps fell under the category of "managing professional and personal stress" (chosen by 88% of supervisors). The second most commonly chosen step was "assisting children in managing overwhelming emotion" (45.7% of supervisors); the third was "maximizing the child's sense of safety" (42.1%). Barriers for full implementation of trauma-informed practice included: time constraints; heavy caseloads/being short-staffed; lack of resources (housing or treatment resources); and foster parents being untrained or unprepared to provide trauma-informed care to the children placed with them.

In 1978 Congress passed the Indian Child Welfare Act (ICWA) to "protect the best interests of Indian children and to promote the stability and security of Indian tribes and families." It is important that child welfare workers address historical trauma in the family using child welfare best practice and incorporate tribal kinship and cultural ways to facilitate healing, resulting in safety, permanency, and well-being of American Indian children and families.

The utilization of peers is becoming increasingly popular in child welfare for parents with substance abuse problems (Berrick, Cohen, and Anthony 2011; Summer et al. 2012). Preliminary results on outcomes of these peer services are promising, including parents experiencing a sense of empowerment that contributed to change, increased compliance with case plans and attendance at court hearings, and support and advice in the face of negative events.

Rockhill and colleagues (2014) presented findings from interviews with parents participating in the *Parenting Mentoring Program (PMPP)*, which focuses upon parents with open child welfare cases and substance abuse issues. Parents spent a great deal of time talking about receiving guidance from mentors that was "clear, dependable, and predictable" (Rockhill, Furrer, and Duong 2014, p. 132). Mentors explained or translated information given to parents by professionals, took the time necessary to put things into words parents could understand, shared insights and advice, and gave information regarding local treatment resources. Mentors also held parents accountable for their actions and commitments, helped parents imagine the outcomes of their behavior before they acted, and allowed them to see choices that were not otherwise evident. Parents reported that mentors showed them respect by listening to their opinions, giving them time to think, and validating their needs. Parents also described feeling hope with their mentors. Results also showed that some things undermined parents' motivation; these included a failure to connect with the peer mentor, lack of follow-through by the mentor, and the mentor being overly directive.

Education

Schools are an excellent entry point for access to mental health services for children. However, most school-based mental health programs do not systematically screen, assess, or provide counseling for trauma. Stein and colleagues (2003) found that, among 769 students in the Los Angeles Unified School District, the average number of violent events experienced in the previous year was 5.9. In addition, 76 percent of the students had witnessed or experienced violence involving a gun or knife. One program, the *Cognitive Behavioral Interventions for Trauma in Schools (CBITS)* (Jaycox et al. 2012), involves: ten weekly group sessions; one to three individual sessions to prepare the child for group; and four parent group sessions to discuss trauma and enhance parenting skills. The program has been shown to reduce PTSD and depression symptoms in a randomized clinical trial and an independent quasi-experimental design study with an ethnocentrically diverse urban sample of middle school children.

Schools can be sites for multi-leveled interventions focused not just on treatment but prevention. Seventy percent of mental health disorders, including substance abuse, depression, schizophrenia, and eating disorders, have their onset before age 24. Approximately 45 percent of children have experienced one adverse childhood event. We need to address issues at the subclinical level, before they turn into a diagnosed illness. That is why we need to pay attention to traumatic exposure. School-based health centers are two-generation programs; delivering healthcare to children in elementary schools means communicating with parents, who often feel more comfortable and more trusting of schools than they do of other community agencies. What is needed is to increase attention to interventions that "nurture" parents, so that they can better nurture their children.

The Trauma and Learning Policy Initiative (TLPI) is a nationally recognized collaboration between Massachusetts Advocates for Children and Harvard Law School. The mission of this initiative is to ensure that children affected by family violence and other adverse childhood events succeed in school. TLPI works directly with schools to help them become trauma-sensitive, providing training and technical assistance. TLPI's publications, *Helping Traumatized Children Learn: A Report and Policy Agenda* and *Helping Traumatized Children Learn: Creating and Advocating for Trauma-Sensitive Schools*, are available on its website, www.traumasensitiveschools.org. In 2012, the Lesley Institute for Trauma Sensitivity (at Lesley University Center for Special Education) and TLPI developed a *Trauma-Sensitive School Checklist* to help schools address their policies and practices and identify areas needing more trauma-informed work. The checklist (available at www.lesley.edu/center/special-education/trauma-and-learning) is divided into five components: (1) school-wide policies and practices (e.g., discipline policies must balance accountability with an understanding of trauma); (2) classroom strategies (e.g., activities are structured in predictable and emotionally safe ways); (3) collaborations and linkages with mental health (e.g., access exists to trauma-competent services for prevention, early intervention, treatment, and crisis intervention); (4) family partnerships (e.g., strategies to involve parents are tailored to meet individual family needs and include flexibility in selecting times and places for meetings, availability of interpreters, and translated materials); and (5) community linkages (e.g., when possible, school and community agencies leverage funding to increase the array of supports available).

Trauma impacts all aspects of a child's development, including emotional regulation, memory, cognitive processing, social skills, and physical health. Trauma-informed practice supports a focus upon making the school space—its routines, its relationships, and its activities in and around its students—facilitative and flexible to the needs of all children and young people, but particularly those who are affected by traumatic experiences. Recognizing this, Australia has begun to make their schools trauma-informed, and its Childhood Foundation Protecting Children (2012) has developed a publication, *Making Space for Learning: Trauma Informed Practice in Schools* (available at www.childhood.org.au). The acronym SPACE represents five key dimensions to trauma-informed practice in the Australian schools: staged, predictable, adaptive, connected, and enabled.

- Staged: Development is sequential, and strategies aimed at helping traumatized children/youth need to follow this staged pattern of conceptualization and implementation for them to succeed.

- Predictable: Uncertainty and unpredictability of routines and reactions from others can amplify the stress responses used by students. Strategies which promote stability and familiarity reduce the stress.
- Adaptive: Traumatized children/youth rely on a limited set of behavioral routines to respond to the challenges of the school environment. They may have considerable difficulty in adapting to new challenges in the school.
- Connected: Traumatized children/youth have learned to perceive relationships as possible sources of harm. At other times, they may have a strong need for attention and love from teachers. They also struggle to interpret social cues and can feel isolated from their peers. Strategies to support these children emphasize relationships with safe and consistent adults as the foundation for change.
- Enabled: Traumatized children/youth find the process of understanding themselves difficult. They are challenged to identify their feelings, understand them, and communicate them to others. Strategies for responding to these children in the school context fall into the category of empowerment; helping them understand their feelings, make sense of what leads to their reactions, and to learn new coping skills.

Some school districts have chosen to utilize the *Positive Behavioral Interventions and Supports (PBIS)* model to support students with a wide range of behavioral and emotional challenges. *PBIS* systems begin with the assumption that approximately 80 percent of students can and will behave well if: (1) there are clear behavioral expectations; and (2) they are taught how to behave in effective and trauma-informed ways. Behaviors may often communicate a student's emotional needs. Some of the coping strategies for responding to trauma may be risky, problematic, truant, or anti-social. Acknowledging and understanding that the student may be acting out in response to adult-caused pain (e.g., witnessing DV) or other factors beyond their control, rather than malicious intent, can help lead to more effective responses.

Chronic trauma can impair the development of a child's ability to regulate her/his emotions and to control impulsive and externalizing behaviors (e.g., aggression, defiance). Trauma-informed approaches can also help schools identify children who have internalized symptoms, such as depression and social withdrawal. Teachers may experience the student's reactions of "fight-flight-freeze"; these should indicate that trauma responses have been triggered. Adopting a trauma-informed perspective helps educators see the importance of implementing discipline in a sensitive, predictable, and respectful manner.

Criminal Justice/Juvenile Justice/Family Drug Treatment Courts

The juvenile justice system is an interconnecting system of multiple organizations, including law enforcement, courts, detention centers, prisons or "training camps," probation and parole systems, residential centers, and group homes. Trauma-informed practice has been slow to take hold in the juvenile justice system, despite the fact that trauma is recognized as an important factor in the origins of delinquency. For example, studies (Abram et al. 2004) have shown that approximately 75 percent of youth in juvenile justice systems have been exposed to trauma and

11 percent to 50 percent of the youths have PTSD. Many justice-involved youth also are involved in Family Drug Treatment Courts systems. A small percent of juvenile offenders (10%) are known as serious, violent, and chronic (SVC) offenders (DeLisi and Piquero 2011; Loeber and Ahonen 2014). One of the most significant findings about the SVC population is that they are disproportionality (90%) victims of childhood trauma as compared to the less severe offender population (Dierkhising et al. 2013; Loeber and Farrington 2000).

Fox and colleagues (2015) studied how effective the ACE questions are in identifying children at high risk of SVC offending. Data were collected on 22,575 delinquent youth, of which 10,714 were SVCs and 11,861 were O&D offenders ("One non-violent felony and done"). Results indicated that there was a significant difference in prevalence of ACEs between the two groups, with SVC offenders showing higher prevalence of individual ACEs, as well as higher composite ACE scores. The total number of ACEs among SVC offenders was more than double that of the O&D group, and the number of juveniles that experienced six or more types of trauma was triple the rate for SVC vs. O&D. Each ACE a youth experienced increased the risk of him/her being a serious, violent, and chronic offender by more than 35 percent, even when controlling for other known risk factors for criminal behavior. Components analysis showed that some ACEs had more impact on risk of SVC offending than indicated in the aggregated model; physical abuse and incarcerated household members raised the SVC risk by 58 percent and 119 percent respectively. The authors recommend that the ACE questions be used as an early screening tool by pediatricians, school personnel, and other providers to identify risk factors before a child is ever involved in the criminal justice system, so that preventive interventions can be implemented.

Complex trauma has been defined as exposure to traumatic stressors during childhood and/or prolonged abuse, torture, or captivity that compromises secure attachment with primary caregivers and the ability to self-regulate emotions (Cook et al. 2005; Cloitre et al. 2009). A hierarchical cluster analysis of a large sample of juvenile detention facilities (Ford, Hawke, and Chapman 2010) showed two complex trauma subgroups: 20 percent reported some combination of sexual or physical abuse or family violence, and 15 percent experienced emotional abuse and family violence, but not physical or sexual abuse.

Exposure to complex trauma in childhood puts youth at risk for PTSD, depression, substance use, and incarceration. Youth with complex trauma are likely to have impairments in the types of emotional regulation that are needed to successfully participate in juvenile justice residential programs. Therefore, interventions that build self-regulation skills are needed, as well as staff who are well trained in self-regulation in their interactions with the youth and in understanding trauma and trauma-related triggers. Youth with complex trauma histories are not trusting of authority and often "test" staff by acting out in ways that trigger intense stress reactions in staff.

There is also a growing number of girls involved in our juvenile justice system. Between 70 and 90 percent of girls placed in secure juvenile justice settings report trauma histories consistent with complex trauma (Abram et al. 2004). The girls are eight to ten times more likely to report sexual abuse and 33 percent more likely to have PTSD than their male counterparts. Self-harm also is more common among girls than boys.

Youth from racial and ethnic minority backgrounds are a population that is over-represented in the juvenile justice system. Placement into ethnically heterogeneous settings may trigger aggression in these youths that is related to trauma experienced with other groups. Trauma-informed approaches are needed for milieu management, rehabilitation, and treatment for youth, as well as re-entry into the community (Ford et al. 2012).

For both juveniles and adults in jails and prisons, we need "inmate-centered, trauma-informed" programs. This means that correctional staff need to be trained in trauma issues, so that they can: (1) watch for signs of emerging problems (e.g., someone who is starting not to shower, showing signs of depression or psychotic process); (2) make a referral to mental health; and (3) use trauma-informed practices to de-escalate any increasing tensions. With regard to "body searches," staff need to explain why they are being done ("We have to do this to keep the jail/prison safe, and I know it can be uncomfortable"). If at all possible, jails and prisons should establish a "Quiet Room" (not isolation) where security can view the person, but the inmate can go in and calm down. Prisons are challenging settings for trauma-informed care; they are full of unavoidable trauma triggers such as strip searches and restricted movement. Trauma-informed principles can help staff play a major role in minimizing triggers, stabilizing offenders, reducing critical incidents, and deescalating situations that could lead to violence.

The vast majority of women in prison have experienced trauma, with estimates as high as 90 percent (Governor's Commission on Corrections Reform 2005). Sexual violence (combined child and adult sexual abuse/assault) is the most commonly reported trauma experience, followed by IPV/DV (Battle et al. 2002; Clements-Nolle, Wolden, and Bargmann-Losche 2009). In studies of male prisoners, the most commonly reported trauma is witnessing someone being killed or seriously injured (Sarchiapone et al. 2009), followed by physical assault and childhood sexual abuse (Weeks and Widom 1999). Men and women may also face a risk of sexual assault in the prison (National Prison Rape Elimination Commission 2009).

One difficulty in implementing trauma-informed practice within the prison setting is that trauma-informed principles of compassionate care, inmate-centered care, etc., may be perceived by staff as "weak," "enabling," and "unsafe." However, when clinical and nonclinical staff members understand their common goals—public safety, safety of inmates, safety of staff, rehabilitation and recovery—they can focus on safety (for both inmates and staff), training on new coping skills, and keeping critical incidents to a minimum. Training that highlights stress management and self-care for staff can be effective in discussing a trauma-informed approach.

Family Drug Treatment Courts (FDTCs) are designed to respond to the multiple needs of families involved in the child welfare system who have substance abuse problems. There are more than 300 FDTCs currently operating in the U.S. Research results suggest that FDTCs are effective in improving treatment outcomes, increasing the likelihood of family reunification, and decreasing the time children spend in foster care (Bruns et al. 2012; Chuang et al. 2012). Families affected by substance abuse disorders who are involved in the child welfare system need a system of care that recognizes the impact of trauma on their recovery.

A paper by Drabble and colleagues (2013) focused upon one FDTC in which a trauma-informed walk-through process was implemented. The authors explored the benefits of, barriers to, and facilitators for the assessment and improvement initiative. Four major facilitating factors emerged: (1) a formal commitment from the system for training, walk-through assessment, and discussion about trauma-informed changes; (2) trauma leaders and champions; (3) support and advocacy through peer mentors; and (4) judicial leadership. In a more recent study, Kellerman and colleagues (submitted for publication) presented the findings of the National Center on Substance Abuse and Child Welfare's (NCSACW) Trauma-Informed Care Assessment Project, funded by SAMHSA, which supported trauma-informed care walk-throughs (Brown, Harris, and Fallot 2013) by myself and NCSACW staff in five FDTCs across the U.S. Six-month and 12-month follow-ups were conducted to assess the changes that occurred after these walk-throughs and the development action plans occurred. Within the Family Drug Treatment Courts, I have worked with some outstanding teams across the country.

Police

The *Child Development Community Policing Program (CD-CP)* is a model program for creating trauma-informed police systems (Marans 1995; Murphy et al. 2005). The program was developed by the Yale Child Study Center and the New Haven, Connecticut Department of Police Service in 1991 after a significant increase in community violence. The program places mental health professionals in the community side by side with the police to intervene when children are exposed to violence or other forms of trauma. All police in New Haven are trained on the intersection of child development, trauma, and community policing; all clinicians are trained in the basics of police procedures and responsibilities and are on call 24/7. The program now includes: the *Domestic Violence Home Visit Intervention*, which provides outreach and advocacy for children; the *Death Notification Protocol*, which assists officers in providing support to families following the loss of a family member; and the *Family Intervention Program*, which offers case management and monitoring for youth at risk for involvement in violent and delinquent behavior.

Military

As it faces increasing numbers of returning military members with posttraumatic stress disorders (PTSD) and traumatic brain injury (TBI), the Veterans Administration (VA) has also been adding innovative practices to the field of trauma-informed practices. The VA's National Center for PTSD is a recognized leader in conducting research and promoting appropriate treatments for veterans suffering from PTSD. Rates of exposure to specific types of combat trauma range from 5 to 50 percent. Direct injuries are reported by 10 to 20 percent. A report from RAND (Tanielian and Jaycox 2008) estimated that approximately 300,000 individuals suffer from PTSD and/or depression and that 320,000 veterans report TBI. The numbers have increased dramatically after the wars in Afghanistan and Iraq.

At a NIH Conference, "Trauma Spectrum Conference: Polytrauma, Recovery and Reintegration for Service Members, Veterans, and Their Families," held in 2010, it was very clear that the focus of the military services' response is a complex of problems, i.e., pain, PTSD, mTBI (minimal traumatic brain injury), TBI, substance use disorders, sleep problems, and suicide. This problem cluster was referred to as "post-deployment multi-symptom disorder" (PMD), and the VA, DoD, and others were looking at various models of integrated care to treat it. One of the speakers (Jim Tackett from the Connecticut Veterans Jail Diversion and Trauma Recovery Initiative) stated, "The hypervigilance that may have kept the veteran alive in Iraq leads him to get arrested when he gets home," because of speeding, bar fights, domestic violence, substance abuse, etc. One of the most poignant presentations was made by Major Ed Purido, who stated that: (1) he didn't want to believe that he had mTBI; (2) he needed to understand and learn about "hypervigilance" before he could begin to understand his problems; (3) a number of mental health and other professionals said things to him that "didn't help" at all; and (4) it was very important to him to "give back" through the Wounded Warrior Program.

One of the other important issues around trauma and the military is military sexual trauma (MST), defined by the U.S. Department of Veteran Affairs (VA) as "experiences of sexual assault or repeated threatening acts of sexual harassment" that occurred while the veteran was serving on active duty or training for active duty. Since the creation of the Army Nurse Corps in 1901, women have served in the U.S. military. In early studies from the 1990s, it was becoming clear that sexual and physical assaults in the military were of considerable concern. In 1996 Coyle and colleagues (1996) reported that 68 percent of 429 women veterans using primary care services in the VA had experienced physical or sexual victimization, and 58 percent reported that it occurred during military service.

Pre-combat sexual and physical abuse was shown to be associated with greater frequency of PTSD as well as trauma symptoms in women in the military. In a study by Butterfield and colleagues (1998) on the impact of physical and sexual assault in 632 veteran women seeking primary care in the VA, it was found that nearly 60 percent reported no trauma history; 40 percent experienced at least one type of trauma, and, of these women, half had multiple traumas. Thirty-three percent of reported rapes and 22 percent of reported battering among this group of women occurred during military service. Increased levels of trauma were associated with a higher prevalence of all mental disorder symptoms (e.g., depression, anxiety, substance use), regardless of military status. Those women with multiple trauma experiences, at least one of which occurred during military service, had a higher prevalence of mental disorder symptoms.

It has been noted that stigmatization and fear of retaliation intensify barriers to reporting MST and to receiving treatment. Reports of MST have risen by approximately 88 percent between 1997 (2,688 reports) and 2013 (5,061 reports) (DoD 2011; DoD 2014). However, the DoD (2013) also acknowledges that less than 15 percent of MST victims reported the assault. In peer-reviewed research (outside military research) examining MST (Turchik and Wilson 2010), between 22 percent and 84 percent of women in the military report having these experiences during military service. Military sexual trauma is now a major concern on the national level.

It has also been reported that women who enlist in the military also have higher rates of childhood sexual abuse than nonmilitary women (Himmelfarb, Yaeger, and Mintz 2006). These experiences, compounded by MST and experiences of trauma in combat areas, can lead to increased risk of PTSD and higher levels of comorbidity (e.g., depression, anxiety, substance use, health problems). A recent study by Kintzle and colleagues (2015), investigating sexual assault in the military among a sample of women veterans from pre-9/11 and post-9/11 service eras, as well as symptoms of PTSD and mental health care utilization, found that approximately 40 percent of the 327 women reported experiencing MST. Almost half of the pre-9/11 veterans (48%) and 30 percent of the post-9/11 veterans reported sexual contact against their will during military service. Only 10 percent of pre-9/11 and 18 percent of post-9/11 veterans indicated receiving help after their sexual assault. While it is encouraging that reported MST post-9/11 was lower than pre-9/11, it certainly does not show a significant difference in the rates of MST at the present time.

One of the unique and unfortunate features of MST is that victims must continue to live and work in close proximity to their perpetrators; this often, and understandably, leads to feelings of helplessness and places the women at risk for further harassment. Victims may have to rely on their perpetrators (or associates of the perpetrator) for approval if they wish to be referred for medical and psychological care for their trauma. Perpetrators are also often supervisors responsible for work-related evaluations and promotions of those attacked. This is also true of male victims on the military. Given the fact that the combat areas in Afghanistan and Iraq have brought higher-than-normal stress and trauma, as well as PTSD and TBI, the additional trauma of MST increases the impact of cumulative trauma on victims (both women and men) and needs to be addressed in a more appropriate way—both for humane and for economic reasons.

The National Defense Authorization Act (NDAA) was passed in 2013. The Act included 19 amendments to significantly reform the Department of Defense sexual assault and sexual harassment policies. These amendments included: (1) mandatory separation from the military of convicted sex offenders from military service; (2) Special Victims Units created to investigate, prosecute, and provide support to the victim; (3) an independent review panel with both civilian and military members to monitor the investigation, prosecution, and adjudication of MST; and (4) required sexual assault prevention training in pre-command and command courses for officers. However, from a trauma-informed perspective, there is also a need for a culture shift in the military away from the idea that these are your comrades and you are obligated "to do no harm" to any of them. When the person who is expected to protect you under all circumstances is the one who victimizes you, there is, added to the mix of traumatic experiences, an intense sense of betrayal and powerlessness. This experience is similar to the betrayal experienced by those who suffer sexual abuse by a family member or clergyman or sport coach. Trauma-informed training needs to be implemented throughout the military.

In a recent book, Berwick and colleagues stated, "Only a trauma care system structured around the patient's experience, one that considers and actively engages the patient, family, and community, can achieve optimal short- and long-term outcomes for injured patients" (Berwick, Downey, and Cornett 2016, p. 272). While not calling it "trauma-informed care" (but patient-centered care in a trauma system), this book shows the need for integration of trauma-informed and patient-centered care for both military and civilian populations. Such integration can lead to preventing many more deaths from injuries, as trauma is the leading cause of death in the U.S. for individuals under the age of 46 and, in 2013 alone, was associated with $670 billion in medical care expenses and lost productivity. The committee convened for the book estimates that, with optimal trauma care, as many as 20 percent of the 147,790 deaths from trauma in 2014 might have been prevented.

A unified effort driven by leadership from military and civilian sectors is needed to address the gaps; the committee offers 11 recommendations toward this goal.

The committee recommends that the White House lead the integration of military and civilian trauma care to establish a national trauma care system and that the Secretaries of the Department of Defense and the Department of Health and Human Services should each identify, within their respective departments, a locus of responsibility and authority to lead and coordinate the efforts.

Some of the gaps addressed highlighted "transition points," i.e., those points in moving patients from acute care to rehabilitation to community re-entry where trauma should be assessed and addressed.

Multiple studies conducted by the military report persistent barriers to effective communication and seamless care transitions (Defense Health Board 2015; Rotondo et al. 2011). While the military sector can establish policies and procedures (through the Department of Defense) that smooth the transition from injury to rehabilitation, in the civilian sector the burden of managing the overwhelming process of transitioning to one of the many different types of rehabilitation facilities or outpatient services most often falls to patients, their families, and their health care providers. In addition, in the civilian system lack of access to high quality rehabilitation care for uninsured and underinsured individuals has been associated with poor long-term outcomes. A growing body of research funded by the National Institute of Health (NIH) shows the effectiveness of a "transition care model," in which an advanced practice nurse assumes responsibility for managing the flow between phases of care. This model shows reduced numbers of readmissions and increased cost savings in patients with chronic illnesses and complex treatment regimens (Coleman et al. 2006; Naylor and Keating 2008).

Trauma (physical/war/combat) patients who have been hospitalized for serious injuries are at high risk for PTSD and depression (O'Donnell et al. 2010). The National Study on the Costs and Outcomes of Trauma found that 20.7 percent of patients with injuries scoring 3 or higher on the Abbreviated Injury Scale screened positive for PTSD one year after injury, and 6.6 percent had symptoms consistent with depression (Zatzick et al. 2008). These findings are echoed in studies of the military sector. For example, Grieger and colleagues (2006) assessed PTSD and depression among seriously injured soldiers at one, four, and seven months after they were injured. At one month, 4.2 percent of the soldiers met the criteria for PTSD and 4.4 percent for depression. At seven months, 12 percent met the criteria for PTSD and 9 percent for depression; 6 percent met the criteria for both. At one month post-injury, the soldiers with high combat exposure were 4.8 times as likely to meet PTSD criteria as those with lower combat exposure; this was not true at seven months post-injury. High severity of physical problems at one month was significantly associated with PTSD and depression at all time points, i.e., one, four, and seven months post-injury. The authors state that assessing the severity of physical problems shortly after the injury may be of value in predicting persistence or later onset of PTSD and depression, and that secondary prevention strategies may be of value in reducing the likelihood of developing both disorders.

In addition to integrating behavioral health specialists, peer support is used in the military sector, particularly for amputees. Peer support can also be obtained through the Trauma Survivors Network online (www.traumasurvivornetwork.org).

The implementation of innovative trauma-informed practices in a range of settings, organizations, and systems offers reassurance that there is considerable movement across the U.S. and other countries toward a trauma-informed system of care. Adopting a trauma-informed approach poses exciting challenges. As can be seen throughout this book, trauma-informed practice takes into account issues of gender and sexual orientation, racial/ethnic diversity, and equity. It is also a critical aspect of the patient-centered, integrated care models being encouraged and supported through health care reform. I hope this book makes a contribution to real transformation in our systems. We owe it to our patients/clients and to ourselves.

References

Abram, KM, Teplin, LA, Charles, DR et al. 2004, Posttraumatic Stress Disorder and Trauma in Youth in Juvenile Detention, *Archives of General Psychiatry*, vol. 61, pp. 403–410.

Administration for Children and Families (ACF), Children's Bureau 2015, *Child Maltreatment 2013*, Washington, DC, U.S. Department of Health and Human Services, www.acf.hhs.gov/programs/cb/research-data-technology/statistics-research/child-maltreatment.

Australian Childhood Foundation Protecting Children 2012, *Making Space for Learning: Trauma Informed Practice in Schools*, Victoria, Australia: Australian Childhood Foundation Protecting Children.

Battle, C, Zlotnick, C, Najavits, LM et al. 2002, Posttraumatic Stress Disorder and Substance Use Disorder Among Incarcerated Women, in P Ouimette and RJ Brown (eds.), *Trauma and Substance Abuse: Causes, Consequences, and Treatment of Comorbid Disorders*, Washington, DC: American Psychological Association, pp. 209–226.

Berrick, JD, Cohen, E, and Anthony, E 2011, Partnering with Parents: Promising Approaches to Improve Reunification Outcomes for Children in Foster Care, *Journal of Family Strengths*, vol. 11, no. 1, article 14.

Berwick, D, Downey, A, and Cornett, E (eds.) 2016, *A National Trauma Care System: Integrating Military and Civilian Trauma Systems to Achieve Zero Preventable Deaths After Injury*, Washington, DC, National Academy of Sciences.

Brown, VB, Harris, M, and Fallot, R 2013, Moving Toward Trauma-Informed Practice in Addiction Treatment: A Collaborative Model of Agency Assessment, *Journal of Psychoactive Drugs*, vol. 45, no. 5, pp. 386–393.

Bruns, E, Pullman, M, Weathers, E et al. 2012, Effects of a Multidisciplinary Family Treatment Drug Court on Child and Family Outcomes: Results of a Quasi-Experimental Study, *Child Maltreatment*, vol. 17, pp. 218–230.

Butterfield, M, McIntyre, L, Stechuchak, K et al. 1998, Mental Disorder Symptoms in Veteran Women: Impact of Physical and Sexual Assault, *Journal of the American Medical Women's Association*, vol. 53, pp. 198–200.

Chuang, E, Moore, K, Barrett, B, and Young, M 2012, Effect of an Integrated Family Dependency Treatment Court on Child Welfare Reunification, Time to Permanency and Re-Entry Rates, *Children and Youth Services Review*, vol. 34, pp. 1896–1902.

Clements-Nolle, K, Wolden, M, and Bargmann-Losche, J 2009, Childhood Trauma and Risk for Past and Future Suicide Attempts Among Women in Prison, *Women's Health Issues*, vol. 19, no. 3, pp. 185–192.

Cloitre, M, Stolbach, BC, Herman, JL et al. 2009, A Developmental Approach to Complex PTSD, *Journal of Traumatic Stress*, vol. 22, pp. 399–408.

Coleman, EA, Parry, C, Chalmers, S, and Min, SJ 2006, The Care Transitions Intervention: Results of a Randomized Controlled Trial, *Archives of Internal Medicine*, vol. 166, no. 17, pp. 1822–1828.

Cook, A, Spinazzola, P, Ford, J et al. 2005, Complex Trauma in Children and Adolescents, *Psychiatric Annals*, vol. 35, pp. 390–398.

Coyle, BS, Wolman, DL, and Van Horn, AS 1996, The Prevalence of Physical and Sexual Abuse in Women Veterans Seeking Care at a Veterans Affairs Medical Center, *Military Medicine*, vol. 161, pp. 588–593.

Defense Health Board 2015, *Combat Trauma Lessons Learned from Military Operations of 2001–2013*, Falls Church, VA, Office of the Assistant Secretary of Defense for Health Affairs.

DeLisi, M and Piquero, AR 2011, New Frontiers in Criminal Careers Research 2000–2011: A State-of-the-Art Review, *Journal of Criminal Justice*, vol. 39, pp. 289–301.

Department of Defense (DoD) 2011, *Annual Report on Sexual Assault in the Military, Fiscal Year 2010*, Washington, DC, U.S. Government Printing Office.

Department of Defense (DoD) 2013, *Annual Report on Sexual Assault in the Military, Fiscal Year 2012*, Washington, DC, U.S. Government Printing Office.

Department of Defense (DoD) 2014, *Annual Report on Sexual Assault in the Military, Fiscal Year 2013*, Washington, DC, U.S. Government Printing Office.

Dierkhising, CB, Ko, SJ, Woods-Jaeger, B et al. 2013, Trauma Histories Among Justice-Involved Youth: Findings from the National Child Traumatic Stress Network, *European Journal of Psychotraumatology*, vol. 4, pp. 1–12.

Drabble, LA, Jones, S, and Brown, V 2013, Advancing Trauma-Informed Systems Change in a Family Drug Treatment Court Context, *Journal of Social Work Practice in the Addictions*, vol. 13, pp. 91–113.

Ford, JD, Chapman, J, Connor, DF, and Cruise, K 2012, Complex Trauma and Aggression in Secure Juvenile Justice Settings, *Criminal Justice & Behavior*, vol. 39, no. 6, pp. 694–724.

Ford, JD, Hawke, J, and Chapman, JC 2010, *Complex Psychological Trauma Among Juvenile Justice-Involved Youth*, Farmington, University of Connecticut.

Fox, BH, Perez, N, Cass, E et al. 2015, Trauma Changes Everything: Examining the Relationship Between Adverse Childhood Experiences and Serious, Violent, and Chronic Juvenile Offenders, *Child Abuse & Neglect*, vol. 46, pp. 163–173.

Governor's Commission on Corrections Reform 2005, *Dedicated External Female Offender Review 2005*, Boston, MA: Commonwealth of Massachusetts Executive Office of Public Safety Department of Corrections.

Grieger, TA, Cozza, SJ, Ursano, RJ et al. 2006, Posttraumatic Stress Disorder and Depression in Battle-Injured Soldiers, *American Journal of Psychiatry*, vol. 163, no. 10, pp. 1777–1783.

Himmelfarb, N, Yaeger, D, and Mintz, J 2006, Posttraumatic Stress Disorder in Female Veterans with Military and Civilian Trauma, *Journal of Traumatic Stress*, vol. 19, pp. 837–846.

Jaycox, LH, Kataoka, SH, Stein, BD et al. 2012, Cognitive Behavioral Intervention for Trauma in Schools, *Journal of Applied School Psychology*, vol. 28, no. 3, pp. 239–255.

Kellerman, A, Brown, VB, and Nguyen, K, Trauma-Informed System Assessment in Family Drug Courts (submitted for publication).

Kintzle, S, Schuyler, AC, Ray-Letourneau, D et al. 2015, Sexual Trauma in the Military: Exploring PTSD and Mental Health Care Utilization in Female Veterans, *Psychological Services*, vol. 12, no. 4, pp. 394–401.

Kramer, TL, Sigal, BA, Conners-Burrow, NA et al. 2013, A Statewide Introduction of Trauma-Informed Care in a Child Welfare System, *Children & Youth Services Review*, vol. 35, pp. 19–24.

Leslie, LK, Hurlburt, MS, Landsverk, J et al. 2004, Outpatient Mental Health Services for Children in Foster Care: A National Perspective, *Child Abuse & Neglect*, vol. 28, pp. 697–712.

Loeber, R and Ahonen, L 2014, What Are the Policy Implications of Our Knowledge on Serious, Violent, and Chronic Offenders, *Criminology & Public Policy*, vol. 13, pp. 117–125.

Loeber, R and Farrington, DP 2000, Young Children Who Commit Crime: Epidemiology, Developmental Origins, Risk Factors, Early Interventions, and Policy Implications, *Development and Psychopathology*, vol. 12, pp. 737–762.

Marans, SR (ed.) 1995, *The Police-Mental Health Partnership: A Community-Based Response to Urban Violence*, New Haven, CT, Yale University Press.

Murphy, RA, Rosenheck, RA, Berkowitz, SJ, and Marans, SR 2005, Acute Service Delivery in a Police-Mental Health Program for Children Exposed to Violence and Trauma, *Psychiatric Quarterly*, vol. 76, pp. 107–121.

National Prison Rape Elimination Commission 2009, *Standards for the Prevention, Detection, Response, and Monitoring of Sexual Abuse in Adult Prisons and Jails*, Washington, DC, National Institute of Justice.

Naylor, M and Keating, SA 2008, Transitional Care: Moving Patients from One Care Setting to Another, *The American Journal of Nursing*, vol. 108, supplement 9, pp. 58–63.

O'Donnell, ML, Creemer, M, Holmes, A et al. 2010, Posttraumatic Stress Disorder After Injury: Does Admission to Intensive Care Unit Increase Risk, *Journal of Trauma*, vol. 69, no. 3, pp. 627–632.

Rockhill, A, Furrer, CJ, and Duong, TM 2014, Peer Mentoring in Child Welfare: A Motivational Framework, *Child Welfare*, vol. 94, no. 5, pp. 125–144.

Rotondo, MT, Scalea, A, Rizzo, K et al. 2011, *The United States Military Joint Trauma System Assessment: A Report Commissioned by the U.S. Central Command Surgeon*, Washington, DC, Department of Defense.

Sarchiapone, M, Carli, V, Cuomo, C et al. 2009, Association Between Childhood Trauma and Aggression in Male Prisoners, *Psychiatry Research*, vol. 165, no. 1–2, pp. 187–192.

Stein, BD, Jaycox, LH, Kataoka, SH et al. 2003, A Mental Health Intervention for School Age Children Exposed to Violence: A Randomized Controlled Trial, *Journal of the American Medical Association*, vol. 290, no. 5, pp. 603–611.

Summer, A, Wood, S, Russell, J, and Macgill, S 2012, An Evaluation of the Effectiveness of a Parent-to-Parent Program in Changing Attitudes and Increasing Parental Engagement in the Juvenile Dependency System, *Children & Youth Services Review*, vol. 34, pp. 2036–2041.

Tanielian, T and Jaycox, LH 2008, *Invisible Wounds of War: Psychological and Cognitive Injuries, Their Consequences, and Services to Assist Recovery*, Los Angeles, RAND.

Taylor, N, Wilson, C, and Igelman, R 2006, In Pursuit of a More Trauma-Informed Child Welfare System, *APSAC Advisor*, vol. 18, no. 2, pp. 4–9.

Turchik, JA and Wilson, SM 2010, Sexual Assault in the Military: A Review of the Literature and Recommendations for the Future, *Aggression and Violent Behavior*, vol. 15, pp. 267–277.

Weeks, R and Widom, CS 1999, *Early Childhood Victimization Among Incarcerated Adult Male Felons*, Washington, DC, U.S. Department of Justice, National Institute of Justice.

Zatzick, D, Jurkovich, GJ, Rivara, FP et al. 2008, A National U.S. Study of Posttraumatic Stress Disorder, Depression, and Work and Functional Outcomes After Hospitalization for Traumatic Injury, *Annals of Surgery*, vol. 248, no. 3, pp. 429–437.

Trauma Resources

1. ACES Too High
   www.acestoohigh.com
2. ACES Connection Network
   www.acesconnection.com
3. Centers for Disease Control and Prevention/ACE Studies
   www.cdc.gov/ACE/index.htm
4. Anna Institute
   www.theannainstitute.org
5. National Center on Domestic Violence, Trauma, and Mental Health
   www.nationalcenterdvtraumamh.org
6. National Center for Children Exposed to Violence
   www.nccev.org
7. National Center on Substance Abuse and Child Welfare
   www.ncsacw.samhsa.gov
8. National Center for Trauma-Informed Care
   www.samhsa.gov/nctic
9. National Child Traumatic Stress Network (NCTSN)
   www.nctsnet.org
10. National Coalition Against Domestic Violence
    www.ncadv.org
11. Rape, Abuse and Incest National Network (RAINN)
    www.rain.org
12. National Native Children's Trauma Center (Institute for Educational Research
    and Service), University of Montana
    www.iers.umt.edu/national_native_childrens_trauma_center
13. National Center for PTSD
    www.ptsd.va.gov
14. After the Injury (Children's Hospital of Philadelphia)
    www.aftertheinjury.org
15. The Centre for Addiction and Mental Health (CAMH)
    www.camh.ca
16. National Trauma Consortium
    www.nationaltraumaconsortium.org
17. Sidran Institute
    www.sidran.org

Screening Instruments

1. *Clinician Administered PTSD Scale (CAPS)*
2. *Impacts of Event Scale-Revised (IES-R)*
3. *Screen for Posttraumatic Stress Symptoms (SPTSS)*
4. *Trauma History Questionnaire (THQ)*
5. *Trauma Symptom Inventory (TSI)*
6. *The PTSD Checklist for Adults (PCL)*
7. *Adverse Childhood Experiences Questionnaire (ACE)*
8. *Life Stressor Checklist-Revised (LSC-R)*
9. *Trauma Symptom Checklist (TSC-40)*
10. *UCLA Child/Adolescent PTSD Reaction Index for DSM-5*
11. *Trauma Symptom Checklist for Children (TSC-C)*
12. *Revised COJAC Screener* (attached as Appendix G)
13. *Commonwealth of Massachusetts Department of Mental Health De-Escalation Form for DMH Facilities/Vendors*

Appendix C

Trauma-Specific Interventions

1. Najavits, LM 2002, *Seeking Safety: A Treatment Manual for PTSD and Substance Abuse*, New York, NY, Guilford Press.
2. Harris, M and the Community Connections Trauma Work Group 1998, *Trauma Recovery and Empowerment: A Clinician's Guide for Working with Women in Groups*, New York, NY, The Free Press.
3. Fallot, R, Harris M, Affolter HU et al. 2001, *Men's Trauma Recovery and Empowerment Model (M-TREM)*, Washington, DC, Community Connections.
4. Covington, SS 2016, *Beyond Trauma: A Healing Journey for Women (Second Edition)*, Center City, MN, Hazelden.
5. Ford, JD and Russo E 2006, Trauma-Focused, Present-Centered, Emotional Self-Regulation Approach to Integrated Treatment for Posttraumatic Stress and Addiction: Trauma Adaptive Recovery Group Education and Therapy (TARGET), *American Journal of Psychotherapy*, vol. 60, no. 4, pp. 335–355.
6. Linehan, MM 2016, *DBT® Skills Training Manual: Second Edition*, New York, Guilford Press.
7. Covington, SS, Griffin, D, and Dauer, R 2011, *Helping Men Recover: A Program for Treating Addiction*, San Francisco, CA, Jossey-Bass.
8. Shapiro, F 2001, *Eye Movement Desensitization and Reprocessing (EMDR): Basic Principles, Protocols, and Procedures, 2nd Edition*, New York, Guilford Press.
9. Cloitre, M et al. 2002, Skills Training in Affective and Interpersonal Regulation Followed by Exposure: A Phase-Based Treatment for PTSD Related to Childhood Abuse, *Journal of Consulting and Clinical Psychology*, vol. 70, no. 5, pp. 1067–1074.
10. Sikkema, KJ et al. 2008, Effects of a Coping Intervention on Transmission Risk Behavior Among People Living with HIV/AIDS and a History of Childhood Sexual Abuse, *Journal of Acquired Immune Deficiency Syndromes*, vol. 47, no. 4, pp. 506–513.
11. Cohen, JA, Mannarino, AP, and Deblinger, E 2012, *Trauma-Focused CBT for Children and Adolescents: Treatment Applications*, New York, Guilford Press.

Appendix D

Self-Assessments for Organizations

1. Fallot, RD and Harris, M 2009, *Creating Cultures of Trauma-Informed Care (CCTIC): A Self Assessment and Planning Protocol*, Washington, DC, Community Connections.
2. Brown, VB, Harris, M, and Fallot, R 2013, Moving Toward Trauma-Informed Practice in Addiction Treatment: A Collaborative Model of Agency Assessment, *Journal of Psychoactive Drugs*, vol. 45, no. 5, pp. 386–393.
3. Guarino, K, Soares, P, Konnath, K, Clervil, R, and Bassuk, E 2009, *Trauma-Informed Organizational Toolkit for Homeless Services*, www.familyhomelessness.org.
4. Institute for Health and Recovery, WELL Project 2012, *Developing Trauma-Informed Organizations: A Tool Kit (2nd Edition)*, Cambridge, MA, Institute for Health and Recovery.
5. University of South Florida, College of Behavioral and Community Service, *Creating Trauma-Informed Care Environments: Organizational Self-Assessment for Trauma-Informed Care Practices in Youth Residential Settings*.

Appendix E

Health Care Training Resources

1. VitalTalk: www.vitaltalk.org.
2. I★CARE: www.mdanderson.org/education-and-research/resources-for-professionals/professonal-educational-resources/i-care/index.html.
3. Green, B et al. 2015, Trauma-Informed Medical Care: CME Communication Training for Primary Care Providers, *Family Medicine*, vol. 47, no. 1, pp. 1–11.
4. Center for Pediatric Traumatic Stress Online Courses: www.CPTS/online-education-for providers.html.

Author's Interview Protocol

1. Could you tell me about your journey into trauma-informed practice? What led you to integrate trauma into your practice? When was that?
2. What do you consider the most important components of a trauma-informed system?
3. What do you see as the major changes you made in your system?

   3a. What physical changes, if any, did you make?
   3b. What new policies and practices have you put in place?
   3b. What trauma screening/assessment tools do you use?

4. What were the easiest things for you to change?
5. What were the most difficult things for you to change? Was there resistance, and how did you handle it?
6. How do you handle training on trauma for staff?
7. Do you employ consumers/peers? What services do they provide?
8. How did staff react to the changes toward integrating trauma? What changes in staff behaviors did you observe?
9. Do you provide a trauma-specific intervention, that is, one that directly helps clients/patients with their trauma symptoms? Which intervention do you use?
10. What were the most significant barriers you met in implementing your trauma-informed practice? How did you overcome these?
11. Have you had much staff turnover? If yes, how has this impacted your program?
12. Who are your collaborators, if any?
13. How are you disseminating your work? Do you have any publications? Have you developed any other products related to your trauma-informed practices?
14. What more are you planning to do with regard to integrating trauma into your practice?
15. What would you recommend to other programs that are thinking of implementing a trauma-informed system?
16. Based on your experience, what do you think would be the best ways of moving your system (e.g., health care) to adopt a trauma-informed approach?
17. What other questions should I have asked you?

Appendix G

Revised COJAC Screening Tool

UNIQUE ID: _____

| A. How administered? Check one: 1☐ In Person   2☐ Phone |

Revised COJAC Screening Tool[1]

<u>Section A. Questions for Mental Health[2]</u>

INTERVIEWER: ASK THE NEXT 3 QUESTIONS. CHECK THE BOX NEXT TO EACH QUESTION ANSWERED "YES".

1☐ 1. Have you ever been worried about how you are thinking, feeling or acting?

1☐ 2. Has anyone ever expressed concerns about how you were thinking, feeling, or acting?

1☐ 3. Have you ever harmed yourself or thought about harming yourself?

____ Number of answers checked for questions 1, 2, and 3

➔ INTERVIEWER: IF NONE OF THE ABOVE QUESTIONS ARE CHECKED, GO TO SECTION B. QUESTIONS FOR ALCOHOL & DRUG USE ON PAGE 2.
  ➔ INTERVIEWER: IF 1 OR MORE QUESTIONS ARE CHECKED IN THIS SECTION, CONTINUE BELOW WITH SECTION A1.

A1. Additional Screening Questions for Mental Health[3]

INTERVIEWER: IF ONE OR MORE QUESTIONS ARE CHECKED IN SECTION A, ASK THE NEXT 5 QUESTIONS.

Over the <u>last 2 weeks</u>, how often have you been bothered by the following problems?

a. **Feeling nervous, anxious or on edge**
   0☐ Not at all   1☐ Several Days   2☐ More than half the days   3☐ Nearly every day

b. **Not being able to stop or control worrying**
   0☐ Not at all   1☐ Several Days   2☐ More than half the days   3☐ Nearly every day

c. **Little interest or pleasure in doing things**
   0☐ Not at all   1☐ Several Days   2☐ More than half the days   3☐ Nearly every day

d. **Feeling down, depressed, or hopeless**
   0☐ Not at all   1☐ Several Days   2☐ More than half the days   3☐ Nearly every day

e. **Thoughts that you would be better off dead or of hurting yourself in some way**
   0☐ Not at all   1☐ Several Days   2☐ More than half the days   3☐ Nearly every day

INTERVIEWER: ENTER THE NUMBERS CORRESPONDING TO THE ANSWERS TO QUESTIONS a, b, c, d, AND e TO SCORE THIS PART OF THE SCREENER.

INTERVIEWER: _____ + _____ = _____   GAD-2 Anxiety Screen
Answer to question a   # Answer to question b   If 3 or more, assess further for anxiety.

INTERVIEWER: _____ + _____ = _____   PHQ-2 Depression Screen
Answer to question c   # Answer to question d   If 3 or more, assess further for depression.

INTERVIEWER: _____   PHQ-9 Suicidality Screen
Answer to question e   *If 1 or more, assess further for suicide risk.*

---

[1] COJAC Screening Subcommittee. November 2012.
[2] Source Questions 1-3: Health Canada Best Practice Report
[3] Source: PHQ4, Spitzer, Williams, Kroenke et al. www.phqscreeners.com

Section B. Questions for Alcohol & Drug Use[4]

INTERVIEWER: ASK THE NEXT 3 QUESTIONS. CHECK THE BOX NEXT TO EACH QUESTION ANSWERED "YES".

₁☐ 4. Have you ever had any problem related to your use of alcohol or other drugs?

₁☐ 5. Has a relative, friend, doctor, or other health worker been concerned about your drinking or other drug use or suggested cutting down?

₁☐ 6. Have you ever said to another person, "No, I don't have an alcohol or drug problem," when around the same time you questioned yourself and felt, maybe I do have a problem?

INTERVIEWER: ASK EITHER 7A OR 7B DEPENDING ON THE PERSON'S GENDER. CHECK THE BOX NEXT TO EACH QUESTION ANSWERED "YES".
NOTE: IF THE PERSON IS A WOMAN, CHECK "N/A" FOR 7A. IF THE PERSON IS A MAN, CHECK "N/A" FOR 7B.

FOR MEN: **7a. In the past year, how many times have you had 5 or more drinks in a day?[5]**
  ₀☐ Never   ₁☐ Once or twice   ₂☐ Monthly   ₃☐ Weekly   ₄☐ Daily or Almost Daily   ☐ N/A [woman]

FOR WOMEN: **7b. In the past year, how many times have you had 4 or more drinks in a day?[5]**
  ₀☐ Never   ₁☐ Once or twice   ₂☐ Monthly   ₃☐ Weekly   ₄☐ Daily or Almost Daily   ☐ N/A [man]

INTERVIEWER: _____ + _____ = [_____]
  # of questions checked for questions 4, 5, & 6   # Answer to question 7a or 7b   If 1 or more, continue below with Section B1

→ *INTERVIEWER: IF THE NUMBER IN THE BOX IS 0, GO TO SECTION C. QUESTIONS FOR TRAUMA/DOMESTIC VIOLENCE ON PAGE 3.*
  → *INTERVIEWER: IF THE NUMBER IN THE BOX IS 1 OR MORE, CONTINUE BELOW WITH SECTION B1.*

B1. Additional Screening Questions for Alcohol and Drug Use[5]

INTERVIEWER: IF ONE OR MORE QUESTIONS ARE CHECKED IN SECTION B, ASK THE NEXT 3 QUESTIONS.

In the past year, how many times have you used the following?

a. **Tobacco products**
  ₀☐ Never   ₁☐ Once or twice   ₂☐ Monthly   ₃☐ Weekly   ₄☐ Daily or Almost Daily

b. **Prescription drugs for nonmedical reasons**
  ₀☐ Never   ₁☐ Once or twice   ₂☐ Monthly   ₃☐ Weekly   ₄☐ Daily or Almost Daily

c. **Illegal drugs**
  ₀☐ Never   ₁☐ Once or twice   ₂☐ Monthly   ₃☐ Weekly   ₄☐ Daily or Almost Daily

INTERVIEWER: "Never" used all drugs in past year for all questions on this page → reinforce abstinence.

"Yes" to one or more days of heavy drinking → screening suggests at-risk drinking. Assess further.

"Yes" to use of tobacco → any current use places individual at risk. Encourage user to quit. Assess further.

"Yes" to use of illegal drugs or prescription drugs for non-medical reasons → Assess further.

INTERVIEWER: CONTINUE TO SECTION C ON PAGE 3.

---

[4] Source Questions 4-6: Health Canada Best Practice Report
[5] Source: NIDA Quick Screen

Section C. Questions for Trauma/Domestic Violence

1☐ 7. Have you ever been in a relationship where your partner has pushed or slapped you?

1☐ 8. Before you were 13, was there any time when you were punched, kicked, choked, or received a more serious physical punishment from a parent or other adult?

1☐ 9. Before you were 13, did anyone ever touch you in a sexual way or make you touch them when you did not want to?

1☐ 10. Have you ever experienced or witnessed or had to deal with an extremely traumatic event that included actual or threatened death or serious injury to you or someone else?[6] [Examples include: serious accidents, sexual or physical assault, terrorist attack, being held hostage, kidnapping, fire, discovering a body, sudden death of someone close to you, war, natural disaster]

____ Number of answers checked for questions 7, 8, 9, and 10

➔ *INTERVIEWER: IF NONE OF THE ABOVE QUESTIONS ARE CHECKED, THE SCREENER IS COMPLETE.*
    ➔ *INTERVIEWER: IF 1 OR MORE QUESTIONS ARE CHECKED IN THIS SECTION, CONTINUE BELOW WITH SECTION C1.*

C1. Additional Screening Questions for Trauma/Violence

INTERVIEWER: IF ONE OR MORE QUESTIONS ARE CHECKED IN SECTION C, ASK THE NEXT 2 QUESTIONS.

a.	Have you re-experienced an awful event in a distressing way in the past month?[7] Examples include: dreams, intense recollections, flashbacks, physical reactions.	1☐ Yes	0☐ No
b.	Have you had significant problems in the past month with becoming very distressed and upset when something reminded you of the past?[7]	1☐ Yes	0☐ No

____ Number of answers checked "Yes" for questions a-b

➔ *INTERVIEWER: IF NONE OF THE ABOVE QUESTIONS ARE CHECKED, THE SCREENER IS COMPLETE.*
➔ *INTERVIEWER: IF 1 OR MORE QUESTIONS ARE CHECKED IN SECTION C OR C1, RECOMMEND FURTHER ASSESSMENT FOR TRAUMA/VIOLENCE/PTSD.*

END OF SCREENING TOOL

---

[6] Source: Modified MINI Screen.
[7] Adapted from the GAIN Short Screener, Chestnut Health Systems.

Index

Lightning Source UK Ltd.
Milton Keynes UK
UKHW021354191222
414112UK00027B/996